The negotiations which led up to the Munich Agreement of September 29, 1938, were the nearest approach in recent years to the settlement of a major international issue by a procedure of peaceful change.

E. H. CARR, *The Twenty Years Crisis* (1939)

The Munich agreement was a tragically misconceived and desperate act of appeasement at the cost of the Czechoslovak state, performed by Chamberlain and the French premier, Daladier, in the vain hope that it would satisfy Hitler's stormy ambition, and thus secure for Europe a peaceful future.

GEORGE F. KENNAN, *Russia and the West Under Lenin and Stalin* (1961)

Peace or Appeasement?

Edited with an Introduction by
FRANCIS L. LOEWENHEIM, *Rice University*

HITLER,

CHAMBERLAIN,

AND THE

MUNICH CRISIS

Houghton Mifflin Company • *Boston*

HOUGHTON MIFFLIN COMPANY • BOSTON
The Riverside Press · Cambridge
PRINTED IN THE U.S.A.

INTRODUCTION

This small volume is intended as an introduction to one of the great historical crises of modern history — the Munich crisis of 1938. It emphasizes the role of the leading protagonists in that crisis. It seeks to show the principal aims and objectives of each, and how they sought to bring about a settlement of the crisis.

I have also sought to show the role played by the French and Czechoslovak Governments, how they saw the principal issues and viewed the peace-making efforts of Prime Minister Chamberlain, the recognized leader of the democratic states; and I have sought to give the reader some impression of what it was like to negotiate with one of the most powerful and ruthless dictators in history. For that, I have drawn on the pertinent British and German documents, as well as on the memoirs of some of the leading diplomatic and political figures of the period.

Finally, I have included some representative examples of important historical writing on the Munich crisis. My purpose here has been to demonstrate not only the diversity of historical opinion, but also the continuity of certain historical judgments over the last two decades.

Each section of this volume is essentially self-contained and self-explanatory. The reader who wishes to do so may well, for instance, begin with the personal memoirs and proceed from there to the historical commentaries. Or he may, to his pleasure and surprise, find himself carried away by the documentary record — the inner history — of Hitler, Chamberlain, and the Munich crisis.

F. L. L.

Houston, Texas
October, 1964

CONTENTS

The Documentary Record, November 5, 1937 to October 2, 1938

A Tale of Four Cities

The Crisis in Historical Perspective

CHRONOLOGY

1937

November 5	Hitler, in conference at the Reich Chancellery, informs German military leaders of his future plans in the realm of foreign policy (Document 1)

1938

March 11-12	Germany annexes Austria; Goering and Neurath reassure Czechoslovak Minister in Berlin that Germany has no hostile intentions toward his country
March 14	Chamberlain, in statement to the House of Commons, takes note of German reassurances to Czechoslovakia (Document 2)
March 24	Chamberlain, in address to House of Commons, rejects the idea of formal British guarantee to Czechoslovakia (Document 4)
March 28	Hitler meets Henlein, and approves his general plan of action (Document 5)
April 21	Hitler and General Keitel agree on plans for "Operation Green" against Czechoslovakia (Document 6)
April 24	Henlein delivers policy address at Karlsbad, setting forth "Eight Demands" of the Sudeten German Nazi Party
April 28-29	Anglo-French ministerial conference in London agrees to press Czechoslovak Government to make maximum concessions to the Sudeten Germans
May 20-22	War scare over unconfirmed reports of alleged German troop movements and possibility of German surprise attack against Czechoslovakia
May 22	Hitler and Henlein meet to discuss future Sudeten German strategy
May 30	Hitler approves revised plans for German attack on Czechoslovakia (Document 8)
June 7	Sudeten German Nazi Party announces Fourteen Point Program, detailing "Eight Demands" set forth April 24
June 18	Final Strategic Directive for attack on Czechoslovakia issued to German army (Document 9)

July 12	Premier Daladier reaffirms French treaty commitments to Czechoslovakia
July 26	Chamberlain, in address to House of Commons, announces forthcoming mission of Lord Runciman (Document 10)
August 27	Sir John Simon, in speech at Lanark, reaffirms British position as stated by Chamberlain on March 24
September 1-2	Hitler and Henlein meet at Berchtesgaden
September 5	Czechoslovak Government submits "Fourth Plan" to Sudeten German negotiators
September 7	*The Times* [London] suggests the desirability of ceding Sudeten territory to Germany
	Sudeten German leaders break off negotiations over alleged incidents at Mährisch-Ostrau
September 12	Hitler, in address to annual Nazi Party Congress at Nuremberg, demands self-determination for Sudeten Germans
September 15	Hitler and Chamberlain meet at Berchtesgaden, and Chamberlain, personally, accepts principle of self-determination for Sudeten Germans (Document 13)
September 18-19	Anglo-French ministerial conference in London agrees to ask Czechoslovakia to accept Hitler's demands
September 20	Czechoslovakia rejects Anglo-French proposal
September 21	Britain and France demand Czechoslovakia accept German terms, and Czechoslovakia does so
September 22	Hitler and Chamberlain meet at Godesberg, and Hitler raises additional demands (Document 15)
September 23-24	Hitler and Chamberlain hold second meeting at Godesberg (Document 16), and Hitler furnishes Chamberlain written statement of his new demands (Document 17)
September 25-26	Anglo-French ministerial conference in London agrees to send Sir Horace Wilson on special mission to Berlin
September 26	President Roosevelt appeals for peaceful settlement of the dispute
	Sir Horace Wilson has first interview with Hitler, and delivers personal letter from Chamberlain (Document 18)
	Hitler, in address at the Sport Palace, delivers violent attack against Czechoslovakia (Document 19)

Chamberlain, in statement to the press, assures Hitler that his demands can be satisfied by "peaceful means" (Document 20)

September 27   Sir Horace Wilson has second interview with Hitler, who hands him reply to Chamberlain's letter (Document 21)

Britain asks Czechoslovakia to make further concessions to Sudeten Germans, and orders mobilization of Royal Navy

Chamberlain makes broadcast to the British people (Document 22)

President Roosevelt sends second appeal to Hitler asking peaceful settlement of the crisis

September 28   Britain and France send Hitler their final proposal, incorporating further concessions

Chamberlain, in personal message, assures Hitler of full satisfaction of his demands, and appeals to Mussolini to intervene with Hitler on behalf of peaceful settlement (Document 23)

Mussolini agrees to Chamberlain's request, and asks Hitler to abstain from military action for twenty-four hours

Chamberlain informs House of Commons of the state of the crisis, and accepts Hitler's invitation to Four Power Conference at Munich

September 29   Hitler, Chamberlain, Mussolini, and Daladier convene for first session at 12.30 P.M. (Document 24), and reconvene for second session at 4.30 P.M. (Document 25)

September 30   Four Power Agreement is signed about 2 A.M. (Document 26)

Hitler and Chamberlain hold private meeting (Document 27), and agree to sign Anglo-German Declaration (Document 28)

Czechoslovakia accepts terms of Four Power settlement

October 1   German troops cross Czechoslovak frontier, and Hitler appoints Henlein High Commissioner of newly ceded Sudeten territory

October 4   French Chamber of Deputies approves the Munich Agreement

October 5   President Benes resigns

October 6   House of Commons approves the Munich Agreement

October 10   German occupation of ceded territory is completed.

A PREFACE TO MUNICH

That is not all. I have something further to say to the House yet. I have now been informed by Herr Hitler that he invites me to meet him at Munich tomorrow morning. He has also invited Signor Mussolini and M. Daladier. Signor Mussolini has accepted and I have no doubt M. Daladier will also accept. I need not say what my answer will be. We are all patriots, and there can be no hon. Member of this House who did not feel his heart leap that the crisis has been once more postponed to give us once more an opportunity to try what reason and good-will and discussion will do to settle a problem which is already within sight of settlement. Mr. Speaker, I cannot say any more. I am sure that the House will be ready to release me now to go and see what I can make of this last effort. Perhaps they may think it will be well, in view of this new development, that the Debate shall stand adjourned for a few days, when perhaps we may meet in happier circumstances.

The House of Commons had rarely seen anything like it. The moment the Prime Minister concluded, there was an enormous outburst of cheers and applause. The Honorable Members down in the packed House chamber, the distinguished guests crowded together in the visitors' galleries, rose almost as one at the wonderful news they had just received. "Thank God for the Prime Minister" someone cried out, and that summed up almost everyone's mood perfectly.[1] Where only a few minutes before, the House had listened in grim, tense silence to Mr. Chamberlain's weary recitation of his long—and it appeared unsuccessful—search for peace, the feeling was now completely transformed. It seemed a happy ending indeed to the gravest international crisis to confront Britain and the world since August 1914.

The time, in London, was four-thirty, Wednesday afternoon, September 28, 1938.

[1] The famous scene is well described, for instance, in Sir John W. Wheeler-Bennett, *Munich—Prologue to Tragedy*, 2nd ed. (New York, 1963), pp. 168-171.

I

Like most other great historical crises, the origins of the Munich crisis went back far into time, and were extraordinarily complex. By 1938, Czechs and Germans had been at odds for many centuries.[2] Ever since the first Germanic and Slavic settlements in Bohemia in the Middle Ages (even the dates of the first settlement by either race were long disputed), relations between the two had been anything but peaceful. On several occasions over the centuries—for instance during the Hussite wars of the fifteenth century and the Thirty Years War in the seventeenth —this conflict had erupted into open warfare of the utmost violence. In 1848 the Austrian general Windischgrätz managed to repress the Prague revolution by armed force. But by the early 1900's the political and intellectual leadership of the Czech minority in the Habsburg Empire had been largely converted to the cause of political independence, and the Austrian disasters during the First World War gave them the opportunity to convert their passionate hopes into political reality.

The Republic of Czechoslovakia, organized in 1918, was not however born under a lucky star. Like the Austro-Hungarian Empire, it was a multi-national state. While the Czechs constituted the single largest nationality in the new state, it also contained substantial Hungarian, Polish, and Slovak minorities. Above all, there were about three and a half million Germans. Though they had never belonged to Germany, they wished now to become part of a German state. The Versailles Peace Conference rejected this demand on three grounds—first, because the Sudeten Germans (as they now called themselves) had never belonged to Germany; second, because they felt that Bohemia's—now Czecho-slovakia's—historical frontiers should remain intact; and, finally, because by separating Czechs and Germans, it would be impossible to create an economically, politically and militarily viable Czechoslovak state. The Czech leaders, in turn, promised that the German minority in the new state would be accorded full and complete political equality.[3]

The German minority was outraged by the Allied decision. There were bloody riots and repeated protests, and for more than six years, until 1926, they refused all participation in the Czechoslovak government.[4] Thereafter, over the next half-dozen years or so, relations between Czechs and Germans seemed to improve; and, although the Great Depres-

[2] See Elizabeth Wiskemann, *Czechs and Germans* (London and New York, 1938), Robert J. Kerner (ed.), *Czechoslovakia* (Berkeley, 1945), and S. Harrison Thomson, *Czechoslovakia in European History*, 2nd ed. (Princeton, 1953), which may be compared with the passionately anti-Czech account of Wenzel Jaksch and Kurt Glazer, *Europe's Road to Potsdam* (New York, 1963).

[3] For a balanced account of the Czechoslovak question at the Paris Peace Conference—long the subject of bitter controversy between Czechs and Germans—see the important new work of Dagmar Perman, *The Shaping of the Czechoslovak State* (Leiden, 1962).

[4] Wiskemann, pp. 118-132.

sion hit the Sudeten German districts particularly hard, as late as November 1933, Dr. Benes, then Foreign Minister, told the American minister in Prague, that he saw no "danger of the German element attempting to leave the Czechoslovak state for incorporation in Germany."[5]

Hitler's rise to power soon changed all that. Himself born into the strife-torn Habsburg Empire in 1889, Hitler had, as a young man in Vienna, developed a bitter hatred of the Czechs and other minorities. "I was repelled," he wrote in *Mein Kampf*, "by the conglomeration of races which the capital showed me, repelled by this whole mixture of Czechs, Poles, Hungarians, Ruthenians, Serbs, and Croats, and everywhere the eternal mushroom of humanity—Jews, and more Jews. . . . The longer I lived in this city the more my hatred grew for the foreign mixture of peoples which had begun to corrode this old site of German culture."[6]

Hitler's political program, as revealed in *Mein Kampf*, was not only frankly Pan-German. It left no doubt that the subjection of the Slavic peoples in Europe was high on the list of his political priorities. "Today," Hitler wrote in *Mein Kampf*, "we count eighty million Germans in Europe! This foreign policy will be acknowledged as correct only if, after scarcely a hundred years, there are two hundred and fifty million Germans on this continent. . . . And so we National Socialists . . . take up where we left off six hundred years ago. We stop the endless German movement to the south and west, and turn our gaze toward the land in the East. If we speak of soil in Europe today, we can have primarily in mind only Russia and her vassal border states."[7]

During his first years in power, Hitler made no overt moves against Czechoslovakia. To be sure, there were repeated demands for greater political freedom for the German minority; vigorous protests against the allegedly anti-German character of the Russo-Czech alliance of 1935;[8] but also discreet overtures for a possible German-Czech détente and non-aggression pact, modelled after the German-Polish treaty of 1934—overtures that came to nothing as soon as the cost of such an accommodation became apparent to the Czechoslovak government.[9]

It seems perfectly clear now that Hitler's diplomatic efforts in this direction amounted to little more than shadow-boxing. His principal objectives, in his first years in office, were directed toward the Western democracies. While professing a deep concern for peace, non-aggression

[5] Dispatch from the United States Minister to Czechoslovakia (Francis White) to the Secretary of State, November 26, 1933 (500.A15 A 4/2395, National Archives).

[6] Boston, 1943, pp. 123-124.

[7] *Ibid.*, pp. 654, 675.

[8] See *Documents on German Foreign Policy 1918-1945*, Series C, Volumes I-IV (Washington, 1958-1961).

[9] These overtures were first officially revealed by President Benes in his *From Munich to New War and Victory* (Boston, 1954). See also Gerhard L. Weinberg, "Secret Hitler-Benes Negotiations, 1936-1937," *Journal of Central European Affairs*, XIX (1960).

pacts, and total disarmament, he sought, first of all, to break the disarmament provisions of the treaty of Versailles, then to remilitarize the
Rhineland, and, finally, to construct a powerful new set of fortifications
on Germany's western frontier, so as to block any possible French military assistance to Czechoslovakia and its other Eastern allies. Once these
objectives had been largely achieved, Hitler was ready to embark on his
Pan-German program in earnest.

II

At the close of the Second World War, most of the records of the
German Foreign Office fell into Allied hands. From these documents
it is possible for us to reconstruct in remarkable detail Hitler's specific
plans and policies in foreign affairs. The great turning point in German
foreign policy came on November 5, 1937. On that date Hitler called
together at the Reich Chancellery in Berlin his Foreign Minister and
his military chiefs. In a talk lasting more than four hours, he placed
before them the program he proposed to follow during the next few
years.

> Germany's future, Hitler declared, could only be safeguarded by acquiring
> additional *Lebensraum*. Such living space was to be sought, not overseas,
> but in Europe, and it could be found only at the risk of conflict. "There had
> never . . . been spaces without a master, and there were none today: the
> attacker always comes up against a possessor. The question for Germany
> was: where could she achieve the greatest gain at the lowest cost."[10]

Hitler left his audience in no doubt that that area was, as he had
written in *Mein Kampf*, in Eastern Europe, and that prominent in his
program of foreign expansion were both the annexation of Austria and
the destruction of Czechoslovakia.[11]

[10] Alan Bullock, *Hitler—A Study in Tyranny*, rev. ed. (New York, 1963), p. 368.

[11] See below, Document 1. There has recently been a tendency among some historians and other writers to downgrade the importance of the Hossbach Protocol, and
to question whether Hitler did indeed proceed from a methodical and carefully
thought-out plan of conquest. A. J. P. Taylor—in his much (and justly) criticized book
The Origins of the Second World War (1961)—was the first historian to question
the importance of the Hossbach Protocol. He was followed by David L. Hoggan,
Der Erzwungene Krieg (Tübingen, 1961), a generally discredited apology for Hitler's
foreign policy. In a heated defense of her husband's foreign policy—and that of
the Third Reich in general—Annelies von Ribbentrop has questioned at great length
both the accuracy and relevance of the Hossbach Protocol, citing among her authorities both Mr. Taylor and Mr. Hoggan. See her *Verschwörung gegen den Frieden*
(Leoni am Starnberger See, 1963), pp. 9-106, esp. 43-49, 101-104. The fact of the
matter is that the top Nazi leaders were well aware of the general direction of German foreign policy, and by late 1937 were increasingly outspoken in discussing the
ideas Hitler summed up at the Reich Chancellery meeting on November 5, 1937. It
is interesting to note—although few historians seem to have done so—that two weeks
after that historic conference Field Marshal Goering talked very frankly about the
future of German foreign policy with William C. Bullitt, the American Ambassador
to France, then visiting Berlin. "We are determined," Goering told Bullitt at that
time, "to join to the German Reich all Germans who are contiguous to the Reich and

Although the outside world of course knew nothing of these proceedings, Hitler soon set to work applying his master plan. By mid-March 1938 he had annexed Austria; and, although both Goering and other German government officials had given Czechoslovakia specific assurances that Germany had no designs whatever on Czechoslovak territory,[12] it was only a few weeks before the Sudeten German Nazis, in full agreement with Berlin, began a process of violent agitation. On the face of it, this agitation was designed to achieve widespread political concessions; in fact, it aimed at nothing less than the complete destruction of Czechoslovakia itself.[13]

Thus began the Sudeten Crisis—the crisis that brought all of Europe increasingly close to war during the summer of 1938; that brought about, in mid-September, two highly dramatic meetings between Hitler and Prime Minister Chamberlain[14]; and that led, in the end, to the historic Four Power Conference at Munich, on September 29-30, 1938.[15]

It was not entirely surprising that it was Mr. Chamberlain who took the lead in seeking to bring about a peaceful settlement of the German-Czechoslovak dispute. To be sure, as he frequently pointed out, Great Britain had no formal treaty commitments to Czechoslovakia—as did France, which was bound, by the terms of its treaty of October 1925, to come immediately to Czechoslovakia's defense, if she was attacked by Germany without provocation. On the other hand, because Great Britain was the leading, if not the most powerful, Western democracy; because France had increasingly come to accept British leadership even on continental affairs; and because a Franco-German war over Czechoslovakia might in the end also involve Great Britain, it was not surprising that it was Great Britain, rather than France, which took the lead, after May 1938, in seeking to bring about a peaceful, if not an amicable, settlement of the German demands.

The British approach was part of its general policy of "appeasement"—a policy that dated back a number of years, and had as its main objective the removal of what were considered to be Germany's legitimate grievances growing out of the Treaty of Versailles. "Appeasement," it was widely held, was the road to lasting peace in Europe.

---

are divided from the great body of the German race merely by the artificial barriers imposed by the treaty of Versailles." Bullitt asked Goering "if he meant that Germany was absolutely determined to annex Austria to the Reich. He replied that this was an absolute determination of the German Government. . . . I asked Goering [Bullitt reported] if the German Government was as decided in its views with regard to the Germans in Bohemia as it was with regard to Austria. He replied there could only be one final solution of this question. The Sudeten Germans must enter the German Reich as all other Germans who lived contiguous to the Reich." *Foreign Relations of the United States, 1937*, Volume I (Washington, 1954), p. 171.

[12] See below, Document 2.

[13] See below, Document 5.

[14] See below, Documents 13, 15, 16.

[15] See below, Documents 24, 25.

Most appeasers [Martin Gilbert and Richard Gott have written] agreed that Hitler was wild, vicious, and unpredictable. But they agreed that his viciousness would be modified, that his aims would eventually clarify, and that his wildness would end. Abrupt criticism would only anger him. Patience and kindness would bring him to reason. . . . If sensible Englishmen would meet Hitler at the right moment, and would speak to him in the right tone, he would be equally sensible. Once he could be persuaded to be reasonable there was a good chance of reaching agreement with him, and an Anglo-German agreement would prove as trustworthy as any agreement between two sovereign states. . . . Such was the logic of appeasement, defended with the fanaticism of a faith.[16]

It should be added at once that Mr. Chamberlain was not the author of this policy. Its origins dated back at least to 1933, when Sir John Simon was Foreign Secretary,[17] and it had been continued under his successors, Sir Samuel Hoare and Anthony Eden, from 1935 to early 1938.[18] But it was under Mr. Chamberlain that the policy was put to its most important test, and it is with his name that "appeasement" is inseparably connected.

But what of Mr. Chamberlain's approach to foreign affairs? Was he, as is sometimes suggested, an "inveterate appeaser," long prepared to accept peace-at-any-price with Hitler? Since 1946, parts of his private diary, and some of his most personal letters, have been published,[19] and we can understand much more fully now the wellsprings of his foreign policy. His foreign policy was motivated by three principal considerations.

In the first place, like many other Englishmen, he was deeply perturbed at some of the inequities of the Treaty of Versailles, and he believed that the time had come for these to be removed, provided such revisions were made peacefully, without the use or threat of force. "I don't see," he wrote to his sisters in November 1937, "why we shouldn't say to Germany, 'Give us satisfactory assurances that you won't use force to deal with the Austrians and the Czechoslovakians and we will give similar assurances that we won't use force to prevent the changes you want if you can get them by peaceful means'."[20]

In the second place, Mr. Chamberlain was deeply troubled by the ravages of the Great Depression, and the great urgency to ameliorate the pressing economic and social needs of the time. But for this to be done, armaments had to be cut and military spending reduced. The

[16] Martin Gilbert and Richard Gott, *The Appeasers* (Boston, 1963), pp. 32-33.

[17] See the thoughtful discussion by Gilbert and Gott, Chapter I, which may be compared with the magisterial account of Winston Churchill, *The Gathering Storm* (Boston, 1948), and A. L. Rowse's brilliant memoir of the 30's, *Appeasement—A Study in Political Decline, 1933-1939* (New York, 1961).

[18] This is borne out not only by the pertinent diplomatic evidence, notably the *Documents on German Foreign Policy 1918-1945*, but also by Eden's own account of these years, *Facing the Dictators* (Boston, 1963).

[19] See Sir Keith Feiling, *Neville Chamberlain* (London, 1946), and Iain Macleod, *Neville Chamberlain* (New York, 1961), and see below, documents 3, 7, 11, 12, 14, 29, 30.

[20] Quoted in Macleod, p. 208.

difference could then be applied to projects of recovery and reform. "To me," the Prime Minister told his Birmingham constituents in April 1938, "the very idea that the hard-won savings of our people, which ought to be devoted to the alleviation of suffering and to the opening out of fresh interests and recreation, to the care of the old and the development of the minds and bodies of the young—to think that all these savings should have to be dissipated on the construction of weapons of war is hateful and damnable."[21]

Finally, Mr. Chamberlain was a profoundly peaceful man. This is not to say that he was unaware of the character and policies of National Socialism, or that he approved of these in the slightest. From 1933 on, he had on numerous occasions expressed himself frankly on this subject.[22] On the other hand, recalling vividly the horrors and losses of the World War of 1914-1918, he deeply believed that another great war would be a catastrophe for Great Britain as well as for Europe, and that it must, therefore, be avoided at—almost—all cost.

But it was one thing to believe deeply in the necessity of peace, and the peaceful settlement of international disputes, and quite another to carry out this policy in practice. It is one of the principal purposes of this volume to show—on the basis of the available British and German documents, as well as other important sources—the nature and progress of German policy toward Czechoslovakia from November 1937 on, and how Mr. Chamberlain sought, month after month, from early 1938 onward, to bring about a peaceful settlement of the German-Czechoslovak dispute.

III

Although it was Hitler and Chamberlain who played the principal roles in the great drama that ended at Munich, it would be misleading to overlook the role played by France and Czechoslovakia, or by the United States.[23] The fact of the matter is that both Paris and Prague played important roles throughout the crisis, though in the end neither was able to influence Chamberlain's course of action decisively. In any case, to understand the Munich crisis fully, to see how the democratic states reacted to the German demands, and how they developed their policies from the first ominous signs in March 1938 to the final denouement at Munich, we must look at how the growing crisis appeared to the governments in Paris and Prague—to men like Paul Reynaud, then Minister of

[21] Quoted in Macleod, p. 208.

[22] Macleod, p. 206.

[23] "The fundamental reason for the Second World War," A. L. Rowse has written, "was the withdrawal of America out of the world system: that, more than anything, enabled the aggressors to get away with things. Not all the mistakes this country [Great Britain] was responsible for in the 1920s and 1930s equalled the one enormous and irreparable mistake America made in contracting out of responsibility." *Appeasement—A Study in Political Decline, 1933-1939*, p. 18.

Justice in the Daladier Cabinet,[24] and Hubert Ripka, a leading journalist and political confidant of President Benes.[25] For their memoirs are among the most revealing sources on the history of these crucial weeks and months.

In the end, however, it was London and Berlin that held the key to the crisis, and it was Hitler and Chamberlain who between them set the tone and terms of the final settlement. What was the atmosphere in London and Berlin in the agonizingly tense days before Munich? What was the role of the British Foreign Office, as the Prime Minister proceeded with his increasingly personal diplomacy? And what took place once Hitler and Mr. Chamberlain sat down at their fateful meetings—first at Berchtesgaden, then at Godesberg, and finally, joined by Daladier and Mussolini, at Munich?

Once it might have taken decades or generations for such records to become available. But not so in our own time. For we have, for instance, among the vast number of personal accounts, the memoirs of William (now Lord) Strang, then head of the Central Department of the Foreign Office, giving us an invaluable account of the inner history of British policy[26]; and the memoirs of the late Sir Ivone Kirkpatrick, then First Secretary of the British Embassy in Berlin, who served as translator at several meetings between Hitler and the Prime Minister, and whose description and comments on the Berlin scene are astute and revealing, and whose account of the atmosphere at Berchtesgaden, Godesberg, and Munich serves as a fresh reminder of what it was like to negotiate, under the threat of war, with one of the most ruthless and power-mad dictators in history.[27]

Above all, we have the stenographic minutes of those meetings, allowing us not only to verify such accounts as those of Lord Strang and Sir Ivone Kirkpatrick, but to follow the tortuous efforts by which the Prime Minister sought to bring about a negotiated settlement, and the way in which he retreated, step by step, from his original position.

IV

But history is something more than documents and memoirs put together. In the last analysis, the views and judgment of historians inevitably exert a powerful influence on our own opinions and attitudes toward particular historical men and events. What, then, of historical opinion of the Munich crisis?

Not surprisingly, perhaps, it has been far from unanimous. It will come as no surprise that Hitler's policies have found no support among responsible historians, though Mr. A. J. P. Taylor has recently argued

[24] See below, pp. 104-119.
[25] See below, pp. 90-103.
[26] See below, pp. 120-147.
[27] See below, pp. 74-89.

that he was less directly responsible for the development of the crisis than is usually thought.[28] On the other hand, historians have differed in their estimate of the Prime Minister's role and policies, and no doubt will continue to do. Most historians, it must be said, have been extremely critical of Mr. Chamberlain[29]—following, to a great extent, Winston Churchill's harsh indictment of him in *The Gathering Storm*. There has also been however, especially in recent years, a growing awareness of the enormous problems—political, military, psychological—that Mr. Chamberlain was confronted with as he carried on his negotiations with Hitler. This is the viewpoint reflected, for instance, in the recent biography by Mr. Iain Macleod.[30] Whatever our own view of the Prime Minister may be, he deserves to be judged on the merit of the evidence.

Most of the pertinent evidence on Hitler, Chamberlain, and the Munich crisis is now available. This little volume is intended as a representative sampler of it. Yet there are many questions that remain. For instance, did the Prime Minister ever intend to support the territorial integrity of Czechoslovakia, or was his policy designed to permit Hitler to achieve his real purposes? Was the Prime Minister's approach—particularly his repeated insistence on his own independence—the best suited to bring about a freely negotiated settlement between Berlin and Prague? Did Mr. Chamberlain, in his conversations with Hitler, overstep his constitutional authority, or was his position, at every important step, in line with official British policy? Ought Mr. Chamberlain to have paid less heed to Hitler's interminable claims, threats, and promises, and consulted more closely and more often with the French Government? Finally, did Mr. Chamberlain genuinely believe in the possibility of a lasting settlement with Hitler, or was his policy—throughout the crisis—based on his conviction that there was nothing that Britain and France could do to keep Hitler from overrunning Czechoslovakia, if he chose to do so, to say nothing of the fact that neither Britain nor France seemed militarily prepared to fight another great war with Germany?

These are some of the important questions that agitated political opinion in September 1938, and that have continued to preoccupy historians ever since. The great debate about Munich—its origins, its history, its meaning—is far from over.[31] This volume is intended as an introduction to that debate. It proceeds from Carl Becker's famous aphorism of more than thirty years ago: "Everyman his own historian"; and finds its meaning in George Santayana's urgent reminder that "those who do not remember the past are condemned to repeat its mistakes."

[28] See below, pp. 158-160. Mr. Taylor has elaborated this thesis at great length in his subsequent work *The Origins of the Second World War*.

[29] See, for example, H. R. Trevor-Roper, "Munich—Ten Years After," *The New York Times Magazine*, August 8, 1948, reprinted below, pp. 150-157.

[30] See below, pp. 161-173.

[31] See, for instance, Edward Whiting Fox, "Munich and Peace for *Our* Time?" *Virginia Quarterly Review*, January 1964.

The Documentary Record

🙣 *November 5, 1937*
to
October 2, 1938

1 MEMORANDUM

Berlin, November 10, 1937.

MINUTES OF THE CONFERENCE IN THE REICH CHANCELLERY, BERLIN,
NOVEMBER 5, 1937, FROM 4:15 TO 8:30 P.M.

PRESENT: The Führer and Chancellor; Field Marshal von Blomberg, War
Minister; Colonel General Baron von Fritsch, Commander in Chief,
Army; Admiral Dr. h. c. Raeder, Commander in Chief, Navy;
Colonel General Goering, Commander in Chief, *Luftwaffe;* Baron
von Neurath, Foreign Minister; Colonel Hossbach.[1]

The Führer began by stating that the subject of the present conference
was of such importance that its discussion would, in other countries, certainly be a matter for a full Cabinet meeting, but he—the Führer—had
rejected the idea of making it a subject of discussion before the wider
circle of the Reich Cabinet just because of the importance of the matter.
His exposition to follow was the fruit of thorough deliberation and the
experiences of his 4½ years of power. He wished to explain to the gentle-
men present his basic ideas concerning the opportunities for the development of our position in the field of foreign affairs and its requirements,
and he asked, in the interests of a long-term German policy, that his
exposition be regarded, in the event of his death, as his last will and
testament.

The Führer then continued:

The aim of German policy was to make secure and to preserve the
racial community [*Volksmasse*] and to enlarge it. It was therefore a
question of space.

The German racial community comprised over 85 million people and,
because of their number and the narrow limits of habitable space in
Europe, constituted a tightly packed racial core such as was not to be
met in any other country and such as implied the right to a greater
living space than in the case of other peoples. If, territorially speaking
there existed no political result corresponding to this German racial core,
that was a consequence of centuries of historical development, and in the
continuance of these political conditions lay the greatest danger to the
preservation of the German race at its present peak. To arrest the decline
of Germanism [*Deutschtum*] in Austria and Czechoslovakia was as little
possible as to maintain the present level in Germany itself. Instead of
increase, sterility was setting in, and in its train disorders of a social

[1] Adjutant to the Führer.

---

1 *Documents on German Foreign Policy 1918-1945* (abbrev. *German Documents*),
Series D, Vol. I (Washington, 1949), no. 19.

character must arise in course of time, since political and ideological ideas remain effective only so long as they furnish the basis for the realization of the essential vital demands of a people. Germany's future was therefore wholly conditional upon the solving of the need for space, and such a solution could be sought, of course, only for a foreseeable period of about one to three generations. . . .

Germany's problem could only be solved by means of force and this was never without attendant risk. The campaigns of Frederick the Great for Silesia and Bismarck's wars against Austria and France had involved unheard-of risk, and the swiftness of the Prussian action in 1870 had kept Austria from entering the war. If one accepts as the basis of the following exposition the resort to force with its attendant risks, then there remain still to be answered the questions "when" and "how." In this matter there were three cases [*Fälle*] to be dealt with:

Case 1: Period 1943-1945.

After this date only a change for the worse, from our point of view, could be expected.

The equipment of the army, navy, and *Luftwaffe,* as well as the formation of the officer corps, was nearly completed. Equipment and armament were modern; in further delay there lay the danger of their obsolescence. In particular, the secrecy of "special weapons" could not be preserved forever. The recruiting of reserves was limited to current age groups; further drafts from older untrained age groups were no longer available.

Our relative strength would decrease in relation to the rearmament which would by then have been carried out by the rest of the world. If we did not act by 1943–45, any year could, in consequence of a lack of reserves, produce the food crisis, to cope with which the necessary foreign exchange was not available, and this must be regarded as a "waning point of the regime." Besides, the world was expecting our attack and was increasing its counter-measures from year to year. It was while the rest of the world was still preparing its defenses [*sich abriegele*] that we were obliged to take the offensive.

Nobody knew today what the situation would be in the years 1943–45. One thing only was certain, that we could not wait longer.

On the one hand there was the great *Wehrmacht,* and the necessity of maintaining it at its present level, the aging of the movement and of its leaders; and on the other, the prospect of a lowering of the standard of living and of a limitation of the birth rate, which left no choice but to act. If the Führer was still living, it was his unalterable resolve to solve Germany's problem of space at the latest by 1943–45. The necessity for action before 1943–45 would arise in cases 2 and 3.

Case 2

If internal strife in France should develop into such a domestic crisis as to absorb the French Army completely and render it incapable of use

for war against Germany, then the time for action against the Czechs
had come.

Case 3

If France is so embroiled by a war with another state that she cannot
"proceed" against Germany.

For the improvement of our politico-military position our first objective, in the event of our being embroiled in war, must be to overthrow
Czechoslovakia and Austria simultaneously in order to remove the threat
to our flank in any possible operation against the West. In a conflict with
France it was hardly to be regarded as likely that the Czechs would
declare war on us on the very same day as France. The desire to join in
the war would, however, increase among the Czechs in proportion to
any weakening on our part and then her participation could clearly take
the form of an attack toward Silesia, toward the north or toward the west.

If the Czechs were overthrown and a common German-Hungarian
frontier achieved, a neutral attitude on the part of Poland could be the
more certainly counted on in the event of a Franco-German conflict. Our
agreements with Poland only retained their force as long as Germany's
strength remained unshaken. In the event of German setbacks a Polish
action against East Prussia, and possibly against Pomerania and Silesia
as well, had to be reckoned with.

On the assumption of a development of the situation leading to action
on our part as planned, in the years 1943–45, the attitude of France,
Britain, Italy, Poland, and Russia could probably be estimated as follows:

Actually, the Führer believed that almost certainly Britain, and probably France as well, had already tacitly written off the Czechs and were
reconciled to the fact that this question would be cleared up in due
course by Germany. Difficulties connected with the Empire, and the
prospect of being once more entangled in a protracted European war,
were decisive considerations for Britain against participation in a war
against Germany. Britain's attitude would certainly not be without
influence on that of France. An attack by France without British support,
and with the prospect of the offensive being brought to a standstill on our
western fortifications, was hardly probable. Nor was a French march
through Belgium and Holland without British support to be expected;
this also was a course not to be contemplated by us in the event of a
conflict with France, because it would certainly entail the hostility of
Britain. It would of course be necessary to maintain a strong defense
[eine Abriegelung] on our western frontier during the prosecution of
our attack on the Czechs and Austria. And in this connection it had to
be remembered that the defense measures of the Czechs were growing
in strength from year to year, and that the actual worth of the Austrian
Army also was increasing in the course of time. Even though the populations concerned, especially of Czechoslovakia, were not sparse, the annexation of Czechoslovakia and Austria would mean an acquisition of food-

stuffs for 5 to 6 million people, on the assumption that the compulsory emigration of 2 million people from Czechoslovakia and 1 million people from Austria was practicable. The incorporation of these two States with Germany meant, from the politico-military point of view, a substantial advantage because it would mean shorter and better frontiers, the freeing of forces for other purposes, and the possibility of creating new units up to a level of about 12 divisions, that is, 1 new division per million inhabitants.

Italy was not expected to object to the elimination of the Czechs, but it was impossible at the moment to estimate what her attitude on the Austrian question would be; that depended essentially upon whether the Duce were still alive.

The degree of surprise and the swiftness of our action were decisive factors for Poland's attitude. Poland—with Russia at her rear—will have little inclination to engage in war against a victorious Germany.

Military intervention by Russia must be countered by the swiftness of our operations; however, whether such an interventio. was a practical contingency at all was, in view of Japan's attitude, more than doubtful.

Should case 2 arise—the crippling of France by civil war—the situation thus created by the elimination of the most dangerous opponent must be seized upon *whenever it occurs* for the blow against the Czechs.

The Führer saw case 3 coming definitely nearer; it might emerge from the present tensions in the Mediterranean, and he was resolved to take advantage of it whenever it happened, even as early as 1938. . . .

If Germany made use of this war to settle the Czech and Austrian questions, it was to be assumed that Britain—herself at war with Italy—would decide not to act against Germany. Without British support, a warlike action by France against Germany was not to be expected.

The time for our attack on the Czechs and Austria must be made dependent on the course of the Anglo-French-Italian war and would not necessarily coincide with the commencement of military operations by these three States. Nor had the Führer in mind military agreements with Italy, but wanted, while retaining his own independence of action, to exploit this favorable situation, which would not occur again, to begin and carry through the campaign against the Czechs. This descent upon the Czechs would have to be carried out with "lightning speed." . . .

HOSSBACH

CERTIFIED CORRECT:
Colonel (General Staff)

2 EXTRACT *from Statement by Prime Minister Chamberlain in the House of Commons*

March 14, 1938.

. . . The Czech Government have officially informed His Majesty's Government that though it is their earnest desire to live on the best possible neighbourly relations with the German Reich, they have followed with the greatest attention the development of events in Austria between the date of the Austro-German Agreement of July, 1936, up to the present day. I am informed that Field-Marshal Goering on March 11 gave a general assurance to the Czech Minister in Berlin[1]—an assurance which he expressly renewed later on behalf of Herr Hitler—that it would be the earnest endeavour of the German Government to improve German-Czech relations. In particular, on March 12, Field-Marshal Goering informed the Czech Minister that German troops marching into Austria had received the strictest orders to keep at least fifteen kilometres from the Czech frontier. On the same day the Czechoslovak Minister in Berlin was assured by Baron von Neurath that Germany considered herself bound by the German-Czechoslovak Arbitration Convention of October, 1925. . . .

3 LETTER *from Neville Chamberlain to Ida Chamberlain*

March 20, 1938.

With Franco winning in Spain by the aid of German guns and Italian planes, with a French government in which one cannot have the slightest

---

[1] The Prime Minister's reference here was to repeated assurances given to M. Mastny, the Czechoslovak Minister to Germany, by Field Marshal Goering, on the evening of March 11, and on the following afternoon, that on "his word of honor" Germany had no evil intentions whatever toward Czechoslovakia. On the second occasion, Goering told Mastny that he spoke in the name of Hitler himself. For records of these conversations, see *German Documents*, Series D, Vol. II, nos. 74, 78.—F.L.L.

2 Monica Curtis (ed.) *Documents on International Affairs*, 1938, Volume II (London and New York, 1943), p. 120.

3 Sir Keith Feiling, *Neville Chamberlain* (London, 1946), pp. 347-348.

confidence and which I suspect to be in closish touch with our Opposition, with the Russians stealthily and cunningly pulling all the strings behind the scenes to get us involved in war with Germany (our Secret Service doesn't spend all its time looking out of the window), and finally with a Germany flushed with triumph, and all too conscious of her power, the prospect looked black indeed. In face of such problems, to be badgered and pressed to come out and give a clear, decided, bold, and unmistakable lead, show "ordinary courage," and all the rest of the twaddle, is calculated to vex the man who has to take the responsibility for the consequences. As a matter of fact, the plan of the "Grand Alliance," as Winston calls it, had occurred to me long before he mentioned it. . . . I talked about it to Halifax, and we submitted it to the chiefs of the Staff and the F.O. experts. It is a very attractive idea; indeed, there is almost everything to be said for it until you come to examine its practicability. From that moment its attraction vanishes. You have only to look at the map to see that nothing that France or we could do could possibly save Czechoslovakia from being overrun by the Germans, if they wanted to do it. The Austrian frontier is practically open; the great Skoda munition works are within easy bombing distance of the German aerodromes, the railways all pass through German territory, Russia is 100 miles away. Therefore we could not help Czechoslovakia—she would simply be a pretext for going to war with Germany. That we could not think of unless we had a reasonable prospect of being able to beat her to her knees in a reasonable time, and of that I see no sign. I have therefore abandoned any idea of giving guarantees to Czechoslovakia, or the French in connection with her obligations to that country.

4   EXTRACTS *from Speech by Prime Minister Chamberlain in the House of Commons*

March 24, 1938.

. . . I now turn to the situation with which we are more particularly concerned this afternoon. His Majesty's Government have expressed the view that recent events in Austria have created a new situation, and we think it right to state the conclusions to which consideration of these events has led us. We have already placed on record our judgment upon the action taken by the German Government [the invasion of Austria]. I have nothing to add to that. But the consequences still remain. There has been a profound disturbance of international confidence. In these

---

4 *Documents on International Affairs,* pp. 121-123.

circumstances the problem before Europe, to which in the opinion of His Majesty's Government it is their most urgent duty to direct their attention, is how best to restore this shaken confidence, how to maintain the rule of law in international affairs, how to seek peaceful solutions to questions that continue to cause anxiety. Of these the one which is necessarily most present to many minds is that which concerns the relations between the Government of Czechoslovakia and the German minority in that country; and it is probable that a solution of this question, if it could be achieved, would go far to re-establish a sense of stability over an area much wider than that immediately concerned.

Accordingly, the Government have given special attention to this matter, and in particular they have fully considered the question whether the United Kingdom, in addition to those obligations by which she is already bound by the Covenant of the League and the Treaty of Locarno, should, as a further contribution towards preserving peace in Europe, now undertake new and specific commitments in Europe, and in particular such a commitment in relation to Czechoslovakia. I think it is right that I should here remind the House what are our existing commitments, which might lead to the use of our arms for purposes other than our own defence and the defence of territories of other parts of the British Commonwealth of Nations. They are, first of all, the defence of France and Belgium against unprovoked aggression in accordance with our existing obligations under the Treaty of Locarno, as reaffirmed in the arrangement which was drawn up in London on 19th March 1936. We have also obligations by treaty to Portugal, Iraq, and Egypt. Those are our definite obligations to particular countries.

There remains another case in which we may have to use our arms, a case which is of a more general character, but which may have no less significance. It is the case arising under the Covenant of the League of Nations which was accurately defined by the former Foreign Secretary[1] when he said:

> In addition, our armaments may be used in bringing help to a victim of aggression in any case where in our judgment it would be proper under the provision of the Covenant to do so.

The case might, for example, include Czechoslovakia. The ex-Foreign Secretary went on to say:

> I use the word "may" deliberately, since in such an instance there is no automatic obligation to take military action. It is moreover right that this should be so, for nations cannot be expected to incur automatic military obligations save for areas where their vital interests are concerned.

[1] Anthony Eden—F.L.L.

His Majesty's Government stand by these declarations. They have acknowledged that in present circumstances the ability of the League to fulfil all the functions originally contemplated for it is reduced; but this is not to be interpreted as meaning that His Majesty's Government would in no circumstances intervene as a member of the League for the restoration of peace or the maintenance of international order if circumstances were such as to make it appropriate for them to do so. And I cannot but feel that the course and development of any dispute, should such unhappily arise, would be greatly influenced by the knowledge that such action as it may be in the power of Great Britain to take will be determined by His Majesty's Government of the day in accordance with the principles laid down in the Covenant.

The question now arises, whether we should go further. Should we forthwith give an assurance to France that, in the event of her being called upon by reason of German aggression on Czechoslovakia to implement her obligations under the Franco-Czechoslovak Treaty, we would immediately employ our full military force on her behalf? Or, alternatively, should we at once declare our readiness to take military action in resistance to any forcible interference with the independence and integrity of Czechoslovakia, and invite any other nations, which might so desire, to associate themselves with us in such a declaration?

From a consideration of these two alternatives it clearly emerges that under either of them the decision as to whether or not this country should find itself involved in war would be automatically removed from the discretion of His Majesty's Government, and the suggested guarantee would apply irrespective of the circumstances by which it was brought into operation, and over which His Majesty's Government might not have been able to exercise any control. This position is not one that His Majesty's Government could see their way to accept, in relation to an area where their vital interests are not concerned in the same degree as they are in the case of France and Belgium; it is certainly not the position that results from the Covenant. For these reasons His Majesty's Government feel themselves unable to give the prior guarantee suggested.

But while plainly stating this decision I would add this. Where peace and war are concerned, legal obligations are not alone involved, and, if war broke out, it would be unlikely to be confined to those who have assumed such obligations. It would be quite impossible to say where it would end and what Governments might become involved. The inexorable pressure of facts might well prove more powerful than formal pronouncements, and in that event it would be well within the bounds of probability that other countries, besides those which were parties to the original dispute, would almost immediately become involved. This is especially true in the case of two countries like Great Britain and France, with long associations of friendship, with interests closely interwoven, devoted to the same ideals of democratic liberty, and determined to uphold them. . . .

So far as Czechoslovakia is concerned, it seems to His Majesty's Government that now is the time when all the resources of diplomacy should be enlisted in the cause of peace. They have been glad to take note of and in no way underrate the definite assurances given by the German Government as to their attitude. On the other side they have observed with satisfaction that the Government of Czechoslovakia are addressing themselves to the practical steps that can be taken within the framework of the Czechoslovak constitution to meet the reasonable wishes of the German minority. For their part, His Majesty's Government will at all times be ready to render any help in their power, by whatever means might seem most appropriate, towards the solution of questions likely to cause difficulty between the German and Czechoslovak Governments. In the meantime, there is no need to assume the use of force, or, indeed, to talk about it. Such talk is to be strongly deprecated. Not only can it do no good; it is bound to do harm. It must interfere with the progress of diplomacy, and it must increase feelings of insecurity and uncertainty. . . .

5 REPORT by Konrad Henlein on his Audience with Hitler[1]

TOP SECRET, MILITARY

TO BE HANDLED ONLY BY OFFICERS

Besides the Führer, Reich Minister Hess, the Führer's Deputy, von Ribbentrop, the Foreign Minister, and *Obergruppenführer* Lorenz were also present, and the conversation lasted for almost three hours. The Führer stated that he intended to settle the Sudeten German problem in the not-too-distant future. He could no longer tolerate Germans being oppressed or fired upon. He told Henlein that he knew how popular he [Henlein] was and that he was the rightful leader of the Sudeten German element, and as a result of his popularity and attractiveness he would triumph over circumstances. To Heinlein's objection that he, Henlein, could only be a substitute, Hitler replied: I will stand by you; from tomorrow you will be my Viceroy *[Statthalter]*. I will not tolerate difficulties being made for you by any department whatsoever within the Reich.

[1] Henlein visited Berlin on March 28, 1938. This document, from the State Secretary's files, was Weizäcker's preliminary report on his conversation with the leader of the Nazi Sudeten Party.—F. L. L.

The purport of the instructions, which the Führer has given to Henlein, is that demands should be made by the Sudeten German Party which are unacceptable to the Czech Government. In spite of the favorable situation created by the events in Austria, Henlein does not intend to drive things to the limit, but merely to put forward the old demands for self-administration and reparation at the Party Rally (April 23–24, 1938).[2] He wishes to reserve for later on a suggestion of the Führer's that he should demand their own German regiments with German officers, and military commands [*Kommandosprache*] to be given in German. The Reich will not intervene of its own accord. Henlein himself would be responsible for events for the time being. However, there would have to be close cooperation. Henlein summarized his view to the Führer as follows: We must always demand so much that we can never be satisfied. The Führer approved this view.

The Führer appreciates the great success which Henlein has had in England[3] and has requested him to go to London again, as soon as he possibly can, and to continue to use his influence with a view to ensuring nonintervention by Britain. As for the position of France, the Führer believes that in certain circumstances the possibility of a revolution in France can be reckoned with. . . .

6 MEMORANDUM *on Operation "Green"*[4]

TOP SECRET, MILITARY   BERLIN, April 22, 1938.

Plan for Operation "Green" [*Fall Grün*].
Summary of Führer—General Keitel conversation on April 21.[5]

A. POLITICAL

(1) Idea of strategic attack out of the blue without cause or possibility of justification is rejected. Reason: hostile world opinion which might lead to serious situation. Such measures only justified for elimination of last enemy on the Continent.

(2) Action after a period of diplomatic discussions which gradually lead to a crisis and to war.

---

[2] The Sudeten German Party Congress at Karlsbad (Karlovy Vary) on April 23-24, 1938.

[3] Henlein last visited London on October 10-15, 1937. His next visit was on May 12.

[4] Operation "Green" (*Fall Grün*) was the German code name for the plan of attack on Czechoslovakia. The word *"Grün"* is similarly used in the documents merely as the code name for Czechoslovakia.

[5] Initialed by the Führer's Adjutant (Schmundt).

6 *German Documents,* Series D, Vol. II, no. 133.

(3) Lightning action based on an incident (for example the murder of the German Minister in the course of an anti-German demonstration).

B. MILITARY CONCLUSIONS

(1) Preparations to be made for political contingencies 2 and 3. Contingency 2 is undesirable because "Green" security measures will have been taken.

(2) The loss of time through transport by rail of the bulk of the divisions—which is unavoidable and must be reduced to a minimum—must not be allowed to divert from lightning attack at the time of action.

(3) "Partial thrusts" toward breaching the defense line at numerous points and in operationally advantageous directions are to be undertaken at once.

These thrusts are to be prepared down to the smallest detail (knowledge of the routes, the objectives, composition of the columns according to tasks allotted them).

Simultaneous attack by land and air forces.

The *Luftwaffe* is to support the individual columns (for instance, dive bombers, sealing off fortification works at the points of penetration; hindering the movement of reserves; destruction of signal communications and thus isolating the garrisons).

(4) The first 4 days of military action are, politically speaking, decisive. In the absence of outstanding military successes, a European crisis is certain to arise. *Faits accomplis* must convince foreign powers of the hopelessness of military intervention; call in allies to the scene (sharing the booty!); demoralize "Green."

Hence, bridging the period between first penetration of enemy's lines and throwing into action the advancing troops by the determined ruthless advance of a motorized army (for instance through Pi past Pr).[6]

(5) If possible, separation of the transport movement "Red" ["*Rot*"][7] from "Green." A simultaneous deployment of "Red" might cause "Red" to adopt undesirable measures. On the other hand operation "Red" must at all times be ready to come into action.

C. PROPAGANDA

(1) Leaflets for the conduct of the Germans in "Green" territory [*Grünland*].

(2) Leaflets with threats to intimidate the "Greens."

SCHM[UNDT]
Written by hand of officer

[6] Presumably meaning "through Pilsen and by-passing Prague."

[7] Operation "Red" (*Fall Rot*) was the German code name for the military plan on the western frontier against France in the event of her mobilizing against the Reich defense of Czechoslovakia. Similarly the word "*Rot*" is used in the documents merely as the code name for France.

7 LETTER *from Neville Chamberlain to Ida Chamberlain*

May 28, 1938

I cannot doubt in my own mind (1) that the German government made all preparations for a coup, (2) that in the end they decided, after getting our warnings, that the risks were too great, (3) that the general view that this was just what had happened made them conscious that they had lost prestige and (4) that they are venting their spite on us because they feel that we have got the credit for giving them a check. . . . But the incident* shows how utterly untrustworthy and dishonest the German government is. . . .

8 DIRECTIVE *for Operation "Green"*[1] *from Hitler to the Commanders in Chief*[2]

BERLIN, May 30, 1938.

TOP SECRET, MILITARY

Supreme Commander of the *Wehrmacht*.
O.K.W. No. 42/38 Top Secret, Military. L I
ONLY TO BE HANDLED BY AN OFFICER
WRITTEN BY AN OFFICER

By order of the Supreme Commander of the *Wehrmacht*, part 2, section II of the directive on the combined preparations for war of the *Wehrmacht* of June 24, 1937 (Supreme Headquarters No. 55/37, Top Secret, Mil. L I a).[3] (War on Two Fronts With Main Effort in the Southeast, Strategic Concentration "Green") is to be replaced by the

---

* Mr. Chamberlain's reference here was to the crisis of May 20-22 brought on by reports of German troop concentrations, a crisis which did much to increase tension between the powers.—F. L. L.

[1] This document is from the Schmundt file (Nuremberg document 388–PS).

[2] With Covering Letter from the Chief of Supreme Headquarters, the Wehrmacht (Keitel).

[3] This directive of June 1937 is not printed.

---

7 Feiling, p. 354.
8 *German Documents*, Series D, Vol. II, no. 221.

attached version. Its execution must be assured by October 1, 1938, at the latest.

Alternations to the other parts of the directive are to be expected during the next few weeks.

KEITEL
Chief of the Supreme Headquarters
of the Wehrmacht

To: C.–in–C. Army
   " " " Navy
   " " " Air Force
    O.K.W. Section L

Certified true copy,
ZEITZLER
Lieut. Colonel, General Staff

[Enclosure]

TOP SECRET, MILITARY   Copy of 4th version.

Appendix to: Supreme Commander of the *Wehrmacht* O.K.W. No. 42/38, Top Secret, Military, L I a, dated May 30, 1938.

ONLY TO BE HANDLED BY AN OFFICER
WRITTEN BY AN OFFICER

II. WAR ON TWO FRONTS WITH MAIN EFFORT IN SOUTHEAST (STRATEGIC CONCENTRATION "GREEN")

1) *Political Assumptions.*

It is my unalterable decision to smash Czechoslovakia by military action in the near future. It is the business of the political leadership to await or bring about the suitable moment from a political and military point of view.

An unavoidable development of events within Czechoslovakia, or other political events in Europe providing a suddenly favorable opportunity which may never recur, may cause me to take early action.

The proper choice and determined exploitation of a favorable moment is the surest guarantee of success. To this end preparations are to be made immediately.

2) *Political Possibilities for Commencing the Operation.*

The following are necessary prerequisites for the intended attack:

a) A convenient apparent excuse and, with it;

b) Adequate political justification,

c) Action not expected by the enemy which will find him in the least possible state of readiness.

Most favorable from a military as well as a political point of view would be lightning action as the result of an incident which would subject Germany to unbearable provocation, and which, in the eyes of at least a part of world opinion, affords the moral justification for military measures.

Moreover, any period of diplomatic tension prior to war must be terminated by sudden action on our part, unexpected in both timing and extent, before the enemy is so far advanced in his state of military readiness that he cannot be overtaken.

3) *Conclusions for the Preparation of Operation "Green."*

a) For the military operations it is essential to make the fullest use of the surprise element as the most important factor contributing to victory, by means of appropriate preparatory measures, already in peace-time, and an unexpected swiftness of action.

Thus it is essential to create a situation within the first two or three days which demonstrates to enemy states which wish to intervene the hopelessness of the Czech military position, and also provides an incentive to those states which have territorial claims upon Czechoslovakia to join in immediately against her. In this case the intervention of Hungary and Poland against Czechoslovakia can be expected, particularly if France, as a result of Italy's unequivocal attitude on our side, fears, or at least hesitates, to unleash a European war by intervening against Germany. In all probability attempts by Russia to give Czechoslovakia military support, particularly with her air force, are to be expected.

If concrete successes are not achieved in the first few days by land operations, a European crisis will certainly arise. Realization of this ought to give commanders of all ranks an incentive to resolute and bold action.

b) *Propaganda warfare* must on the one hand intimidate the Czechs by means of threats and wear down their power of resistance; and on the other hand it must give the national racial groups indications as to how to support our military operations and influence the neutrals in our favor. Further instructions and determination of the appropriate moment are reserved to me.

4) *Tasks of the Wehrmacht.*

Wehrmacht preparations are to be carried out on the following principles:

a) The whole weight of all forces must be employed against Czechoslovakia.

b) In the West, a minimum strength is to be provided as cover for our rear, as may become necessary; the other frontiers in the East against Poland and Lithuania are only to be held defensively; the southern frontier to remain under observation.

c) The army formations capable of rapid employment must force the frontier fortifications with speed and energy, and must break very boldly into Czechoslovakia in the certainty that the bulk of the mobile army will be brought up with all possible speed.

Preparations for this are to be made and timed in such a way that the army formations most capable of rapid movement cross the frontier at the appointed time *simultaneously* with the penetration by the *Luftwaffe,* before the enemy can become aware of our mobilization.

To this end a timetable is to be drawn up by the Army and *Luftwaffe* in conjunction with O.K.W. and submitted to me for approval. . . .

ADOLF HITLER

Certified true copy
ZEITZLER
Lieut. Colonel, General Staff

9   GENERAL STRATEGIC DIRECTIVE[1]

BERLIN, June 18, 1938.

TOP SECRET—MILITARY
L I a
ONLY TO BE SEEN BY OFFICERS
WRITTEN BY AN OFFICER
1ST DRAFT FOR THE NEW DIRECTIVE

GENERAL GUIDING PRINCIPLES

1) There is no danger of a preventive war by foreign states against Germany.

Germany has not committed herself to any military alliance which would automatically draw Germany into a warlike conflict between foreign powers.

The settlement of the Czech question by my own free decision stands as the immediate aim in the forefront of my political intentions. I am resolved, as from October 1, 1938, onward, to make full use of every favorable political opportunity for the realization of this aim.

Friends, interested parties, and enemies could thereby be brought in and other powers remain indifferent, although they could not be included with absolute certainty in any one of these categories beforehand.

[1] This is a document drafted for Hitler's signature by the General Staff, and is taken from the Schmundt file produced as document No. 388–PS at the Nuremberg trials.

I shall, however, only decide to take action against Czechoslovakia if, as in the case of the occupation of the demilitarized zone and the entry into Austria, I am firmly convinced that France will not march and therefore Britain will not intervene either.

2) The preparations by the *Wehrmacht* must cover:

(*a*) Thorough preparations for action against Czechoslovakia (Operation "Green"). . . .

(*b*) The maintenance of the existing Operation "Red" (strategic concentration with the main effort against the West). . . .

(*c*) Special preparations mainly in the form of studies and planning within the Supreme Headquarters. . . .

Z[EITZLER]

K[EITEL]

10 EXTRACTS *from Speech by Prime Minister Chamberlain in the House of Commons*

July 26, 1938.

. . . In recent weeks the attention of His Majesty's Government has necessarily been particularly directed to two areas in Europe. One is that with which I have been dealing, the other is Czechoslovakia. In dealing with Czechoslovakia, it is very difficult for people in this country, with the exception of a comparatively small number who have made a special study of the position, to arrive at a just conclusion as to the rights and wrongs of the dispute between the Czechoslovakian Government and the Sudeten Germans. Many of us would have been very glad if we could have left this matter to be decided by the two parties concerned; but, unfortunately, here again we are only too conscious that there are all the materials present for a breach of the peace, with incalculable consequences, if the matter is not handled boldly and with a reasonable amount of speed. Therefore, in accordance with our general policy, and in close association with France, we have done everything that we could to facilitate a peaceful solution of the dispute. It is a problem which, in one form or another, has existed for centuries, and it would perhaps be unreasonable to expect that a difficulty which has been going on so long should be capable of solution in a few short weeks.

The right hon. Gentleman spoke of one of the many rumours which he has collected, without very much authority behind them. This was to the effect that we were hustling the Czech Government. . . . I should

---

10 *Documents on International Affairs*, pp. 166-168.

like to assure the right hon. Gentleman that there is no truth in it.
Indeed, the very opposite is the truth. Our anxiety has been rather lest
the Czechoslovakian Government should be too hasty in dealing with a
situation of such delicacy that it was most desirable that the two sides
should not get into a position where they were set, and unable to have
any further give-and-take between them. . . .

But while we have felt that an agreement voluntarily come to, if it
could be reached between the Sudeten Germans and the Czech Government, would be the best solution, nevertheless, as time has gone on it
has begun to appear doubtful whether, without some assistance from
outside, such a voluntary agreement could take place. In those circumstances, His Majesty's Government have been considering whether there
were some other way in which they could lend their help to bring the
negotiators together, and, in response to a request from the Government
of Czechoslovakia, we have agreed to propose a person with the necessary experience and qualities to investigate this subject on the spot and
endeavour, if need be, to suggest means for bringing the negotiations
to success. Such an investigator and mediator would, of course, be independent of His Majesty's Government—in fact, he would be independent
of all Governments. He would act only in his personal capacity, and it
would be necessary, of course, that he should have all the facilities and
all the information placed at his disposal in order to enable him to carry
through his task.

I cannot assert that a proposal of that kind will necessarily bring
about a solution of this problem, but I think it may have two valuable
results. First of all, I think it would go far to inform public opinion
generally as to the real facts of the case, and, secondly, I hope that it
may mean that issues which hitherto have appeared intractable may
prove, under the influence of such a mediator, to be less obstinate than
we have thought. But it is quite obvious that the task of any one who
undertakes this duty is going to be a very exacting, very responsible,
and very delicate one, and His Majesty's Government feel that they are
fortunate in having secured from Lord Runciman a promise to undertake it, provided he is assured of the confidence of the Sudeten
Germans—I hope he will be—as well as the assistance of the Czechoslovakian Government. Lord Runciman was a Member of this House so
long that he is well known to many hon. Members. I think they will
agree with me that he has outstanding personal qualifications for the
task he has undertaken. He has a long experience of public affairs and
of men of all sorts and conditions. He is characterized by fearlessness,
freedom from prejudice, integrity, and impartiality, and I am quite
certain that every one here will wish him all success. . . .

He is an investigator and mediator—that is what I called him. He will
try to acquaint himself with all the facts and the views of the two sides,
and he will no doubt see them separately, and perhaps later on he will
be able to make some proposals to them which will help them. He is in

the position, so well known to the hon. Member, of a man who goes down to assist in settling a strike. He has to see two sides who have come to a point when they cannot go any further. He is there as an independent, impartial person. . . .

We have impressed upon the Government of Czechoslovakia, and also upon the German Government, our own sense of the desirability of restraint. We have noted with satisfaction the efforts which the Czech Government have made, and we have also been very happy to receive assurances, only recently renewed, from the German Government of their own desire for a peaceful solution. . . .

If only we could find some peaceful solution of this Czechoslovakian question, I should myself feel that the way was open again for a further effort for a general appeasement—an appeasement which cannot be obtained until we can be satisfied that no major cause of difference or dispute remains unsettled. We have already demonstrated the possibility of a complete agreement between a democratic and a totalitarian State, and I do not myself see why that experience should not be repeated. When Herr Hitler made his offer of a Naval Treaty[1] under which the German fleet was to be restricted to an agreed level bearing a fixed ratio to the size of the British fleet, he made a notable gesture of a most practical kind in the direction of peace, the value of which it seems to me has not ever been fully appreciated as tending towards this general appeasement. There the treaty stands as a demonstration that it is possible for Germany and ourselves to agree upon matters which are vital to both of us. Since agreement has already been reached on that point, I do not think that we ought to find it impossible to continue our efforts at understanding, which, if they were successful, would do so much to bring back confidence. . . .

11 PRIVATE DIARY, *Neville Chamberlain*

September 3, 1938.

Is it not positively horrible to think that the fate of hundreds of millions depends on one man, and he is half mad? I keep racking my brains to try and devise some means of averting a catastrophe, if it should seem to be upon us. I thought of one so unconventional and daring that it rather took Halifax's breath away. But since Henderson thought it might save the situation at the 11th hour, I haven't abandoned it, though I hope all the time that it won't be necessary to try it.

[1] Refers to the Anglo-German Naval Agreement of June 1935.—F. L. L.

11 Feiling, p. 357.

12 PRIVATE DIARY, *Neville Chamberlain*

September 11, 1938.

I fully realise that, if eventually things go wrong and the aggression takes place, there will be many, including Winston, who will say that the British government must bear the responsibility, and that if only they had had the courage to tell Hitler now that, if he used force, we should at once declare war, that would have stopped him. By that time it will be impossible to prove the contrary, but I am satisfied that we should be wrong to allow the most vital decision that any country could take, the decision as to peace or war, to pass out of our hands into those of the ruler of another country, and a lunatic at that. I have been fortified in this view by reading a very interesting book on the foreign policy of Canning.[1] . . . Over and over again Canning lays it down that you should never menace unless you are in a position to carry out your threats, and although, if we have to fight I should hope we should be able to give a good account of ourselves, we are certainly not in a position in which our military advisers would feel happy in undertaking to begin hostilities if we were not forced to do so.

There is another consideration which, of course, our critics cannot have in mind, and that is the plan,[2] the nature of which I think you have guessed correctly. The time for this has not yet arrived, and it is always possible that Hitler might act so unexpectedly as to forestall it. That is a risk which we have to take, but in the meantime I do not want to do anything which would destroy its chance of success because, if it came off, it would go far beyond the present crisis, and might prove the opportunity for bringing about a complete change in the international situation.

---

[1] Professor Harold Temperley's *Foreign Policy of Canning.*
[2] Mr. Chamberlain's reference here was to his plan to pay a personal visit to Hitler.—F. L. L.

---

12 Feiling, pp. 360-1.

13

MEMORANDUM *on the Conversation Between Hitler and Prime Minister Chamberlain at the Obersalzberg (Berchtesgaden)*[1]

Mr. Chamberlain mentioned in his introductory remarks that since he had become Prime Minister of Great Britain he had always worked for an Anglo-German *rapprochement* and had always been on the lookout for opportunities to put his intentions into practice. In spite of occasional difficulties in Anglo-German relations, he had nevertheless again and again had the feeling that there was the possibility of strengthening mutual relations by a direct exchange of views. During the last weeks the situation had now become so difficult and grave that the danger of a conflict had seemed to him extremely close. Yet, even if both countries avoided becoming directly involved, the tension in Europe would have developed in a fashion anything but conducive to a *rapprochement* between the two countries.

Quite apart from the Czechoslovak question there were today much greater problems down for discussion and, conscious of this tension, he had therefore undertaken the journey to Germany in order, by means of a direct conversion with the Führer, to attempt to clarify the situation.

The Führer replied that he was well aware of the significance of the British Prime Minister's journey. The whole German nation welcomed this journey, as Mr. Chamberlain could, of course, have gathered from the demonstrations of sympathy which he had received from the German population on his arrival in Munich and on the way to Berchtesgaden.

He (the Führer) could definitely state that since his youth he had had the idea of Anglo-German cooperation. The war had come as a great internal spiritual shock to him. However, he had since 1918

---

[1] On the evening of September 13th Mr. Chamberlain sent Hitler the following message: "In view of the increasingly critical situation, I propose to come over at once to see you with a view to trying to find peaceful solution. I propose to come across by air and am ready to start tomorrow. Please indicate earliest time at which you can see me and suggest place of meeting. Should be grateful for very early reply." The following afternoon Ribbentrop telephoned Sir Nevile Henderson, the British ambassador in Berlin, informing him of Hitler's acceptance of the proposal, and suggesting that Chamberlain fly to Munich the next day. Hitler's joyous reaction at the news of Chamberlain's message was "Ich bin wie vom Himmel gefallen [I fell from Heaven]."—F. L. L.

13 *German Documents*, Series D, Vol. II, no. 487.

kept the idea of Anglo-German friendship constantly in mind. The reason why he had thus taken up the cause of this friendship was that since his nineteenth year he had developed certain racial ideals within himself, which had caused him immediately at the end of the war to have the *rapprochement* between both nations systematically in view as one of his aims. He had to admit that in recent years this idealistic belief in Anglo-German racial affinity had suffered very severe blows. He would, however, count himself fortunate if he could succeed at the eleventh hour, in spite of all this, in leading back the whole political development into channels laid down by the theories which he had advocated again and again in his speeches and writings for a decade and a half.

Mr. Chamberlain replied that he fully valued the words of appreciation which the Führer had spoken to him. It was, in fact, no easy thing for a man of his age to undertake a journey of this kind. The fact that he had embarked on this journey to Germany should serve as proof, for the Führer and the German people, both of the importance which he (Mr. Chamberlain) attached to an Anglo-German *rapprochement* and also of his sincere desire to attempt everything possible to find a way out of the present difficulties.

This first conversation might best be utilized for the exchange of general ideas on the situation, so that each party could understand the other aright and ascertain between themselves whether agreement was possible or not. He (Mr. Chamberlain) had frankly to admit that many Englishmen regarded the Führer's speeches solely as words behind which carefully prepared plans were concealed. He (Mr. Chamberlain), however, looked on the Führer as a man who, from a strong feeling for the sufferings of his people, had carried through the rebirth of the German nation with extraordinary success. He had the greatest respect for this man, and had come to Germany in order to attempt to solve the present difficulties by means of a frank exchange of views at the fountainhead of the German return to prosperity. He hoped that as a result of this exchange of views with the Führer both parties would be precisely informed of the views of the other, and that on the basis of this precise knowledge of the Führer's attitude he could then with redoubled confidence continue to work for an Anglo-German *rapprochement*.

The Führer then declared that at the head of all the problems to be discussed there stood the Sudeten German question, which had at the moment gone beyond the stage of theoretical discussion, since the situation was moving from hour to hour toward an open crisis. It therefore seemed appropriate to him to begin with this question, since it was also decisive for the future development of Anglo-German relations. He did not wish to linger too long over the past, for there were many points on which the two countries differed and few which they had in common. What was decisive was whether and how far agreement could be reached between the two countries on a common attitude in this question.

The situation was very grave. On the basis of the latest information, 300 fatal casualties and many hundreds of injured were to be expected among the Sudeten Germans.[1] There were entire villages from which the population had fled. In these circumstances a decision must be reached in some way or another within a very short time. In this state of affairs he was obliged to state quite frankly that there would be no point in carrying on a conversation in the manner of previous diplomatic discussions. The long journey which the Prime Minister had made would not have proved worth while if they were to stop short at mere formalities. . . .

Germany, had, nevertheless, put forward a general demand in all clarity. The 10 million Germans who lived in Austria and Czechoslovakia, and whose earnest desire it was to return to the Reich to which they had belonged for a thousand years, must be enabled in all circumstances to return to it. In the case of the 7 million Germans in the Ostmark this demand had been met. The return to the Reich of the 3 million Germans in Czechoslovakia he (the Führer) would make possible at all costs. He would face any war, and even the risk of a world war, for this. Here the limit had been reached where the rest of the world might do what it liked, he would not yield one single step.

Mr. Chamberlain asked in this connection whether the difficulties with Czechoslovakia would then be at an end with the return of 3 million Sudeten Germans to the Reich. The question was being asked in Britain whether this was all that Germany was demanding, or whether she was not aiming over and above this at the dismemberment of the Czechoslovak State.

The Führer replied that, apart from the demands of the Sudeten Germans, similar demands would, of course, be made by the Poles, Hungarians, and Ukranians living in Czechoslovakia, which it would be impossible to ignore in the long run, but that he was, of course, not their spokesman. . . .

With regard to the Czechs, he was obliged, however, to assert once more that he would solve this question by one means or another. He did not wish that any doubts should arise as to his absolute determination not to tolerate any longer that a small, second-rate country should treat the mighty thousand-year-old German Reich as something inferior. . . .

---

[1] This was one of Hitler's numerous—but remarkably successful—prevarications. The situation, in fact, was exactly the opposite. On September 23rd, Carr, the American Minister in Prague, telegraphed the Department of State: "Henlein's Freikorps are conducting a campaign of provocation and murderous attack at various points on the frontier. German radio and press exaggerate and wholly misrepresent incidents and unjustly place complete blame on the Czechs. Often the facts are completely reversed by the German press. There is clearly a German effort to provoke trouble and have the world believe the Czechs are responsible." *Foreign Relations of the United States 1938,* Volume I (Washington, 1955), p. 640.—F. L. L.

Mr. Chamberlain thanked the Führer for his clear and frank exposition of the German attitude. He believed he had rightly understood the Führer to say that he had made the demand for the return of 10 million Germans to the German Reich for racial reasons. Seven million Germans had returned to the Reich through the incorporation of Austria. Three million Sudeten Germans must in any circumstances be restored to the Reich. But the Führer had given the assurance that thereafter no territorial demands could exist any longer in other regions, which might give rise to conflicts between Germany and other countries. He (the British Prime Minister) had also understood the Führer to say that he was prepared even to run the risk of a world war in order to secure the return of these 3 million Germans to the Reich. At the moment he did not wish to make any further observation on this than that it ought to be possible for the Führer and himself to prevent a world war on account of these 3 million Sudeten Germans. . . .

The British Prime Minister went on to say that as a practical man he had set himself the question as to how an eventual decision regarding the inclusion of the Sudeten Germans in the Reich was to be carried out in practice. For the Sudeten Germans did not live in a compact area but were fairly scattered, and even if those areas were allotted to Germany in which 80 percent of the total population was German, there would always remain quite a number of inhabitants of German descent in the remaining part of the Czechoslovak State. It was, therefore, not only a question of a new delimitation of frontiers but also, if that were the case, of a transfer of certain sections of the population.

The Führer replied that, in his opinion, of course only the Sudeten German region as a whole could be taken into consideration, and that in every place where there was a majority for Germany, the territory in question would have to go to Germany. In this connection there would have to be an exchange of minorities after that, and in particular with due regard also to the German language enclaves in Czech territory.

He (the Führer) was, however, afraid that all these discussions were of a purely theoretical nature, since the march of events was continuing at a rapid pace. Whole villages in the Sudeten German region had been evacuated by their inhabitants, 10 thousand refugees were already on German soil, places had been attacked with gas, the number of dead already amounted to 300. It was clear that he (the Führer) could not tolerate these proceedings any longer. He had made his intentions plain at Nuremberg, and it was a mistake to assume that these had been merely empty phrases. He could in no circumstances tolerate this persecution of Germans, and he was firmly resolved to act quickly.

The British Prime Minister then proposed to address a joint appeal to both parties in Czechoslovakia, so as to provide the opportunity for mutual discussions to be carried out in a calmer atmosphere. It was clear that, if the information received by the Führer was correct, conditions in the Sudeten German region were almost untenable. However, experience often showed that reports which first seemed grave proved on closer examination to be less serious.

The Führer then replied that he could not possibly address an appeal of this kind to the Sudeten German population. He could not be expected to give the victims of Czechoslovak persecution admonitions as well. One should also take into consideration the fact that the nervous tension among the inhabitants of the frontier regions had so increased as to be almost unbearable. From German territory there could be heard the sound of artillery fire directed against defenseless Sudeten German villages, and at the same time whole divisions were concentrated on the German side and the air force units stood in readiness, and it constituted an immense degree of nervous tension, if, in face of all these preparations, Germany was obliged to look on while old German towns, such as Eger, were attacked by the Czechs. . . .

After the Führer had once more emphatically rejected the idea of an appeal to the two parties, the British Prime Minister stated that he would now drop this proposal, but he was obliged to ask himself why the Führer had let him come to Germany when he (the Führer) was apparently firmly resolved to proceed in a quite definite direction and not to consider the idea of an armistice.

The Führer replied that he thought it necessary today or tomorrow to go into the question whether perhaps a peaceful settlement of the question was still possible after all. He was obliged, however, to emphasize once more that he was firmly determined in any circumstances to decide this question in one way or another within the shortest possible time.

Moreover, he pointed out that Czechoslovakia had made use of the British Prime Minister's journey to order mobilization and call up ten age groups.

The British Prime Minister emphasized afresh that when it was a matter of saving human lives all chances must be explored to the very last. He was, therefore, repeating his proposal to bring about a kind of armistice and added that he was prepared to agree to a breathing space of this kind of limited duration.

The Führer replied that an immediate pacification of the Sudeten region could be achieved if the Czech State police were withdrawn and confined to barracks. Furthermore, it seemed to him important —and this in answer to the question as to the further course of the conversations—what attitude Britain was adopting with regard to the Sudeten region. Would Britain agree to the secession of these areas and an alteration in the present constitution of Czechoslovakia, or would she not? If Britain could assent to a separation of this kind, and this could be announced to the world as a fundamental decision of principle, then, no doubt, it would be possible by this means to bring about a large degree of pacification in the regions in question. It was, therefore, a matter of knowing whether Britain was now prepared to assent to the detachment of the Sudeten German districts on the basis of the right of national self-determination, and in this connection he (the Führer) was obliged to observe that this right of self-determination had not just been invented by him in 1938 specially for the Czechoslovak question, but that it had already been brought into being in 1918 in order to create a moral basis for the changes made under the Treaty of Versailles. The conversations could continue on these lines, but the British Prime Minister must first of all state whether he could accept this basis or not, namely, the secession of the Sudeten German region by virtue of the right of self-determination.

The British Prime Minister expressed his satisfaction that they had now got down to the crux of the matter at last. He was not in a position to make categorical statements for the whole of the British Government. Besides, he was obliged, of course, to consult France and Lord Runciman also. But he could give it as his own personal view that, now that he had heard the Führer's motives and now that he saw the whole situation in a clearer light, he was prepared to ascertain whether his personal opinion was also shared by his colleagues in the Cabinet. He could state personally that he recognized the principle of the detachment of the Sudeten areas. The difficulty seemed to him to lie in the implementation of this principle in actual practice. In these circumstances he wished to return to England in order to report to the Government and secure their approval of his personal attitude. At the same time he was proposing that on both sides they should be perfectly clear in their own minds about the practical methods of implementing this principle, for it involved the solution of a whole series of problems of organization and administration.

The Führer stated that he would gladly spare the British Prime Minister a second journey to Germany, for he was much younger and could undertake journeys of this kind, but he was afraid that, if he were to come to England, anti-German demonstrations would complicate rather than simplify the situation. But, in order to shorten the Prime Minister's journey somewhat, he was proposing for their next meeting the Lower Rhine district, Cologne or Godesberg.

The British Prime Minister then asked the Führer what would happen in the meantime, and whether it would not be possible to ensure that the situation did not deteriorate any further.

The Führer replied that the danger of such a deterioration in the situation of course existed, with the result that the mighty military machine which Germany had built up would have to be set in motion. But once this machine was in motion it would no longer be possible to stop it. If major incidents, cases of frontier violation and the like, were to occur, the danger would be increased to the utmost limits.

But even at the risk of this being interpreted as weakness, as perhaps the British press would interpret it, he was prepared to give an assurance that, if at all possible, he would not give the order to set the military machine in motion during the next few days, unless a completely impossible situation should arise. In that case, of course, all further discussions would be useless. . . .

The British Prime Minister replied that he understood from the Führer's words that both he and the Führer wished to do everything in their power in order to keep the political situation as calm as possible during the days in question. The Führer had declared to him that he could do little in the actual situation. He hoped, nevertheless, that he would do what lay in his power in order to keep developments in peaceful channels, and he could say, on his part, that he himself would make every possible effort in that direction.

The Führer declared that he would also do everything; nevertheless, he could not issue a public proclamation.

After an observation by the Führer on the value of German friendship, the Prime Minister stated in conclusion that Britain was not so much concerned about the advantages accruing to her from friendship with Germany, but that she rather yielded to a natural tendency on the part of the British toward friendship with Germany.

Finally, the following brief press communiqué on the conversation was agreed upon:

"The Führer and Reich Chancellor had a conversation with Mr. Chamberlain, the British Prime Minister, on the Obersalzberg today, during the course of which there was a comprehensive and frank exchange of views on the present situation. The British Prime Minister is returning to England tomorrow to confer with the British Cabinet. In a few days a new conversation will take place."

Submitted herewith to the Führer in accordance with instructions.

SCHMIDT
Counselor of Legation

BERCHTESGADEN, September 15, 1938.

14 LETTER *from Neville Chamberlain to Ida Chamberlain*

September 19, 1938.

In my last letter I wondered what might happen before I wrote again, for I knew the hour must be near, if it was to come at all. Two things

---

14 Feiling, pp. 363-364.

were essential, first, that the plan should be tried just when things looked blackest, and second that it should be a complete surprise . . . on Tuesday night I saw that the moment had come and must be taken, if I was not to be too late. So I sent the fateful telegram and told the Cabinet next morning what I had done. . . . At last during the afternoon my anxiety was relieved. Hitler was entirely at my disposal, and would not Mrs. Chamberlain come too! Afterwards I heard from Hitler himself, and it was confirmed by others who were with him, that he was struck all of a heap, and exlaimed "I can't possibly let a man of his age come all this way; I must go to London." Of course, when he considered it further, he saw that wouldn't do, and indeed it would not have suited me, for it would have deprived my coup of much of its dramatic force. But it shows a side of Hitler that would surprise many people in this country.

15   NOTES *of a Conversation Between Prime Minister Chamberlain and Herr Hitler at Godesberg*[1]

September 22, 1938.

The Prime Minister said that at the end of the last conversation at Berchtesgaden the situation was as follows: After he had expressed his personal opinion on the principle of self-determination he had promised to consult his colleagues. He had gone home and had succeeded in getting not only his colleagues but the French Government and also the Czechoslovak Government to agree to self-determination in principle. It appeared that the simplest plan was to tell the Chancellor what were the British proposals, and then perhaps to consider how they could be carried out.

The Führer had said at the last meeting that the question of the Sudeten was urgent, and that a solution could not be delayed, but that a settlement must be reached before any other question could be discussed. This accordingly was the problem which he, Mr. Chamberlain, had set himself to attack. He did not know how much importance the Führer attached to the principle of self-determination as such. But the Führer had said at Berchtesgaden that a distinction must be drawn

[1] These notes were made by Mr. Kirkpatrick.

15 *Documents on British Foreign Policy 1919-1939* (abbrev. *British Documents*), Third Series, Vol. II (London, 1949), no. 1033.

between the possible and the impossible. The Prime Minister's colleagues had agreed in the course of their deliberations in London, and were also of the opinion that the principle of self-determination need not necessarily be the basis of the existing system in all countries and in all circumstances; otherwise it might cause difficulties all over the world.

Once the principle of self-determination had been admitted, however, in the case of the Sudeten, and it was agreed that they should be given the opportunity to return to Germany, the question arose of how this was to be achieved. The first solution which came to mind was that of a plebiscite, but this method gave rise to difficulties, delays, and possibly disorders. Since the Führer had emphasised his desire for a quick solution, it had therefore seemed to all simpler to achieve a settlement not by a plebiscite, but by the agreed cession of territory to the Reich, subject to the proviso that measures should be laid down to enable people to be transferred from one area to another.

Some of the districts where there was an enormous preponderance of Germans presented no difficulties; but there were also mixed populations to consider. In the circumstances, when drawing up a new frontier, it seemed that some body must be set up for the purpose of frontier delimitation. They must be given a principle on which to work, and must at the same time have discrimination to draw a line having regard to political, geographical and military considerations, etc., as well as to the wishes of the local inhabitants.

He, Mr. Chamberlain, accordingly proposed that we should agree on a guiding principle and appoint a commission to carry it out. One could take as a basis a given proportion of Germans to the whole population, although that was a rough-and-ready calculation, since some Germans might prefer to remain in Czechoslovakia. Where it was established that, for example, 80 per cent. of the population were Germans, there would of course be no discussion. But a figure to be agreed upon might be established as a guiding principle for the commission, say, 65 per cent., subject to the use of their discrimination as defined above. The commission would consist of one German, one Czech, and one neutral chairman, with power to make a decision in the event of disagreement between the two other members.

We thought it important that an option should be given to populations to transfer, because it was practically impossible to draw a line which absolutely divided Czechs from Germans. There were thus two problems to consider, namely, the transfer of territory and the transfer of populations. The second presented some difficulty, because of the fact that there were obviously a number of persons with property or fixed interests in the territories concerned. In view of this difficulty, it would be necessary to draw such a line as to minimise to the greatest possible degree the necessity for transfer, but, as the Führer had himself recognised during the last conversation, it was impossible to avoid leaving certain minorities behind, and there must accordingly be adequate safeguards for these people. There was also the question of State property, although this was not an immediate matter. He desired only to mention it, as it would have to be considered later, and he presumed that the German Government would take over such property as buildings, belonging to the Czechoslovak Government, banks, public works, etc., at a valuation. There was similarly the ancillary question of the public debt, and he thought that the German Government would not refuse to take over an agreed proportion of the Czech public debt corresponding to the amount of territory which they received.

There was, finally, one more matter which he desired to raise. The cession of the proposed property meant that the existing frontier fortifications would no longer be in Czechoslovakia, and her security would be *pro tanto* diminished. He recollected that the Führer had said that he only wished to get this Sudeten question settled and did not want any further territory. Nevertheless, we felt it not unreasonable that Czechoslovakia should want to substitute some other security for the loss of her strategic frontier. We had also considered what the Führer had said at Berchtesgaden about the threat to Germany of the Czechoslovak spear-head at her side. It seemed that the Führer's objections could be met and the Czech requirements satisfied at the same time, if we substituted [? for] the existing Czech alliances, with their military obligations, by [sic] a condition of guaranteed security against unprovoked aggression. Consequently, the British Government had agreed to join in guaranteeing Czechoslovakia against unprovoked aggression in the place of her existing treaties involving military obligations. Czechoslovakia would thus be a neutral State, under no military obligations, and would only be guaranteed against unprovoked aggression. He desired to add that this guarantee would not necessarily mean that the present Czech frontiers would be guaranteed in perpetuity. They could be altered by negotiation, as was being done in the present case.

Herr Hitler said that he would like to thank the Prime Minister for his great efforts to reach a peaceful solution. He was not clear, however, whether the proposals, of which the Prime Minister had just given him an outline, were those submitted to the Czechoslovak Government.

The Prime Minister replied: Yes.

Herr Hitler said that he was sorry, since these proposals could not be maintained.

It was not a question now of doing an injustice to Czechoslovakia, but of redressing grave injustices committed in the past. As a matter of principle a man who has committed an injustice can have no reason for complaint at the restoration to the victim of the rights of which he has been unlawfully deprived. Czechoslovakia was an artificial construction, which was called into being and was established solely on the grounds of political considerations. For this purpose a great wrong had been done to a number of other countries. Three and a half million Germans, against their will, which they vociferously proclaimed at the time, were forcibly incorporated into Czechoslovakia, as well as several million Slovaks together with a territory which was torn by violence from Hungary and which contained almost a million Hungarians. Furthermore, the Czechs, at a time when the Poles were fighting the Bolsheviks, took advantage of the situation to tear the Teschen territory, containing about 100,000 Poles, from the Motherland. That was the genesis of a State which possessed neither a history nor tradition, nor, indeed, conditions of existence. These other nationalities did not want in any circumstances to be under Czech rule. Representatives of Poland and Hungary had recently visited him and said that they would not in any circumstances agree to their nationals remaining under Czech rule. During the course of 20 years the Czechs had in point of fact been unable to conquer the sympathy of any of these nationals. However that might be, he declared that as Führer of Germany he spoke in the first place of Germans. He had been obliged, owing to the provisions of the Peace Treaties to leave so many Germans in other countries that the interests of Germans were his first care. It was, however, his duty to say that demands were being made by others which had his full sympathy, and peace could not be firmly established until these claims had been settled.

The Prime Minister said that he did not wish to dissent. He, the Führer, had said that the Sudeten question was of the utmost urgency and that was why he had addressed himself to this particular problem. The others had not the same urgency.

Herr Hitler retorted that, of course, for him as a German this problem was most urgent. But a Pole or an Hungarian would, of course, have maintained that theirs was the most urgent question.

However this might be, he (the Chancellor) must emphasise that the problem was now in a most critical stage. In his view no delay was possible, and there seemed to be a slight difference between them as to the urgency of the matter. In his own view, a settlement must be reached within a few days. There were, as the whole world knew, military preparations on both sides, but this situation could not be held for very long and a solution must be found one way, or another, either by agreement or by force. He desired to say, categorically, that the problem must be settled definitely and completely by the 1st October at the latest. . . .

The Prime Minister said that he was both disappointed and puzzled at the Führer's statement. The Führer had said during their previous conversation that if he, the Prime Minister, could arrange for a settlement on the basis of self-determination he would be prepared then to discuss procedure. He (Mr. Chamberlain) had then expressed his personal opinion as being in favour of the principle of self-determination;

he had recognised the basis of the German claim and the fact that it was not possible to expect the Sudetens to remain as citizens of Czechoslovakia. He had induced his colleagues, the French and the Czechs to agree to the principle of self-determination, in fact he had got exactly what the Führer wanted and without the expenditure of a drop of German blood. In doing so, he had been obliged to take his political life into his hands. As an illustration of the difficulties which he had had to face, he mentioned that when he undertook his first flight to Germany he was applauded by public opinion. Today he was accused of selling the Czechs, yielding to dictators, capitulating, and so on. He had actually been booed on his departure today. Herr Hitler interjected that he had only been booed by the Left, and the Prime Minister replied that he did not mind what the Left thought, but that his serious difficulties came from the people in his own party, some of whom had actually written to protest to him against his policy.

Why, continued Mr. Chamberlain, were [? had] the proposals which he had made not been regarded as acceptable? It was, of course, inevitable that there should be incidents and faults on both sides. At this point, Mr. Chamberlain read a note which he had just received to the effect that Sudeten bands supported by military had entered Eger. Herr Hitler declared that whatever the report might say, he could declare categorically that German troops had not crossed the border. It was quite out of the question.

The Prime Minister then picked up the thread of his argument and said that what he had hoped was to show the world that the orderly operation of treaty revision could be achieved by peaceful means. If the Führer had any proposal to make to this end, he would of course be pleased to consider it.

Herr Hitler declared that there was only one possibility: A frontier line must be drawn at once—he did not hold with commissions, committees, etc., he declared parenthetically—from which the Czechs must withdraw the army, police and all State organs; this area would be at once occupied by Germany. The line he proposed to draw would be that of the language frontier, based on existing reliable maps. The Czechs might declare—and from his knowledge of them would certainly declare—that his line did not represent the real minority situation. If so, he would hold a plebiscite (he did not ask for gifts, nor did he desire to steal territory which did not belong to Germany) on the basis of the situation in 1918 when the Czechs took over the territory; that is to say, the Germans who had since left the territory would be entitled to vote and the Czechs who had since been planted there would not be entitled to vote. In this he would only be following the precedent set by the Saar plebiscite. He was perfectly ready for the plebiscite to be carried out by an international plebiscite commission. The territory would be occupied by German troops at once. But international commissions could be sent out, and, since the plebiscite would not take place for some time—he mentioned October or November—there would be ample time for proper preparations to be made. . . .

Herr Hitler said that, as regards the proposed guarantee, it was, of course, as far as the British guarantee was concerned, the affair of the British Government, and he had no observations to offer. But Germany would only join in such a guarantee if all Czechoslovakia's neighbours and all the Great Powers, including Italy, also agreed to join in the guarantee.

The Prime Minister said that he had not asked Germany to join in the guarantee; in fact, he had foreseen this objection, but he thought that perhaps Herr Hitler would agree to the conclusion of a non-aggression Pact with Czechoslovakia, as he had done with other countries.

Herr Hitler said that only if Czechoslovakia succeeded in placing her relations with Poland and Hungary on a proper footing could he agree. The Czechs would regard a non-aggression Pact with Germany as protecting them from any possible pressure on his part, and this would merely encourage them to flout Poland and Hungary and to maltreat the Polish and Hungarian minorities to their hearts' content. His relations with Poland and Hungary were excellent, and he did not desire to stab them in the back.

As the spokesman of Germany, he must emphasise that there were only two solutions. First, peace and the establishment of a frontier on a national basis; or secondly, a military solution, which meant a frontier not on a national but on a strategic basis. As for the remainder of Czechoslovakia, it simply did not interest Germany.

(At this point I left the room to take a message.)

The Prime Minister said that his proposed guarantee was against *unprovoked* aggression and both Great Britain and France would object to Czechoslovakia resisting legitimate claims.

Herr Hitler retorted that it was impossible to define provocation or to know who in any given case was the provoker.

The Prime Minster said that many people represented that Herr Hitler wanted to annex Czechoslovakia. He personally did not believe this, but he wished Herr Hitler to help him to prove to his critics that they were wrong. Moreover, he, the Prime Minster, was not a party to these negotiations, but rather only a mediator seeking to achieve a peaceful solution. As it was, public opinion in England was not favourably disposed towards the proposals now under consideration, and they would be less favourably disposed if it were known that Herr Hitler was increasing his pretensions. What he would like to be able to do would be to prove that the proposed solution was fair and that the plebiscite was to be held in conditions which ensured freedom from military or other pressure. Again he asked why it was necessary to hold a plebiscite everywhere.

Herr Hitler said it was because the Czechs (and he knew them better than anyone) would question everything, and because he, Herr Hitler, wanted a plebiscite to show the Czechs how numerous were the solid blocks which did not want to stay in Czechoslovakia. Furthermore, a plebiscite would enable a fair frontier to be fixed. One would have to take into account regions rather than isolated villages. One particular village might have a Czech majority, but might have to be in a German region, and *vice versa*. . . .

Herr Hitler said that in any event a plebiscite would prove that the German map and the proposed German line was fair. The population maps of 1910, 1920 and 1930, as well as the latest communal elections, showed how far the Czechs had succeeded in encroaching into Sudeten territory. But under his proposal for the plebiscite, the Germans—as they had done in the Saar—would come back to vote. The following were the numbers of Germans who had left Czechoslovakia since 1918: Overseas 150,000; in Austria 400,000; in Germany 270,000. All these would be entitled to vote, whilst the the 200,000 Czechs planted by the Czechoslovak Government would not be entitled to vote. This was not a revolutionary or unfair proposal. It was based on the model of the Saar plebiscite, which was evolved not by himself or by the German Government, but by high international authorities. . . .

The Prime Minister replied that of course Germany could get what she wanted by the exercise of her might. But such a course would involve loss of life. Moreover, in war there was always an element of hazard, and it was difficult to see why, if Herr Hitler could obtain all that he wanted by peaceful means with complete certainty, he should elect to adopt a course which involved the loss of German lives and a certain element of risk.

Herr Hitler replied that he personally would much prefer a good understanding with England to a good military strategic frontier with Czechoslovakia.

The Prime Minister said that he would not get a good friendship with England if he resorted to force, but that he would if he agreed to achieve his aims by peaceful means.

Herr Hitler said that the decisive element was speed, because whilst they were sitting there they were at the mercy of events, and an irreparable incident could occur at any moment. His solution was the best, because it was the quickest. After the plebiscite which would follow, he would at once return any territory which did not opt for Germany.

At this point it was agreed to inspect the map showing the line which Herr Hitler proposed to draw, based on the language boundary. [Herr von Ribbentrop, Sir Horace Wilson and Sir Nevile Henderson joined the discussions at this stage.]

Herr Hitler, in reply to a question by the Prime Minister, said that he would be prepared to abide by a bare majority vote in the plebiscite. In reply to a further question, he said that if the plebiscite showed that Germans opted for Czechoslovakia, he would only be too glad to get rid of them. He did not want such Germans in the Reich. If the Prime Minster knew the territory and the people as well as he did, he would agree that the idea of a conflict between Great Britain and Germany on account of such people was simply absurd.

The Prime Minister asked what exactly Herr Hitler meant by applying the result of the plebiscite by regions rather than by towns, villages, etc. Did he have in mind voting by communes, or what were the districts he had in mind?

At this moment Herr Hitler received a message to the effect that twelve German hostages had been shot in Eger. This led him to a disquisition on the iniquity of the Czechs, and on the difficulty he had in refraining from military action against Czechoslovakia.

The Prime Minister further sought to elucidate Herr Hitler's statement that the result of the voting would have to be considered regionally rather than locally.

Herr Hitler vociferated, in reply, that after their behaviour during the last twenty years, the Czechs had no reason to complain of any solution. The essential element, he continued, was speed. If Prague fell under Bolshevik influence, or if hostages continued to be shot, he would intervene militarily at once.

The Prime Minister reverted to the question of the plebiscite, and under pressure Herr Hitler agreed that he would have no objection to a plebiscite on both sides of the disputed border.

The Prime Minister then asked Herr Hitler if he would take steps to control the Sudetens whilst we took similar action at Prague.

Herr Hitler said that he could give instructions to his army, his S.S. and his police, and they would be obeyed. But he could not communicate with or control the hordes of refugees on the frontier. The solution was for the Czechs to withdraw from [sic] the army and police.

The Prime Minister said that if he could not appeal to the Sudetens, he would make a personal appeal to them himself.

Herr Hitler replied that this was practically impossible, since there was no Sudeten leadership, no telephonic communication and no one with whom one could get into touch. The Czechs had destroyed the whole organization, and the Sudeten refugees were now a leaderless rabble. So long as shooting affrays continued on the frontier, nothing could prevent the Sudetens from endeavouring to rescue their comrades and kith and kin involved in these affrays.

The Prime Minister said that of course it was impossible wholly to prevent these incidents; they were, indeed, inevitable. But they could do their best and appeal to Prague, and he—Herr Hitler—could appeal to such Sudeten leaders and organizations as existed.

Herr Hitler replied that he would do his best, but that it was an intolerable strain on his nerves to hold his hand in view of constant Czech provocation, when he knew that he could at any moment rout the Czechs with one armoured battalion. The friends of the shot hostages would be shouting tonight for revenge.

After further argument, Herr Hitler said that he would give instructions at once to General Keitel that no military action was to be taken. But Mr. Chamberlain must understand that the Czechs must be spoken to sharply and firmly, or an admonition would have no effect. He never believed himself that a peaceful solution could be reached, and he admitted that he never thought that the Prime Minister could have achieved what he had. That was why he had made his military preparations and Germany was ready today to move at a moment's notice.

After some further desultory discussion the Prime Minister and the Chancellor agreed to adjourn the conversation until the following day.

16 NOTES *of a Conversation Between Prime Minister Chamberlain and Herr Hitler at Godesberg*[1]

There were also present:

Sir Horace Wilson   Herr von Ribbentrop
Sir Nevile Henderson   Herr von Weizsäcker
Mr. Kirkpatrick

September 23–4, 1938.

Herr Hitler said that he and the German people gratefully thanked Mr. Chamberlain for his efforts to secure a peaceful solution of this problem. He, Herr Hitler, knew that it had been a great physical effort for Mr. Chamberlain, and that, in addition, great political courage had been required on his part. Their negotiations were perhaps difficult. But

[1] These notes were made by Mr. Kirkpatrick. This conversation took place during the night of September 23-4.

16 *British Documents*, Third Series, Vol. II, no. 1073.

he, Mr. Chamberlain, was an Englishman, and he, Herr Hitler, came from Nieder Sachsen, so that possibly they could in the distant past claim a common ancestry. Nevertheless, however this might be, it was difficult for them to regard this problem on a common basis, for they were obliged to look at it from different angles. For England it was perhaps a matter of general policy; but for Germany it was not only a national question of life and death, but also a question of national honour. All the same, he, Herr Hitler, still entertained the hope of a peaceful solution, and he could only say that, if this happy result were achieved, it would be largely due to the Prime Minister and his efforts.

The Prime Minister said that he much appreciated the words of the Führer, and his reference to his own efforts. He had listened with hope to what Herr Hitler had said regarding the possibility of finding a peaceful solution, but perhaps Herr Hitler could tell him more about that as it had been agreed that afternoon that we were going to have a memorandum to consider.

At this point Herr von Ribbentrop produced the German memorandum, stating the German desiderata in regard to the execution of the agreement, already reached in principle, for the application of self-determination for the Sudetens.[2]

Herr Hitler said that the memorandum represented essentially the ideas which he had expressed in his letter to Mr. Chamberlain of the 23rd September, supplemented by the verbal statements which he had made.

Herr Hitler went on to say that during the last years Germany had had a series of national problems to solve which were absolutely vital to her. Unfortunately, England in each case had been either disinterested or had taken up an attitude opposed to that of Germany, particularly so far as the press was concerned. This was the first occasion on which Germany had had a feeling that England had endeavoured to solve the problem in favour of Germany's legitimate interests. If the efforts they were now making to reach a peaceful solution achieved their object, it might well represent a turning point in Anglo-German relations. He added that this was the last question that remained open.

The Prime Minister said that Herr Hitler must know that it was or had been his ambition to get a peaceful solution. If it proved possible to achieve this peaceful solution—even if it were not agreeable to sections of British public opinion—he was hopeful that the agreement so reached might, as Herr Hitler had described it, be a turning point in Anglo-German relations. But he, Mr. Chamberlain, must be able to show to his people that his efforts had met with some response on the German side. He must, however, say that hitherto he had had no such response. He had been told at Berchtesgaden that if he could get the

[2] For the text of this memorandum, see Document 17.—F. L. L.

principle of self-determination accepted by the parties concerned, we could then discuss method and procedure. He had succeeded in his task, not only at home, but with the French and Czechoslovak Governments, and he thought that on his arrival at Godesberg Herr Hitler would have been prepared to discuss the application of the principle to the Sudetens. But unfortunately Herr Hitler had categorically refused to consider the proposals which he had submitted. Instead Herr Hitler had adopted the line that this and that must be done, and done quickly, including not merely the immediate cession of both the Sudeten German areas and the mixed areas, but also their occupation forthwith by German military forces. . . .

The Prime Minister . . . went on to say that if the memorandum only represented what Herr Hitler had said the previous day, public opinion would not be satisfied. He emphasised the risks of a solution by warlike methods and the loss and suffering to vast numbers of people without adequate cause. He could not believe that Herr Hitler would deliberately gamble away all chances of working together, the prospect of peace and a happy future for Europe merely for the sake of avoiding a delay of a few days. He, Mr. Chamberlain, was not an unreasonable person, and he understood the Führer's desire for a speedy settlement, but to rush things like this was to take fearful chances.

Herr Hitler asked what the Prime Minister meant by gambling everything away for the sake of avoiding a delay of a few days.

The Prime Minister referred to the memorandum and pointed out that it demanded that the Czech evacuation of the Sudeten area should begin on the 26th September. Apart from anything else this was a quite impracticable date. Then there followed the timetable for German occupations. The whole thing was in terms of dictation, not in terms of negotiation.

Herr Hitler retorted that he sincerely believed that the shorter the time limit the greater the chances of definite acceptance.

At this point a message was brought in to Herr von Ribbentrop, who announced in a portentous tone that M. Benes had ordered general mobilisation.

Herr Hitler said that in that event things were settled.

The Prime Minister asked why things must be regarded as settled. Mobilisation was a precaution, but not necessarily an offensive measure. He must point out that there was mobilisation on the other side also.

Herr Hitler said that when he talked of things being settled, he meant that the Czech mobilisation was a clear indication that Czechoslovakia did not intend to cede territory.

The Prime Minister dissented categorically. Czechoslovakia, he said, with the assent of the British and French Governments had agreed to the principle of self-determination, and they would not go back on it.

Herr Hitler maintained that if Czechoslovakia was sincerely determined to abide by her acceptance of the principle of self-determination, she would not mobilise.

The Prime Minister asked who mobilised first?

Herr Hitler said: The Czechs.

The Prime Minister retorted that on the contrary Germany had mobilised first; she had called up reservists and moved troops to the frontier.

Herr Hitler replied that when mobilisation was ordered here, Mr. Chamberlain would see the difference between the peace and war strength of the German army.

The Prime Minister replied that Herr Hitler had placed 1½ million men under arms, and had moved his tanks, his aeroplanes and his troops to their appropriate stations. In the circumstances it was not surprising that the Czechs felt themselves threatened. Herr Hitler might declare that he had no confidence in the Czechs, but the latter, in view of what had been done, could not be expected to have much confidence in Herr Hitler's intentions.

Herr Hitler said that he had already declared that the situation could not be held very much longer. No responsible statesman would assent to its indefinite perpetuation.

The Prime Minister agreed that there must be an early settlement.

Herr Hitler said that the attempts to get a peaceful solution had been going on now for eighteen years.

The Prime Minister said that Herr Hitler had emphasised that he was faced with an unbearable situation. He himself did not dissent. But did the Führer not think that if he decided to achieve a settlement by war, many more persons would be shot? There would be many more refugees and much more property would be irretrievably lost, even if it were only a localised war. He asked again whether the memorandum represented [Herr] Hitler's last word and whether recourse to force was worth the sacrifice when the objective was already completely within his grasp.

Herr Hitler said he would quote a German proverb to the effect that "An end, even with terror, is better than terror without end." He added that the memorandum did, in fact, represent his last word. But quite independently of the problem before them, he must take the appropriate military measures to meet the Czech mobilisation.

The Prime Minister said in that event there was no purpose in negotiating any further. He would go home with a heavy heart, since he saw the final wreck of all his hopes for the peace of Europe. But his conscience was clear; he had done everything possible for peace. Unfortunately, he had not found an echo in Herr Hitler.

Herr von Ribbentrop intervened to say that he did not understand what the Prime Minister meant by declaring that there was no purpose in further negotiation. The Prime Minister had that very afternoon asked for a memorandum, which he proposed to submit to the Czech Government for their immediate reply. The memorandum had now been drafted, but without even looking at it the Prime Minister had decided that the memorandum did not represent a possible basis for a peaceful solution. That seemed to him, Herr von Ribbentrop, an altogether novel procedure. . . .

Sir Horace Wilson, who meanwhile had been perusing the German memorandum, called attention to the fact that it provided for a detailed timetable for the Czech evacuation of the Sudeten districts and for the immediate occupation by German troops, with dates and even hours. The evacuation must begin on the 26th September and be completed by the 28th.

Herr Hitler asked how long he considered the time limit should be.

Sir Horace Wilson replied that communication of the Memorandum meant publication; and this peremptory time limit for the immediate military occupation of territory which was to be ceded by agreement would make the most profound impression on public opinion throughout the world.

Herr Hitler replied that if the dates were taken out there would be no end to the ensuing negotiations. Now that Czechoslovakia had mobilised, Germany would take appropriate military measures, and other States might well follow suit. It was quite impossible for such a state of affairs to last indefinitely.

The Prime Minister said that it was his definite opinion that the time limit, as set forth in the Memorandum, would produce a deplorable effect on public opinion in England and probably elsewhere. The Memorandum was an ultimatum and not a negotiation.

Herr Hitler said that it bore the word "Memorandum" on the top.

The Prime Minister retorted that he was more impressed by the contents than by the title.

Herr Hitler said that they had now been negotiating for two days. Surely it was not unreasonable that at some point or other, a concrete proposal must be made which would have to be taken or rejected. He repeated that things could not be left as they were.

The Prime Minister said that it was to some extent a matter of form. The way in which the proposals were put would inevitably make people say that Herr Hitler was behaving like a conqueror. (Herr Hitler interjected: "No, like an owner of his property.") It was the behavior of a victor to a defeated foe. No time was given for the slightest discussion; there was no time even for the practical execution of the necessary measures. When Herr Hitler said that there was no time to lose, he would agree.

Herr Hitler then asked the Prime Minister if he had read the memorandum.

The Prime Minister replied that he had already seen a penciled translation of the most important passages written for him by Sir Nevile Henderson; he did not want to read any more of the memorandum, and if he did it would not make him change his opinion.

Herr von Ribbentrop asked what exactly were the Prime Minister's objections to the document. General agreement had now been reached in principle to cede the territory. Evacuation, followed by occupation, must come some time or other. The only question was the question of time. Why did they object to the time?

At this point, after some discussion, it was decided that Herr Schmidt should translate the memorandum orally into English. . . .

The Prime Minister, when the memorandum had been read, said that he would like to repeat that as an intermediary his duty was to transmit proposals and he would do this. He had said from the first that the memorandum would have a bad effect on public opinion. The Führer had asked him to read the document first and then tell him why. After hearing the memorandum read he could say once more that the insertion of the dates would have a deplorable effect. The dates in themselves were wholly impracticable; it was now already the 24th September, and the Czechs were being required between the evening of the 24th, when the memorandum would reach them, and the morning of the 26th, to accept it and to issue the necessary orders to enable the withdrawal of the troops to begin. But he did not wish to lay stress on the impracticability of the dates, and it would not really help him if the time-table were put forward by a day. The fact remained that laying down a peremptory and rigid time-table of this nature would have a bad effect on public opinion.

If Czechoslovakia accepted the memorandum, he, Mr. Chamberlain, agreed that no time should be lost in carrying it into effect. If they accepted, he would do his best to see that they carried it out in a reasonable time, and in this matter he would feel a certain responsibility.

Herr Hitler asked what exactly he regarded as a reasonable time?

The Prime Minister replied that he could not say now what would be a reasonable time, but he meant a reasonable time, and Herr Hitler could safely trust his sincerity in this respect.

Herr Hitler said that the Czech mobilisation was the second of its kind. The first had taken place in May when Germany had not moved a single man. The action of the Czech Government meant counter military measures. Quite apart from the constant incidents on the frontier, to which he had drawn urgent attention, it was manifestly impossible for the German Government to wait indefinitely with 90 or 100 Divisions under arms. Other considerations apart, the cost was prohibitive.

He would not be fulfilling his duty to his country if he did not take these military measures. The Czechs might at any moment change their Government and the new Government might reverse the decision of their predecessors in regard to the acceptance of self-determination of the Sudetens and cession of the territory to Germany. In that event His Majesty's Government would doubtless regard the action of the Czech Government as regrettable, and would condemn it. But the German Government would have to act. In the meantime he would omit the two sets of dates and substitute the 1st October.

The Prime Minister said that he could not, of course, either accept or reject the memorandum; he could only transmit. He appreciated the spirit in which his objections to the form had been made [sic, ? met], and he thought that from this point of view, but of course from that point alone, the effect on public opinion would be better.

The Prime Minister said that he would like to ask one more question, and he would put it to Herr Hitler for his own satisfaction. Big things were at stake and it would be wrong to forgo the slightest opportunity merely for the sake of a few minutes' talk.

Herr Hitler had said that the memorandum represented his last word, but he had made a number of alterations of form. The question he now wished to put to Herr Hitler related to the occupation of the territory by troops. Under the proposals of the memorandum the whole territory would be immediately occupied by troops. Could the occupation by German troops be confined to that part of the territory only which had a considerable German preponderance, say, for example, 80 per cent.? Acceptance of this suggestion could not possibly make any difference in the end, but it might possibly be found helpful.

Herr Hitler replied that the suggestion had, in fact, been previously mooted, and he had discussed it that very morning with his military advisers. In their view such a partial occupation was technically impossible in view of the character of the frontier and the distribution of the population. In some parts the doubtful areas were in pockets, and not on the border at all. If they were not to be entered by troops, troop movements in the whole Sudeten area would be gravely hampered, if not rendered impossible. Many vital roads and railways required by the military authorities passed through some of these so-called doubtful areas, where the total number of Germans was less than 80 per cent. . . .

The Prime Minister said that there was one last question he wanted to put. If the memorandum were accepted, German troops would occupy areas in which there would be Czechs and possibly even some Germans who had worked against the "Anschluss" with the Reich. What would happen to these people, and how would they be protected? He did not suggest that they would be necessarily beaten and mishandled, but the question would certainly be addressed to him in England, and he would be grateful if Herr Hitler would provide him with an answer.

Herr Hitler said he could only refer him to the experience of the Saar plebiscite. Critics of Germany had averred at the time that at least 100,000 persons would be the victims of revenge. But Herr Hitler was not aware of one single complaint against Germany on this score. The Germans bore no grudge against a Czech for wishing to be incorporated in his own country; that was the attitude they expected Germans to adopt. If any man in the Sudeten area, however, had murdered a German, he would be well advised to flee in time before the local population wreaked their vengeance on him. As regards Communists, it was high treason to indulge in Communist activities in Germany, and this would apply to the Sudeten territory; but he did not mind and had never minded what a Communist had been before, provided that he abandoned his Communist activities. In general, his object was to exchange populations on both sides as quickly as possible.

The Prime Minister then said he would submit the proposals to the Czech Government as soon as possible, and the conversation terminated.

17 MEMORANDUM *handed by Hitler to Prime Minister Chamberlain*

GODESBERG, September 24, 1938.

Reports which are increasing in number from hour to hour regarding incidents in the Sudetenland show that the situation has become completely intolerable for the Sudeten German people and, in consequence, a danger to the peace of Europe. It is therefore essential that the separation of the Sudentenland agreed to by Czechoslovakia should be effected without any further delay. On the attached map the Sudeten German area which is to be ceded is shaded red. The areas in which over and above the areas which are to be occupied a plebiscite is also to be held, are drawn in and shaded green.

The final delimitation of the frontier must correspond to the wishes of those concerned. In order to determine these wishes a certain period is

17 *British Documents*, Third Series, Vol. II, no. 1068.

necessary for the preparation of the plebiscite during which disturbances must in all circumstances be prevented. A situation of parity must be created. The area designated on the attached map as a German area is to be occupied by German troops without taking account as to whether in the plebiscite there may prove to be in this or that part of the area a Czech majority. On the other hand, the Czech territory is to be occupied by Czech troops without taking account as to whether, within this area, there lie large German language islands, in which, in the plebiscite, a majority will without doubt give expression to its German national feeling.

With a view to bringing about an immediate and final solution of the Sudeten German problem the following proposals[1] are submitted by the German Government.

1. Withdrawal of the whole Czech armed forces, the police, the gendarmerie, the customs officials and the frontier guards from the area to be evacuated as designated on the attached map, this area to be handed over to Germany on October 1st.

2. The evacuated territory is to be handed over in its present condition (see further details in appendix). The German Government agree that a plenipotentiary representative of the Czech Government and of the Czech Army should be attached to the headquarters of the German military forces to deal with the details of the modalities for the evacuation.

3. The Czech Government discharges at once all Sudeten Germans serving in the military forces or the police anywhere in Czech State territory and permits them to return home.

4. The Czech Government liberates all political prisoners of German race.

5. The German Government agrees to permit a plebiscite to take place in those areas, which will be more definitely defined, before at latest the 25th November. Alterations to the new frontier arising out of the plebiscite will be settled by a German-Czech or an international commission.

The plebiscite itself will be carried out under the control of an international commission. All persons who were residing in the areas in question on the 28th of October 1918, or who where born in those areas prior to this date will be eligible to vote. A simple majority of all eligible male and female voters will determine the desire of the population to belong to either the German Reich or to the Czech State. During the plebiscite both parties will withdraw their military forces out of areas which will be defined more precisely. The date and duration will be settled mutually by the German and Czech Governments.

[1] In the text shown to Mr. Chamberlain the word "demands" was used in this sentence; and, in the following paragraph, September 26 was laid down as the date for the commencement and September 28 for the completion of the withdrawal of Czech troops and police, and in paragraph 5 the words "or an international" were not included. The modifications in the text were made by Herr Hitler as a result of the strongest remonstrances by Mr. Chamberlain. [See Document 16.]

6. The German Government proposes that an authoritative German-Czech commission should be set up to settle all further details.

Godesberg, September 23rd, 1938.

Appendix.

The evacuated Sudeten German area is to be handed over without destroying or rendering unusable in any way military, economic or traffic establishments (plants). These include the ground organisation of the air service and all wireless stations.

All economic and traffic materials, especially the rolling stock of the railway system, in the designated areas, are to be handed over undamaged. The same applies to all utility services (gas-works, power stations, etc.).

Finally no foodstuffs, goods, cattle, raw materials etc. are to be removed.

18 LETTER *from Prime Minister Chamberlain to Herr Hitler*[1]

September 26, 1938.

MY DEAR REICHSKANZLER: In my capacity as intermediary I have transmitted to the Czechoslovakian Government the Memorandum which Your Excellency gave me on the occasion of our last conversation.

The Czechoslovakian Government now inform me that, while they adhere to their acceptance of the proposals for the transfer of the Sudeten-German areas on the lines discussed by my Government and the French Government and explained by me to you on Thursday last, they regard as wholly unacceptable the proposal in your Memorandum for the immediate evacuation of the areas and their immediate occupation by German troops, these processes to take place before the terms of cession have been negotiated or even discussed.

Your Excellency will remember that in my letter to you of Friday last I said that an attempt to occupy forthwith by German troops areas which will become part of the Reich at once in principle and very shortly afterwards by formal delimitation, would be condemned as an unnecessary display of force and that in my opinion if German troops moved into the

[1] This letter was delivered by Sir Horace Wilson. The text of the letter was telegraphed to Sir R. Lindsay at 6.45 p.m. on September 27 for communication to President Roosevelt.

areas that you had proposed, I felt sure that Czechoslovakian Government would resist and that this would mean the destruction of the basis upon which you and I a week ago agreed to work together, namely, an orderly settlement of this question rather than a settlement by the use of force. I referred also to the effect likely to be produced upon public opinion in my country, in France and, indeed, in the world generally.

The development of opinion since my return confirms me in the views I expressed to you in my letter and in our subsequent conversation.

In communicating with me about your proposals, the Government of Czechoslovakia point out that they go far beyond what was agreed to in the so-called Anglo-French plan. Czechoslovakia would be deprived of every safeguard for her national existence. She would have to yield up large proportions of her carefully prepared defences and admit the German Armies deep into her country before it had been organised on the new basis or any preparations had been made for its defence. Her national and economic independence would automatically disappear with the acceptance of the German plan. The whole process of moving the population is to be reduced to panic flight.

I learn that the German Ambassador in Paris has issued a communiqué which begins by stating that as a result of our conversations at Godesberg Your Excellency and I are in complete agreement as to the imperative necessity to maintain the peace of Europe. In this spirit I address my present communication to you.

In the first place, I would remind Your Excellency that as the Czechoslovakian Government adhere to their acceptance of the proposals for the transfer of the Sudeten-German areas there can be no question of Germany "finding it impossible to have the clear rights of Germans in Czechoslovakia accepted by way of negotiation." I am quoting the words at the end of Your Excellency's letter to me of Friday last.

On the contrary a settlement by negotiation remains possible and, with a clear recollection of the conversations which you and I have had and with an equally clear appreciation of the consequences which must follow the abandonment of negotiation and the substitution of force, I ask Your Excellency to agree that representatives of Germany shall meet representatives of the Czechoslovakian Government to discuss immediately the situation by which we are confronted with a view to settling by agreement the way in which the territory is to be handed over. I am convinced that these discussions can be completed in a very short time and if you and the Czechoslovakian Government desire it, I am willing to arrange for the representation of the British Government at the discussions.

In our conversation, as in the official communiqué issued in Germany, you said that the only differences between us lay in the method of carrying out an agreed principle. If this is so, then surely the tragic consequences of a conflict ought not to be incurred over a difference in method.

A conference such as I suggest would give confidence that the cession of territory would be carried into effect but that it would be done in an orderly manner with suitable safeguards.

Convinced that your passionate wish to see the Sudeten-German question promptly and satisfactorily settled can be fulfilled without incurring the human misery and suffering that would inevitably follow on a conflict I most earnestly urge you to accept my proposal.

I am,

Yours faithfully,

NEVILLE CHAMBERLAIN

19 EXTRACTS *from Speech by Hitler, at the Sport Palace, in Berlin*

September 26, 1938.

❊   ❊   ❊   ❊   ❊

[Czechoslovakia: Attack on President Benes]

And now before us stands the last problem that must be solved and will be solved. It is the last territorial claim which I have to make in Europe, but it is the claim from which I will not recede and which, God willing, I will make good.

The history of the problem is as follows: in 1918 under the watchword "The Right of the Peoples to Self-Determination" Central Europe was torn in pieces and was newly formed by certain crazy so-called "statesmen." Without regard for the origin of the peoples, without regard for either their wish as nations or for economic necessities Central Europe at that time was broken up into atoms and new so-called States were arbitrarily formed. To this procedure Czechoslovakia owes its existence. This Czech State began with a single lie and the father of this lie was named Benes. This Mr. Benes at that time appeared in Versailles and he first of all gave the assurance that there was a Czechoslovak nation. He was forced to invent this lie in order to give to the slender number of his own fellow-countrymen a somewhat greater range and thus a fuller justification. And the Anglo-Saxon statesmen, who were, as always, not very adequately versed in respect of questions of geography or nationality, did not at that time find it necessary to test these assertions of Mr. Benes. Had they done so, they could have established the fact that there is no such thing as a Czechoslovak nation but only Czechs and Slovaks and that the Slovaks did not wish to have anything to do with the Czechs but . . . *(the rest of the sentence was drowned in a tumultuous outburst of applause).*

---

19 *Documents on International Affairs*, pp. 254-260.

So in the end through Mr. Benes these Czechs annexed Slovakia. Since this State did not seem fitted to live, out of hand three and a half million Germans were taken in violation of their right to self-determination and their wish for self-determination. Since even that did not suffice, over a million Magyars had to be added, then some Carpathian Russians, and at last several hundred thousand Poles.

That is this State which then later proceeded to call itself Czecho-slovakia—in violation of the right of the peoples to self-determination, in violation of the clear wish and will of the nations to which this violence had been done. When I speak to you here it goes without saying that I should sympathize with the fate of all these oppressed peoples, with the fate of Poles, Hungarians, and Ukrainians. I am naturally spokesman only for the fate of my Germans.

At the time that Mr. Benes lied this State into being, he gave a solemn pledge to divide it on the model of the Swiss system into cantons; for amongst the democratic statesmen there were some who still had some twinges of conscience. We all know how Mr. Benes has redeemed his pledge to introduce this cantonal system. He began his reign of terror. Even at that time the Germans already attempted to protest against this arbitrary violence. They were shot down. After that a war of extermina-tion began. In these years of the "peaceful" development of Czechoslo-vakia nearly 600,000 Germans had to leave Czechoslovakia. This hap-pened for a very simple reason: otherwise they would have had to starve!

The whole development from the year 1918 up to 1938 showed one thing clearly: Mr. Benes was determined slowly to exterminate the German element. And this to a certain extent he has achieved. He has hurled countless people into the profoundest misery. He has managed to make millions of people fearful and anxious. Through the continous em-ployment of his methods of terrorism he has succeeded in reducing to silence these millions while at the same time it also became clear what were the "international" duties of this State.

No longer was any secret made of the fact that this State was intended, if necessary, to be employed against Germany. A French Minister for Air, Pierre Cot, has expressed this wish quite soberly: "We need the State," he said, "because from this State German business life and German in-dustry can be most easily destroyed with bombs." And then Bolshevism uses this State as the gateway through which it can find entry. It is not we who have sought this contact with Bolshevism, but Bolshevism uses this State in order to possess a canal leading into Central Europe. . . .

Germany had not called a man to the colours: it never thought for a moment to solve this problem by military intervention. Still I always hoped that the Czechs at the last minute would realize that this tyranny could not be maintained any longer. But Mr. Benes adopted the stand-point that, protected by France and by England, one could do anything with Germany with impunity—nothing could happen to him. And above all: when all other strings failed, behind him stood Soviet Russia.

[Germany's Demands]

And so the answer of this man was now more than before: Shoot down, arrest, imprison—the fate of all those who in any way failed to please him. Thus it was that there came my demand in Nuremberg. This demand was quite clear: for the first time I there expressed the claim that now at last—almost twenty years since the statements of President Wilson—for these three and a half millions the right of self-determination must come into force. And once again Mr. Benes gave his answer: more deaths, more imprisonments, more arrests. The Germans began perforce to flee.

And then came England. I have told Mr. Chamberlain quite distinctly what we regard now as the sole possibility of a solution. It is the most natural solution that there can be. I know that *all* nationalities no longer wish to remain with Dr. Benes, but I am in the first place spokesman of the Germans, and for these Germans I have now spoken and asserted that I am no longer willing to look on calm and inactive and see how this madman in Prague thinks that he can undisturbed ill-treat three and a half million human beings. And I have left him in no doubt that now at last German patience has really come to an end: I have left him in no doubt that, though it is a characteristic of our German mentality to bear something for a long time and again and again to raise no protest, yet one day the moment comes when it has to stop! And now England and France have sent to Czechoslovakia the only possible demand—to set free the German area and to surrender it to the Reich.

We are now accurately informed on the conversations which Dr. Benes conducted at that time. Faced by the declaration of England and of France that they would no longer support Czechoslovakia if at last the fate of these peoples was not changed and the areas liberated Mr. Benes found a way of escape. He conceded that these districts must be surrendered. That was what he stated, but what did he do? He did not surrender the area but the Germans he now drives out! And that is now the point at which the game comes to an end. Mr. Benes had hardly spoken when he began his military subjugation afresh—only with still greater violence. We see the appalling figures: on one day 10,000 fugitives, on the next 20,000, a day later, already 37,000, again two days later 41,000, then 62,000, then 78,000: now 90,000, 107,000, 137,000 and today 214,000. Whole stretches of country were depopulated, villages are burned down, attempts are made to smoke out the Germans with hand-grenades and gas. Mr. Benes, however, sits in Prague and is convinced: "Nothing can happen to me: in the end England and France stand behind me.". . .

[The Godesberg Memorandum]

I have now placed a memorandum containing a last and final German proposal in the hands of the British Government. This memorandum contains nothing save the putting into effect of what Mr. Benes has already promised. The content of this proposal is very simple:

That area which in its people is German and has the wish to be German comes to Germany, and that, too, not only when Mr. Benes has succeeded in driving out perhaps one or two million Germans, but now, and that immediately! I have here chosen that frontier which on the basis of the material which has existed for decades on the division of people and language in Czechoslovakia is the just frontier-line. But in spite of this I am more just than Mr. Benes and I have no wish to exploit the power which we possess. I have therefore laid it down from the outset that this area will be placed under German supremacy (*Oberhoheit*) because it is essentially settled by Germans, the final delimitation of the frontier, however, I then leave to the vote of our fellow-countrymen themselves who are in the area! I have therefore laid down that in this area there must then be held a plebiscite. And in order that no one can say that the procedure of the plebiscite might be unjust, I have chosen as the basis for this plebiscite the Statute that governed the Saar Plebiscite.

Now I am and was prepared, so far as I am concerned, to allow a plebiscite to be held throughout the area. But Mr. Benes and his friends objected. They wished that a plebiscite should be allowed only in certain parts of the area. Good, I have yielded the point. I was even prepared to allow the plebiscite to be subject to the inspection of international Commissions of Control. I went even further and agreed to leave the delimitation of the frontier to a German-Czech Commission. Mr. Chamberlain suggested: might it not be an international Commission? To this, too, I agreed. I even wished during this period of the plebiscite to withdraw again the troops, and I have today declared my readiness to invite for this period the British Legion, which offered me its services, to go into these district and there maintain calm and order. And I was further ready to allow the international Commission to fix the final frontier and to hand over all details of procedure to a Commission composed of Germans and Czechs.

The content of this memorandum is nothing else than the practical execution of what Mr. Benes has already promised and that too under the most complete international guarantees. Mr. Benes now says that this memorandum is "a new situation." And in what in fact does this "new situation" consist? It consists in this: that this time—exceptionally—the promise made by Mr. Benes must also be kept! That is for Mr. Benes the "new situation." What is there that Mr. Benes has not promised at some time in his life? And no promise has been kept! Now for the first time he has got to keep to something.

Mr. Benes says: "We cannot go back from this area." Mr. Benes has then understood the transfer of this area to mean that the legal title is recognized as belonging to the German Reich but the area is still to be subject to the violence of the Czechs. That is now past!

I have demanded that now after twenty years Mr. Benes should at last be compelled to come to terms with the truth. On 1 October he will have to hand over to us this area. . . .

[*Denial of Further Territorial Claims*]

I have only a few statements still to make: I am grateful to Mr. Chamberlain for all his efforts. I have assured him that the German people desires nothing else than peace, but I have also told him that I cannot go back behind the limits set to our patience. I have further assured him, and I repeat it here, that when this problem is solved there is for Germany no further territorial problem in Europe. And I have further assured him that at the moment when Czechoslovakia solves her problems, that means when the Czechs have come to terms with their other minorities, and that peaceably and not through oppression, then I have no further interest in the Czech State. And that is guaranteed to him! We want no Czechs!

[*Ultimatum*]

But in the same way I desire to state before the German people that with regard to the problem of the Sudeten Germans my patience is now at an end! I have made Mr. Benes an offer which is nothing but the carrying into effect of what he himself has promised. The decision now lies in his hands: Peace or War! He will either accept this offer and now at last give to the Germans their freedom or we will go and fetch this freedom for ourselves. The world must take note that in four and a half years of war and through the long years of my political life there is one thing which no one could ever cast in my teeth: I have never been a coward!

Now I go before my people as its first soldier and behind me—that the world should know—there marches a people and a different people from that of 1918!

If at that time a wandering scholar was able to inject into our people the poison of democratic catchwords—the people of today is no longer the people that it was then. Such catchwords are for us like wasp-stings: they cannot hurt us: we are now immune.

In this hour the whole German people will unite with me! It will feel my will to be its will. Just as in my eyes it is its future and its fate which give me the commission for my action. And we wish now to make our will as strong as it was in the time of our fight, the time when I, as a simple unknown soldier, went forth to conquer a Reich and never doubted of success and final victory. Then there gathered close about me a band of brave men and brave women, and they went with me. And so I ask you, my German people, take your stand behind me, man by man, and woman by woman. In this hour we all wish to form a common will and that will must be stronger than every hardship and every danger. And if this will is stronger than hardship and danger, then one day it will break down hardship and danger.

We are determined!

Now let Mr. Benes make his choice!

20 STATEMENT *by Prime Minister Chamberlain*[1]

September 26, 1938.

I have read the speech of the German Chancellor[2] and I appreciate his references to the efforts I have made to save the peace. I cannot abandon those efforts since it seems to me incredible that the peoples of Europe who do not want war with one another should be plunged into a bloody struggle over a question on which agreement has already been largely obtained.

It is evident that the Chancellor has no faith that the promises made will be carried out. These promises were made, not to the German Government direct, but to the British and French Governments in the first instance. Speaking for the British Government we regard ourselves as morally responsible for seeing that the promises are carried out fairly and fully, and we are prepared to undertake that they shall be so carried out with all reasonable promptitude, provided that the German Government will agree to the settlement of terms and conditions of transfer by discussion and not by force.

I trust that the Chancellor will not reject this proposal, which is made in the same spirit of friendliness as that in which I was received in Germany and which, if it is accepted, will satisfy the German desire for the union of Sudeten Germans with the Reich without the shedding of blood in any part of Europe.

[1] The Prime Minister's statement was issued to the press in the middle of the night. During the afternoon of the 26th the following official statement had been authorized by Lord Halifax at the Foreign Office, and it was broadcast just before 10 P.M. at night:

"During the last week Mr. Chamberlain has tried with the German Chancellor to find the way of settling peacefully the Czechoslovak question. It is still possible to do so by negotiation."

"The German claim to the transfer of the Sudeten areas has already been conceded by the French, British, and Czechoslovak Governments, but if in spite of all efforts made by the British Prime Minister a German attack is made upon Czechoslovakia the immediate result must be that France will be bound to come to her assistance, and Great Britain and Russia will certainly stand by France."

"It is still not too late to stop this great tragedy, and for the peoples of all nations to insist on settlement by free negotiation." *British Documents*, Third Series, Vol. II, no. 1111, note 1.—F. L. L.

[2] This was a reference to Hitler's address at the Sport Palace earlier in the evening. See document 19.—F. L. L.

20 *Documents on International Affairs*, pp. 260-261.

21 LETTER *from Hitler to Prime Minister Chamberlain*[1]

BERLIN, September 27, 1938.

DEAR MR. CHAMBERLAIN: I have in the course of the conversations once more informed Sir Horace Wilson, who brought me your letter of September 26, of my final attitude. I should like, however, to make the following written reply to certain details in your letter:—

The Government in Prague feels justified in maintaining that the proposals in my memorandum of September 23 went far beyond the concession which it made to the British and French Governments and that the acceptance of the memorandum would rob Czechoslovakia of every guarantee for its national existence. This statement is based on the argument that Czechoslovakia is to give up a great part of her prepared defensive system before she can take steps elsewhere for her military protection. Thereby the political and economic independence of the country is automatically abolished. Moreover, the exchange of population proposed by me would turn out in practice to be a panic-stricken flight.

I must openly declare that I cannot bring myself to understand these arguments or even admit that they can be regarded as seriously put forward. The Government in Prague simply passes over the fact that the actual arrangement for the final settlement of the Sudeten German problem, in accordance with my proposals, will be made dependent, not on a unilateral German decision or on German measures of force, but rather, on the one hand, on a free vote under no outside influence, and, on the other hand, to a very wide degree on German-Czech agreement on matters of detail to be reached subsequently. Not only the exact definition of the territories in which the plebiscite is to take place, but the execution of the plebiscite and the delimitation of the frontier to be made on the basis of its result, are in accordance with my proposals to be met independently of any unilateral decision by Germany. Moreover, all other details are to be reserved for agreement on the part of a German-Czech commission.

In the light of this interpretation of my proposals and in the light of the cession of the Sudeten population areas, in fact agreed to by Czechoslovakia, the immediate occupation by German contingents demanded by me represents no more than a security measure which is intended to guarantee a quick and smooth achievement of the final settlement.

---

[1] Document No. 10 in the British White Paper, Cmd. 5847. The copy found in the Foreign Ministry file is an unsigned and undated draft, amended in Weizsäcker's handwriting.

This security measure is indispensable. If the German Government renounced it and left the whole further treatment of the problem simply to normal negotiations with Czechoslovakia, the present unbearable circumstances in the Sudeten German territories, which I described in my speech yesterday, would continue to exist for a period, the length of which cannot be foreseen. The Czechoslovak Government would be completely in a position to drag out the negotiations on any point they liked, and thus to delay the final settlement. You will understand after everything that has passed that I cannot place such confidence in the assurances received from the Prague Government. The British Government also would surely not be in a position to dispose of this danger by any use of diplomatic pressure.

That Czechoslovakia should lose part of her fortifications is naturally an unavoidable consequence of the cession of the Sudeten German territory agreed to by the Prague Government itself. If one were to wait for the entry into force of the final settlement, in which Czechoslovakia had completed new fortifications in the territory which remained to her, it would doubtless last months and years. But this is the only object of all the Czech objections. Above all, it is completely incorrect to maintain that Czechoslovakia in this manner would be crippled in her national existence or in her political and economic independence. It is clear from my memorandum that the German occupation would only extend to the given line, and that the final delimitation of the frontier would take place in accordance with the procedure which I have already described. The Prague Government has no right to doubt that the German military measures would stop within these limits. If, nevertheless, it desires such a doubt to be taken into account, the British and, if necessary, also the French Government can guarantee the quick fulfillment of my proposal. I can, moreover, only refer to my speech yesterday in which I clearly declared that I regret the idea of any attack on Czechoslovak territory and that, under the condition which I laid down, I am even ready to give a formal guarantee for the remainder of Czechoslovakia. There can, therefore, be not the slightest question whatsoever of a check to the independence of Czechoslovakia. It is equally erroneous to talk of an economic rift. It is, on the contrary, a well-known fact that Czechoslovakia, after the cession of the Sudeten German territory, would constitute a healthier and more unified economic organism than before.

If the Government in Prague finally evinces anxiety also in regard to the state of the Czech population in the territories to be occupied, I can only regard this with surprise. It can be sure that, on the German side, nothing whatever will occur which will preserve for those Czechs a similar fate to that which has befallen the Sudeten Germans consequent on the Czech measures.

In these circumstances, I must assume that the Government in Prague is only using a proposal for the occupation by German troops in order, by distorting the meaning and object of my proposal, to mobilize those forces in other countries, in particular in England and France, from which they hope to receive unreserved support for their aim, and thus to achieve the possibility of a general warlike conflagration. I must leave it to your judgment whether, in view of these facts, you consider that you should continue your effort, for which I should like to take this opportunity of once more sincerely thanking you, to spoil such maneuvers and bring the Government in Prague to reason at the very last hour.

22 BROADCAST SPEECH *by Prime Minister Chamberlain*

September 27, 1938.

Tomorrow Parliament is going to meet, and I shall be making a full statement of the events which have led up to the present anxious and critical situation. An earlier statement would not have been possible when I was flying backwards and forwards across Europe, and the position was changing from hour to hour. But today there is a lull for a brief time, and I want to say a few words to you, men and women of Britain and the Empire, and perhaps to others as well.

First of all I must say something to those who have written to my wife or myself in these last weeks to tell us of their gratitude for my efforts and to assure us of their prayers for my success. Most of these letters have come from women—mothers or sisters of our own countrymen. But there are countless others besides—from France, from Belgium, from Italy, even from Germany, and it has been heart-breaking to read of the growing anxiety they reveal and their intense relief when they thought, too soon, that the danger of war was past.

If I felt my responsibility heavy before, to read such letters has made it seem almost overwhelming. How horrible, fantastic, incredible it is that we should be digging trenches and trying on gas-masks here because of a quarrel in a far-away country between people of whom we know nothing. It seems still more impossible that a quarrel which has already been settled in principle should be the subject of war.

I can well understand the reasons why the Czech Government have felt unable to accept the terms which have been put before them in the German memorandum. Yet I believe after my talks with Herr Hitler that, if only time were allowed, it ought to be possible for the arrange-

22 *Documents on International Affairs,* pp. 270-1.

ments for transferring the territory that the Czech Government has agreed to give to Germany to be settled by agreement under conditions which would assure fair treatment to the population concerned.

You know already that I have done all that one man can do to compose this quarrel. After my visits to Germany I have realized vividly how Herr Hitler feels that he must champion other Germans, and his indignation that grievances have not been met before this. He told me privately, and last night he repeated publicly, that after this Sudeten German question is settled, that is the end of Germany's territorial claims in Europe.

After my first visit to Berchtesgaden I did get the assent of the Czech Government to proposals which gave the substance of what Herr Hitler wanted, and I was taken completely by surprise when I got back to Germany and found that he insisted that the territory should be handed over to him immediately, and immediately occupied by German troops without previous arrangements for safeguarding the people within the territory who were not Germans, or did not want to join the German Reich.

I must say that I find this attitude unreasonable. If it arises out of any doubts that Herr Hitler feels about the intentions of the Czech Government to carry out their promises and hand over the territory, I have offered on the part of the British Government to guarantee their words, and I am sure the value of our promise will not be underrated anywhere. I shall not give up the hope of a peaceful solution, or abandon my efforts for peace, as long as any chance for peace remains. I would not hesitate to pay even a third visit to Germany if I thought it would do any good. But at this moment I see nothing further that I can usefully do in the way of mediation.

Meanwhile there are certain things we can and shall do at home. Volunteers are still wanted for air-raid precautions, for fire brigade and police services, and for the Territorial units. I know that all of you, men and women alike, are ready to play your part in the defence of the country, and I ask you all to offer your services, if you have not already done so, to the local authorities, who will tell you if you are wanted and in what capacity.

Do not be alarmed if you hear of men being called up to man the anti-aircraft defences or ships. These are only precautionary measures such as a Government must take in times like this. But they do not necessarily mean that we have determined on war or that war is imminent.

However much we may sympathize with a small nation confronted by a big and powerful neighbour, we cannot in all circumstances undertake to involve the whole British Empire in war simply on her account. If we have to fight it must be on larger issues than that. I am myself a man of peace to the depths of my soul. Armed conflict between nations is a nightmare to me; but if I were convinced that any nation had made up its mind to dominate the world by fear of its force, I should feel that it must be resisted. Under such a domination life for people who believe in liberty would not be worth living; but war is a fearful thing, and we must be very clear, before we embark on it, that it is really the great issues that are at stake, and that the call to risk everything in their defence, when all the consequences are weighed, is irresistible.

For the present I ask you to await as calmly as you can the events of the next few days. As long as war has not begun, there is always hope that it may be prevented, and you know that I am going to work for peace to the last moment. Good night.

23 TELEGRAM *from Viscount Halifax to Sir Nevile Henderson*[1]

September 28, 1938, 11:30 A.M.

You should seek immediate interview with German Chancellor and deliver to him the following personal message from the Prime Minister:—

After reading your letter I feel certain that you can get all essentials without war and without delay.

I am ready to come to Berlin myself at once to discuss arrangements for transfer with you and representatives of Czech Government, together with representatives of France and Italy if you desire.

I feel convinced we could reach agreement in a week. However much you distrust Prague Government's intentions, you cannot doubt power

---

[1] British Ambassador in Berlin. At the same time Lord Halifax sent the following telegram, by telephone, to the Earl of Perth, the British Ambassador in Rome:

"You should immediately communicate the following personal message from the Prime Minister to the Duce:—

I have today addressed last appeal to Herr Hitler to abstain from force to settle Sudeten problem which I feel sure can be settled by a short discussion and will give him the essential territory, population and protection for both Sudetens and Czechs during transfer. I have offered myself to go at once to Berlin to discuss arrangements with German and Czech representatives and, if the Chancellor desires, representatives also of Italy and France.

I trust Your Excellency will inform German Chancellor that you are willing to be represented and urge him to agree to my proposal which will keep all our peoples out of war. I have already guaranteed that Czech promises shall be carried out and feel confident full agreement could be reached in a week.

Repeated to Paris, Washington, Prague, and Berlin."

British Documents, Third Series, Vol. II, no. 1159.—F.L.L.

of British and French Governments to see that promises are carried out fairly and fully and forthwith. As you know I have stated publicly that we are prepared to undertake that they shall be so carried out.

I cannot believe that you will take responsibility of starting a world war which may end civilisation for the sake of a few days' delay in settling this long standing problem.

Repeated to Paris, Washington, Prague and Rome.

24 MEMORANDUM *on the First Meeting Between the British and French Prime Ministers, Mussolini, and Hitler at Munich*

MUNICH, September 29, 1938—7 P.M.

IMMEDIATE
STRICTLY SECRET

For the Under State Secretary, the Foreign Ministry, Berlin.
By special messenger.
Send Under State Secretary's certificate of receipt.

The Führer opened the discussion at 12:45 p.m. and expressed his thanks to the Heads of Government present for accepting his invitation to come to Munich. He added that he wished first of all to give a brief summary of the Czech question as it appeared at the present time. The existence of Czechoslovakia in her present form threatened the peace of Europe. The German, Hungarian, Slovak, Polish, and Carpatho-Russian minorities, which had been forced into this State against their will, revolted against its continued existence. He, the Führer, could only come forward as spokesman for the German minorities.

In the interest of European peace, the problem must be settled in the shortest possible time and, particularly, by the Czech Government's fulfillment of their promises of cession [of territory]. Germany could no longer contemplate the distress and misery of the Sudeten German population. Reports of the destruction of property were coming in in increasing numbers. The population was exposed to a barbaric persecution. Since he, the Führer, had last spoken with Mr. Chamberlain, the number of refugees had risen to 240,000, and there seemed to be no end to the flood. Moreover, it was necessary that the political, military, and economic tension, which had become intolerable, should end. This tension made it necessary to settle the problem in a few days as it was to postpone mobilization in Germany for 24 hours. Further delay would be a crime. In order to settle the problem, the responsible statesmen of Europe had assembled here, and he observed that their differences were really very small, for, in the first place, it was agreed that the territory must be ceded to Germany and, secondly, that Germany claimed nothing more than this territory. However, in order to ascertain exactly what territory was involved, it could not be left to a commission to decide. It was much rather a plebiscite that was necessary, especially as for 20 years no free election had taken place in Czechoslovakia. He had now declared in his speech in the Sport Palace that he would in any case march in on October 1. He had received the answer that this action would have the character of an act of violence. Hence the task arose to absolve this action from such a character. Action must, however, be taken at once; in the first place, because the persecutions could no longer be tolerated, and, in addition, because, in face of the vacillating attitude of Prague, no further delay could be suffered. From the military aspect the occupation presented no problem, for the depths on all fronts were comparatively small. With a little good will it must consequently be possible to evacuate the territory in 10 days; indeed, he was convinced, in from 6 to 7 days. In order to conciliate public opinion in England and France he wished to leave open the question of whether Germany would also march into the territory in which the Plebiscite was to be held. In this case, however, the Czechs would have to do the same, so that a situation of parity would be brought about. The conditions governing the transfer could be discussed, but action must soon be taken. The fact that armed powers were lined up against each other in Europe, as at this present time, would be unbearable over a prolonged period.

Mr. Chamberlain, the Prime Minister, thanked the Führer first of all for the invitation to the discussions, and extended these thanks to the Duce also, to whose initiative, if he had understood rightly, today's discussions were in part to be ascribed. Today's discussions gave Europe new breathing space, whereas yesterday catastrophe seemed to be immediately impending. He fully comprehended that action must be taken quickly, and he particularly welcomed the Führer's declaration that he did not wish to apply force, but to establish order. If the problem was approached in this spirit he was sure that results would be obtained.

The Head of the Italian Government observed at this point that theoretical agreement had already been reached and that it was now only a matter of translating this theoretical agreement into practice. The question of time was of particular importance in this connection. Every delay was a source of danger. He therefore particularly insisted on speedy action, because in this case speed fully coincided with justice. It was better to come to an agreement this very day, as an adjournment of only 24 hours would produce new unrest and new mistrust. In order to bring about a practical solution of the problem, he wished to make the following proposal. . . . [1]

Daladier, the French Prime Minister, thanked the Führer also for his initiative. He was delighted to have the opportunity now of meeting him personally. The plan for such a meeting had, indeed, already existed before, but circumstances had unfortunately prevented its realization until the present. However, there was a French proverb: "Better late than never."

M. Daladier, the French Prime Minister, then also expressed to the Duce his personal admiration for the latter's step which would, it was to be hoped, lead to a solution of the question. He was of the opinion, even as was Mr. Chamberlain, that measures would have to be taken with the utmost promptitude. He particularly welcomed the Duce's proposal which had been made in an objective and realistic spirit, and which he accepted as a basis for discussion. This naturally did not signify that he agreed on all points, as for one thing, economic points of view would have to be considered, in order that the foundation of future war should not be laid. Finally, there still remained the question of the organization of the plebiscite and the demarcation of the zone. He mentioned these points only because he had not yet carefully studied the proposal which had just been read through. He wished to accept it at once, however, as a basis for discussion.

Chamberlain, the Prime Minister of Great Britain, also welcomed the Duce's proposal and declared that he himself had conceived of a solution on the lines of this proposal. As regards the guarantee demanded of Great Britain he would welcome it if a representative of the Czech Government were available, for Great Britain could naturally undertake no guarantee that the territory would be evacuated by October 10, and that no demolition would be carried out, if no assurance of this was forthcoming from the Czech Government.

[1] The Italian proposals, which formed the basis of the subsequent discussions, do not accompany the memorandum printed, and it has not been possible to trace a copy in the German files. They were, however, identical with [German Documents]. Erich Kordt has given the following account of the history of these demands:

"He [Weizsäcker] got hold of Neurath and Goering and elaborated with them a short paper with possible conditions of a compromise, for a plebiscite to be taken in the regions, for evacuation dates in the case that the plebiscite should be favorable to Germany. Then Goering submitted this draft to Hitler, who took a quick look at this paper and said, well, it might perhaps be acceptable to him. Now this paper has a special significance because the moment afterward I was asked to have Schmidt translate it into French. The State Secretary passed it on to Ambassador Attolico, Attolico rushed to meet Mussolini on his way to Munich. And when the meeting opened in Munich, to the great surprise of Ribbentrop and others present, Mussolini presented this suggestion as his own, and therefore the whole proceedings of the Munich Conference were conducted on the basis of this paper." (Official Transcript of Evidence Given at Nuremberg on June 4, 1948, Before U. S. Military Tribunal IV in the Matter of *U.S.A.* v. *Ernst Weizsäcker.*) Cf. also E. Kordt, *Wahn und Wirklichkeit* (Stuttgart, 1947), pp. 129-131.

[A provisional translation of the Italian proposals is printed in *British Documents*, no. 1227, Appendix A—F. L. L.]

The Führer answered this by saying that he was not interested in an assurance from the Czech Government, as it was this very Government which was already carrying out demolition work. The real question was how to bring the Czech Government to accept the proposal. It was agreed that Germany should receive the territory ceded. The Czechs maintained, however, that they could not undertake an evacuation before new fortifications were established and economic decisions had been taken.

Daladier, the French Prime Minister, answered that the French Government would in no wise tolerate procrastination in this matter by the Czech Government. The Czech Government had given its word and must honor it. There could be no talk of postponing the evacuation of the territory until new fortifications were installed. He asked that these ideas should be completely excluded from the discussions, since the Czech Government were receiving a guarantee in return for their cession. In general, however, he was of the opinion, as was Mr. Chamberlain, that the presence of a Czech representative, who could be consulted if necessary [*eventuell*], would be of advantage. This seemed to him to be of advantage above all because it would obviate confusion which could so easily arise in a matter so delicate as a cession of territory. Everything must be done to avoid chaos.

The Führer replied that, if the Czech Government's consent had first to be sought on every detail, a solution could not be expected before a fortnight had passed. The Duce's proposal contemplated a commission on which a representative of the Czech Government would also sit. What interested him most was a guarantee by the Great Powers, who should exercise their authority to prevent the Czech Government from their continuing persecutions and demolitions.

Chamberlain, the Prime Minister, replied that he was not of the opinion, either, that there should be any further delay. However, before he undertook a guarantee he must know whether he could honor it, and for this reason he would welcome the presence of a Prague representative in the next room, in order that assurances could be obtained from him.

The Führer replied that no Czech representative was available who could speak with authority for his Government. The interesting question for him was what would happen if the Czech Government did not accept the proposal of the Great Powers. Up to the present time 247 bridges and a still greater number of houses had been destroyed.

The Italian Prime Minister declared that he too thought that it was not possible to await a Czech representative. The Great Powers must undertake a moral guarantee as regards the evacuation and prevention of work of destruction. They must point out in Prague that the Czech Government must accept the demands, or would otherwise have to bear the military consequences. It was a question of a kind of request by the Great Powers, who were under a moral obligation to prevent this territory from being handed over as a desert.

Chamberlain, the Prime Minister, replied that he would like to have a

Czechoslovak representative present. For the rest, the timetable proposed by the Duce seemed to him quite reasonable. He was ready to set his hand to it and to inform the Czech Government that they should accept it. He could, however, undertake no guarantee until he knew how far he could honor it. There were, besides, a few other details to clarify:— What powers would the international commission have and what authority would prevail in the territory when it was evacuated? He had no doubt but that the Führer would maintain order and would also take care that those inhabitants who were against the union should not be persecuted. A few points in the German memorandum were, however, misunderstood in Britain. Thus, the question had been asked as to what the regulation signified which stated that no cattle should be taken out of this territory. Did this mean that the farmers would be expelled but that their cattle would be retained?[2]

The Führer replied that, in the territory to be ceded to Germany, German laws would naturally be applied; moreover, the facts were completely the reverse. At present it was the Czechs who were driving the German farmers' cattle away and not the converse. What seemed decisive was whether the question should be regarded as a German-Czech conflict which could be settled in a fortnight, or whether it should be regarded as a problem of European significance. If a European problem was in question, then the Great Powers would have to throw their authority into the scales and accept the responsibility for the correct completion of the transfer. If, that is to say, the Czech Government did not wish to accept these proposals, it was clear that the greatest moral authority which could possibly exist, that is to say the authority which was incorporated by the signatures of the four statesmen here assembled, would not suffice. In this case, application of force alone could solve the question.

Mr. Chamberlain, the Prime Minister, replied that he had no objections to raise against the proposed time limits. The Czech question was a European question, and the Great Powers had not only the right to settle it, but the duty also. They also had to ensure that the Czech Government did not repudiate the evacuation of the territory from unreasonableness and obstinacy. It was his wish to apply the authority of the Great Powers in the correct manner; and therefore he proposed first of all to distribute the Duce's plan, and to adjourn the meeting for a short while so that this plan could be studied. Such a procedure did not mean delay.

Daladier, the French Prime Minister, explained that he had already assumed responsibility in London when, without consulting the Czech Government, he had accepted the cession of the German territory in principle. He had adopted the point of view in spite of the fact that France had a treaty of alliance with Czechoslovakia. If the inclusion of a Prague representative would cause difficulties he was ready to forego

---

[2] Cf. the letter from the Czech Minister in London, M. Jan Masaryk, to the British Foreign Secretary on September 25, printed as document No. 7 in the British White Paper, Cmd. 5847.

this, for it was important that the question should be settled speedily.

The Führer replied that if a document bearing the signatures of the four statesmen was, notwithstanding, rejected by the Prague Government, then, in the final analysis, Prague only respected force.

25 MEMORANDUM *on the Second Meeting Between the British and French Prime Ministers, Mussolini, and Hitler at Munich,* at 4:30 P.M.[1]

MUNICH, September 29, 1938.

At the Duce's suggestion it was first decided to discuss point by point the Italian proposal submitted to the delegations in the morning.

Point 1) (beginning of evacuation on October 1) was at once agreed to unanimously.

On point 2) the Führer stated that, if agreement could be reached on this point too, the question of procedure would no longer present any great difficulties. His proposal was first to define on the map certain stages of the German occupation, the procedure of which could then be established by a commission, on which there would also be a Czech representative.

Prime Minister Chamberlain expressed his agreement with the date fixed in point 2) for the completion of the evacuation of the German area, October 10. However, he expressed doubts on the possibility of giving a guarantee to Germany as long as he did not know Czechoslovakia's attitude to the question of evacuation.

On the question whether Czechoslovakia's previous agreement had to be obtained for the granting of the guarantee provided for in the Italian proposal, as Mr. Chamberlain seemed to suggest, Daladier stated that such agreement did not seem necessary to him. At the time he had agreed with Great Britain to the principle of cession of territory by Czechoslovakia, in spite of the Franco-Czech pact, without first consulting the Czechoslovak Government, and now took the view that what had once been promised must be adhered to. With reference to the Anglo-French guarantee, Daladier likewise rejected the Czechoslovak objection previously mentioned in the discussion, that the evacuation

[1] This memorandum was prepared by Erich Kordt, an official of the German Foreign Minister's staff. For the text of Sir Horace Wilson's Note on the first and second meetings, see *British Documents*, Third Series, Vol. II, no. 1227—F.L.L.

could only take place when new defenses had been completed on Czech territory. An evacuation of the purely German area could thus take place quickly; difficulties would only arise where there were language enclaves. It seemed to him that in this district an international occupation by British, Italian, and French forces was appropriate. Moreover, in his opinion, geographical, economic, and political realities must be taken into consideration, as additions to Wilson's principle of self-determination. Furthermore, the principle of exchange of populations used in Greece, Turkey, Bulgaria, and Poland could be applied with regard to the language enclaves.

The Führer agreed that districts with a doubtful German majority should not be occupied by German troops, but should at first be occupied by international units. If point 2) were accepted, he was prepared to act generously when determining the frontier as far as territory was concerned. The proposition put forward by Daladier, that economic, geographical, and political factors should also be taken into consideration in delimiting the frontier seemed to him dangerous, for it was to this very idea that the Czechoslovak State owed its creation in 1918. At that time a structure economically, but not nationally, viable had been created. Moreover, economic difficulties were more easily overcome than national difficulties, all the more so as Czechoslovakia, which was not an old cultural nation, could not assimilate German elements.

After a lengthy discussion on the different meaning of the word "guarantee" in Great Britain and on the Continent, the point was referred to a drafting committee for rewording. This committee, after lengthy deliberation, agreed on the preamble appearing in the text of the agreement as well as a rewording of paragraph 2).

At this point the meeting broke up into individual discussions, the subject of which, with the aid of maps, was particularly the zones to be evacuated and the area in which a plebiscite was to be held. In the course of these discussions Daladier proposed the exchange of a comparatively large zone of predominantly German territory on the Silesian frontier in which Czech fortifications were situated for a corresponding strip of Czech territory in the Böhmerwald, remarking that the existence of the Czech fortifications was not the only reason for this proposal, but that he was making it on grounds of communication policy and for psychological reasons.

The Führer rejected this proposal because of the purely German character of the territory in question, but, after lengthy negotiations, expressed his willingness to accept a formula appearing in the text of the agreement (see paragraph 6 of the Munich Agreement) on frontier adjustments.

Daladier expressed his sincere thanks to the Führer for this and said that the acceptance of this formula would considerably ease the position in France. He would report in France that the Führer had made this personal gesture to him (Daladier).

The decisions reached as a result of the individual discussions between the statesmen were then finally formulated by a drafting committee of the Four Powers, in collaboration with the legal advisers of the delegations, and submitted for the first reading about 10 o'clock in the evening. The final text of the agreement was submitted at 11 o'clock and signed in four languages between 11 and 12 o'clock. At the same time were accepted: a supplementary statement originating in a suggestion by Mussolini on the solution of the problem of the Polish and Magyar minorities; also an additional agreement on a guarantee to be given for the new frontiers of the Czech State; a supplement, stating that all questions arising out of the transfer of territory were within the competence of the new international committee which was to be formed, as well as a further supplement on the composition of the international commission in Berlin.

In conclusion, the Führer thanked the foreign statesmen for their acceptance of his invitation to Munich for the Four-Power talks, and also for their efforts to achieve the happy result of the negotiations. The German people, as well as the other peoples concerned, would welcome this result with the greatest joy, and, in expressing his thanks, he did so at the same time in the name of the German people.

Chamberlain replied on behalf of the foreign statesmen and associated himself with the Führer's remarks on the satisfaction of the peoples concerned with the outcome of Munich. Furthermore he stressed the importance of the agreement for the future development of European politics.

ERICH KORDT

26 AGREEMENT *Signed at Munich Between Germany, the United Kingdom, France, and Italy*[1]

September 29, 1938.

Germany, the United Kingdom, France, and Italy, taking into consideration the agreement, which has been already reached in principle for the cession to Germany of the Sudeten German territory, have agreed on the following terms and conditions governing the said cession and the measures consequent thereon, and by this agreement they each hold themselves responsible for the steps necessary to secure its fulfillment.

[1] The text reproduced is in English in the original and is identical with document No. 4 in the British White Paper, Great Britain, Cmd. 5848: *Further Documents Respecting Czechoslovakia, Including the Agreement Concluded at Munich on September 29, 1938.* Both it and the German version were signed.

26 *German Documents*, Series D, Vol. II, no. 675.

1) The evacuation will begin on October 1st.

2) The United Kingdom, France, and Italy agree that the evacuation of the territory shall be completed by October 10th, without any existing installations having been destroyed, and that the Czechoslovak Government will be held responsible for carrying out the evacuation without damage to the said installations.

3) The conditions governing the evacuation will be laid down in detail by an international commission composed of representatives of Germany, the United Kingdom, France, Italy, and Czechoslovakia.

4) The occupation by stages of the predominantly German territory by German troops will begin on October 1st. The four territories marked on the attached map will be occupied by German troops in the following order: the territory marked number I on the 1st and 2d of October, the territory marked number II on the 2d and 3d of October, the territory marked number III on the 3d, 4th, and 5th of October, the territory marked number IV on the 6th and 7th of October. The remaining territory of preponderantly German character will be ascertained by the aforesaid international commission forthwith and be occupied by German troops by the 10th of October.

5) The international commission referred to in paragraph 3) will determine the territories in which a plebiscite is to be held. These territories will be occupied by international bodies until the plebiscite has been completed. The same commission will fix the conditions in which the plebiscite is to be held, taking as a basis the conditions of the Saar plebiscite. The commission will also fix a date, not later than the end of November, on which the plebiscite will be held.

6) The final determination of the frontiers will be carried out by the international commission. This commission will also be entitled to recommend to the four Powers, Germany, the United Kingdom, France, and Italy, in certain exceptional cases, minor modifications in the strictly ethnographical determination of the zones which are to be transferred without plebiscite.

7) There will be a right of option into and out of the transferred territories, the option to be exercised within 6 months from the date of this agreement. A German-Czechoslovak commission shall determine the details of the option, consider ways of facilitating the transfer of population and settle questions of principle arising out of the said transfer.

8) The Czechoslovak Government will, within a period of 4 weeks from the date of this agreement, release from their military and police forces any Sudeten Germans who may wish to be released, and the Czechoslovak Government will within the same period release Sudeten German prisoners who are serving terms of imprisonment for political offenses.

ADOLF HITLER
ED. DALADIER
MUSSOLINI
MUNICH, September 29, 1938.   NEVILLE CHAMBERLAIN

ANNEX TO THE AGREEMENT

His Majesty's Government in the United Kingdom and the French Government have entered into the above agreement on the basis that they stand by the offer, contained in paragraph 6 of the Anglo-French proposals of September 19th, relating to an international guarantee of the new boundaries of the Czechoslovak State against unprovoked aggression.

When the question of the Polish and Hungarian minorities in Czechoslovakia has been settled, Germany and Italy for their part will give a guarantee to Czechoslovakia.

ADOLF HITLER
NEVILLE CHAMBERLAIN
MUSSOLINI
ED. DALADIER

MUNICH, September 29, 1938.

27 NOTE *of a Conversation Between Prime Minister Chamberlain and Herr Hitler, at the Latter's Flat in Munich*[1]

September 30, 1938.

Prime Minister: He was very pleased at the result of yesterday's proceedings, and he hoped that Herr Hitler was equally happy.

Herr Hitler: He was particularly happy, especially that the hopes of many millions of Germans had now been fulfilled and that the 3½ millions of Sudeten Germans were now going to be once more secure. Their sufferings had indeed been terrible, but now they would be the happiest of all about the result of the conference. In this connection he would like to thank the British Prime Minister once more for his great efforts to bring about a peaceful solution. The most difficult problem of all had now been concluded and his own main task had been happily fulfilled.

Prime Minister: He warmly appreciated Herr Hitler's words, but there was now something he wished to say to him by way of an appeal. He had

[1] This record was made by Dr. Schmidt. The record was sent to Mr. Chamberlain after he had left Munich, and was generally confirmed by him, but this confirmation cannot be taken as an acceptance of the verbal accuracy of the record.

been told that Herr Hitler intended, if the Czechs accepted the proposals, to treat them very generously. This was what he (the Prime Minister) would have expected from Herr Hitler, but he was obliged to consider the possibility that the Czech Government might be mad enough to refuse the terms and attempt resistance. In such an eventuality he wanted to ask Herr Hitler to make sure that nothing should be done which would diminish the high opinion of him which would be held throughout the world in consequence of yesterday's proceedings. In particular, he trusted that there would be no bombardment of Prague or killing of women and children by attacks from the air.

Herr Hitler: Before answering that specific question, he would like to say something on a point of principle. Years ago he made proposals for the restriction of the use of the air arm. He himself fought in the Great War and has a personal knowledge of what air bombardment means. It had been his intention, if he had to use force, to limit air action to front line zones as a matter of principle, but even if the Czechs were mad enough to reject the terms and he had consequently to take forcible action, he would always try to spare the civilian population and to confine himself to military objectives. He hated the thought of little babies being killed by gas bombs. . . .

Now, he would not keep Herr Hitler any longer, but he wished to say that he thought it would be a pity if this meeting passed off with nothing more than the settlement of the Czech question, which had been agreed upon yesterday. What he had in mind was to suggest to Herr Hitler that it would be helpful to both countries and to the world in general if they could issue some statement which showed the agreement between them on the desirability of better Anglo-German relations, leading to a greater European stability. Accordingly, he had ventured to draft a short statement which he would now ask Herr Hitler to read and to consider whether he would be disposed to issue such a statement over the signatures of himself and the Prime Minister to the public. As these observations were translated to Herr Hitler he ejaculated at intervals "Ja! Ja!" and when it was finished he said he would certainly agree to sign this document. When did the Prime Minister wish to do so?

The Prime Minister: Immediately.

Herr Hitler: Then let us sign.

At this point, they both rose, went to a writing table and, without any further words, appended their signatures to the document (copy attached as Appendix), of which the Prime Minister handed Herr Hitler one copy to keep and retained the other.

28 TEXT *of Anglo-German Declaration*

We, the German Führer and Chancellor and the British Prime Minister, have had a further meeting today and are agreed in recognising that the question of Anglo-German relations is of the first importance for the two countries and for Europe.

We regard the agreement signed last night and the Anglo-German Naval Agreement as symbolic of the desire of our two peoples never to go to war with one another again.

We are resolved that the method of consultation shall be the method adopted to deal with any other questions that may concern our two countries, and we are determined to continue our efforts to remove possible sources of difference and thus to contribute to assure the peace of Europe.

(Signed) A. HITLER
(Signed) NEVILLE CHAMBERLAIN

September 30, 1938.

29 LETTER *from Neville Chamberlain to his Sisters*

October 2, 1938.

In these strenuous days I have lost all sense of time and recollection of days, and I hardly know, and certainly have now no wish to recall, where I was a week ago. I only know that, as the hours went by, events seemed to be closing in, and driving us to the edge of the abyss with a horrifying certainty and rapidity. Only Annie knows what I went through in those agonising hours, when hope seemed almost extinguished, and only I know how heroically she maintained her courage and her confidence. . . . For me, I confess that it seemed only too possible that all the prayers of all the peoples of the world, including Germany herself, might break against the fanatical obstinacy of one man. I daresay Annie

28 *British Documents*, Third Series, Vol. II, no. 1228 Appendix.
29 Feiling, pp. 375-377.

has told you, or will tell you, of the birth of the last desperate snatch at the last tuft of grass on the very verge of the precipice. That the news of the deliverance should come to me in the very act of closing my speech in the House, was a piece of drama that no work of fiction ever surpassed.

The events of the next 48 hours entailed terrific physical and mental exertions. I was up the night before till after 2 A.M. preparing my speech. Then came the early rising, the scenes at the aerodrome, and the long flight to Munich. The rest of that day, till after 2 o'clock next morning, was one prolonged nightmare, and I have only gradually been able since then to sort out my impressions.

Hitler's appearance and manner when I saw him appeared to show that the storm signals were up, though he gave me the double hand-shake that he reserves for specially friendly demonstration. Yet these appearances were deceptive. His opening sentences, when we gathered round for our conference, were so moderate and reasonable, that I felt instant relief.

Mussolini's attitude all through was extremely quiet and reserved. He seemed to be cowed by Hitler, but undoubtedly he was most anxious for a peaceful settlement, and he played an indispensable part in attaining it. . . . His manner to me was more than friendly; he listened with the utmost attention to all I said, and expressed the strong hope that I would visit him early in Italy, where I should receive a very warm welcome.

I found an opportunity of talking to him about Spain, and suggesting that the Four-Power Conference should call on the 2 sides to observe a truce, while we helped them to find terms of settlement. He promised to think over this suggestion, which I afterwards made also to Hitler, but he told me that he was "fed up" with Spain, where he had lost 50,000 men in dead and wounded, that he was sick of Franco, who continually threw away all chances of victory, that he had no territorial claims there whatever, that he was satisfied that there was now no chance of Bolshevism getting the upper hand, and that he was very shortly going to withdraw 10,000 men.

I asked Hitler about 1 in the morning, while we were waiting for the draftsmen, whether he would care to see me for another talk. He jumped at the idea, and asked me to come to his private flat, in a tenement house where the other floors are occupied by ordinary citizens. I had a very friendly and pleasant talk: on Spain (where he too said he had never had any territorial ambitions), economic relations with S.E. Europe, and disarmament. I did not mention colonies, nor did he. At the end I pulled out the declaration, which I had prepared beforehand, and asked if he would sign it. As the interpreter translated the words into German, Hitler frequently ejaculated "*ja, ja,*" and at the end he said "yes, I will certainly sign it; when shall we do it?" I said "now," and we went at once to the writing-table, and put our signatures to the two copies which I had brought with me.

Even the descriptions of the papers give no idea of the scenes in the streets as I drove from Heston to the Palace. They were lined from one end to the other with people of every class, shouting themselves hoarse, leaping on the running board, banging on the windows, and thrusting their hands into the car to be shaken. The scenes culminated in Downing St., when I spoke to the multitudes below from the same window, I believe, as that from which Dizzy announced peace with honour 60 years ago.

We came here yesterday immediately after lunch, and walked up through Crow's Close to the Chequers church way. I came nearer there to a nervous breakdown than I have ever been in my life. I have pulled myself together, for there is a fresh ordeal to go through in the House. After that I *must* make an effort to get away, if only for a week.

30 LETTER *from Prime Minister Chamberlain to the Archbishop of Canterbury*[1]

October 2, 1938.

You will, I know, realise that I am almost overwhelmed with what I have to do, and will excuse a brief reply to your moving letter. The knowledge of all the heartfelt prayers that were going up for the success of my efforts has helped to sustain me in the terrible hours through which I have passed. I am sure that someday the Czechs will see that what we did was to save them for a happier future. And I sincerely believe that we have at last opened the way to that general appeasement which alone can save the world from chaos.

---

[1] Cosmo Gordon Lang—F. L. L.

30 Feiling, p. 375.

A Tale of
Four Cities

 THE VIEW FROM BERLIN: *Sir Ivone Kirkpatrick*

THE VIEW FROM PRAGUE: *Hubert Ripka*

THE VIEW FROM PARIS: *Paul Reynaud*

THE VIEW FROM LONDON: *Lord Strang*

Sir Ivone Kirkpatrick · (1897-1964) Educated at Downside College, Cambridge, and at the Sorbonne. He entered the British Foreign Service in 1919, and following posts at Rio de Janeiro, Rome, and the Vatican, he became First Secretary of the British Embassy in Berlin in 1933, where he remained until his recall in December 1938. From 1937 he served directly under Sir Nevile Henderson. He served subsequently as British High Commissioner for Germany, 1950-1953, and as Permanent Under Secretary of State for Foreign Affairs, 1953-1957, when he retired. He has published an account of his diplomatic experiences *The Inner Circle* (1957)—from which the following is taken—and a biography of Benito Mussolini (1964). Present at the Hitler-Chamberlain meetings at Bad Godesberg, and at the Munich conference, Kirkpatrick's account remains one of the most atmospheric reports of those historic events, and of the weeks and months that preceded them.

The successful assimilation of Austria whetted the German appetite. Hitler was stiffened in his belief that he could get away with anything; protests once more only served to irritate him. And so it was only natural that a mere matter of hours separated the disappearance of the Austrian and the emergence of the Czechoslovak problem. The military occupation of Austria had opened up a long Czech border-line and the Western Powers, even if so disposed, could bring no immediate help to Czechoslovakia. Now was the time to strike. It would be wearisome to recapitulate the moves in the game: the Sudeten German demand for autonomy in April, the crisis of May 21st, the fruitless negotiations between the Czechoslovak Government and the Sudeten leader Henlein, who at every stage obtained his orders from Berlin, the appointment of Lord Runciman as mediator, further negotiations in Prague. These events put a heavy strain on the staff of the Embassy; most of us worked a twelve-hour day during the summer months. Nevertheless I managed to get away in August to make a trip through Bayreuth, Braunau (Hitler's birthplace, a place of pious pilgrimage), Innsbruck, Lindau, the Black Forest and Frankfurt, where I stopped to play in the annual German Golf Championship. I received a message there instructing me to return to Berlin at once. Our expedition was nearly over and I had been knocked out of the golf tournament, so it was no hardship to have to make tracks for home. I was not to see Frankfurt again until I returned there as British Political Adviser to General Eisenhower after the war.

From *The Inner Circle*, by Sir Ivone Kirkpatrick. Reprinted by permission of the author and Macmillan & Company, London, Publishers.

On arrival in Berlin I found that the negotiations there were going as badly as they could. By the beginning of September there was deadlock, and on September 12th Hitler made an exceedingly truculent speech at the party rally in Nuremberg. The poor Arabs in Palestine, he shouted, were defenceless and abandoned, but the Sudeten Germans were neither defenceless nor abandoned. Encouraged by this overt promise of support and by the covert introduction of German agents and S.S. troops, the Sudeten Germans began to demonstrate. There were riots and attacks on Czech officials, with serious loss of life. In the light of previous experience it looked as if Hitler would very shortly intervene. In the midst of these events we suddenly received on September 14th a telegram in which the Prime Minister offered to fly to Germany to discuss the situation with Hitler. Arrangements were hurriedly put in hand and on the following day Mr. Chamberlain flew to Berchtesgaden. Henderson went down to meet him, whilst I was instructed to remain behind, inform the South African Minister (the only Dominion Representative in Berlin) of this development and look after the Embassy. Hitler made it clear that he insisted on self-determination for the Sudeten Germans; provided this were acceptable he would be ready to discuss ways and means. Mr. Chamberlain undertook to consult the Cabinet and the French Government,[1] and on the following day he returned to London.

Meanwhile things were going from bad to worse in Czechoslovakia. The incursions of armed bands of S.S. from Germany had created a state of civil war and streams of refugees, who were represented by the German press as victims of Czech oppression, were pouring into Saxony. The ordinary German, however, had little sympathy with the Sudeten Germans, whom he regarded as an inferior brand of German. Austria and the Polish corridor meant something, but there was little stomach for a general war over Czechoslovakia. Dr. Goebbels did his best, but his efforts were not an unqualified success and there was in every quarter a fervent hope that Hitler would get what he required without force. This was the atmosphere to which Mr. Chamberlain returned on September 22nd.

In order to spare the Prime Minister the fatigue of the long journey to Berchtesgaden it had been arranged that the meeting should take place at Godesberg on the Rhine. I should have missed this and subsequent conversations if it had not been for a characteristic piece of knavery. When Mr. Chamberlain reached Berchtesgaden it was represented to him that the best course would be for him to have a heart-to-heart talk with Hitler. The interpretation would be entrusted to the famous Schmidt, who would supply both parties with a record of the conversation. This record was not available by the time Mr. Chamberlain left for London and he had to rely on his memory for his account to the

[1] For the official German minutes on this point, see Document 13. A slightly—but not significantly—varying translation of these minutes is printed in *British Documents*, Third Series, Vol. II, no. 896.—F. L. L.

Cabinet. This was unsatisfactory enough, but worse was to come, for the Germans, after several attempts at equivocation, flatly refused to part with the record. I was instructed to make representation to the State Secretary, and he replied in a most offensive manner that Ribbentrop had ruled that the Schmidt record was an unofficial German document and was on no account to be given to the Prime Minister. In consequence of this behaviour Mr. Chamberlain decided to be fortified at any further meeting by the presence of a British official who could be trusted to keep an eye on Schmidt's interpreting and supply a record for use in London.

During the weeks of the crisis I had been living at the Embassy so as to be on the spot to deal with the ceaseless flow of messages. From September 1st to the 21st I do not think I put my foot outside the building, and almost every night was broken by the arrival of urgent telegrams. The Embassy itself was the gloomiest house I have ever inhabited, and it was something of a relief to have a change of treadmill. The Ambassador and I left Berlin by train on the evening of September 21st. On arrival at Cologne early next morning we were driven to the Petersberg Hotel, overlooking the Rhine opposite Godesberg. Magnificent rooms were reserved for us; fruit, cigars and cigarettes were laid out on every table and the proprietor (the owner of the famous Eau de Cologne) had provided no fewer than fifteen samples of his products: hair lotion, shaving-cream, soap, bath salts, pomades and so on. A discreet number of these objects I appropriated as compensation to my wife, whom I had sent to England with the children. The Prime Minister was due to arrive by air about noon and Henderson I and I drove out to the aerodrome to meet him. We were joined by Ribbentrop, the Gauleiter of Cologne, a galaxy of officials and a guard of honour and band provided by the Leibstandarte Adolf Hitler. With reasonable punctuality Mr. Chamberlain's machine arrived. Grasping the symbol of peace, his umbrella, that symbol which so annoyed Hitler, he emerged followed by Sir Horace Wilson and Strang of the Foreign Office. After inspecting the guard Chamberlain drove to the Petersberg with us, whilst Ribbentrop joined his master at the Hotel Dreesen in Godesberg.

The British party all lunched hurriedly together off a cold buffet and left the hotel as soon as possible for the first meeting at the Dreesen. We crossed the Rhine on ferries. It was characteristic of German thoroughness that two police launches were provided to escort us. There was also a luxury yacht in which Hitler was to take us for a trip on the Rhine; but it turned out that the conversations did not go well enough to cause us to deserve this treat. So far as the eye could see both banks of the Rhine were thronged with spectators. In the streets of Godesberg crowds stood silently; a few waved, and it was easy to see there was no desire for war. On arrival at the Dreesen we were taken into the hall, already filled with a mob of Third Reich nabobs in variegated uniforms. There was an air of expectancy; I thought that an ante-room at the court of the Roman emperors must have looked rather like that. Suddenly there was a murmur: "Der Führer kommt." Conversation stopped, everyone shrank towards the walls, a door opened and Hitler strode in, looking neither to the right nor the left. He walked up to Mr. Chamberlain, shook hands and led him up a staircase preceded by an S.S. guard. Schmidt and I, clasping pencils and paper, followed. Behind me I heard the buzz of conversation resume. We walked along a passage, the guard threw open a door and we entered a room containing a long table covered with green baize. It was a very long table, which could conveniently have sat twenty people or more. Hitler stalked to the top of the table, Mr. Chamberlain sat on his right, Schmidt and I on his left. Beyond, a long vista of green baize and empty chairs. There was a moment of silence and Hitler then gestured to the Prime Minister as if to say: "Your move."

Mr. Chamberlain then made a fairly long prepared statement. It and Hitler's reply were, I fancy, the only prepared statements made during that long and painful session. Mr. Chamberlain recalled that at Berchtesgaden Hitler had declared that he would be satisfied with nothing but self-determination, that was to say Anschluss, for the Sudeten Germans. He himself had been unable to give an immediate reply, but he had undertaken to consult his Cabinet and the French Government. He had done so and was happy to say that the British and French Governments agreed in principle. Moreover they had been able just in time to secure the assent of the Czechoslovak Government. The question of principle having been settled, it only remained to discuss the ways and means of transferring the territory in an orderly manner. On this point he had proposals to make which would doubtless be the subject of discussion at the present meeting. The statement was translated into German. As Schmidt finished speaking Mr. Chamberlain looked enquiringly at Hitler. But Hitler merely gazed down the table and said in a dry rasping voice: "Es tut mir leid, aber das geht nicht mehr." And with these words, he pushed his chair back from the table, crossed his legs, folded his arms and turned to scowl at Mr. Chamberlain. Schmidt translated: "I am very sorry, but all that is no longer any use." There was a long pause of pained silence.

That was the atmosphere in which the Godesberg peace negotiations began. Mr. Chamberlain, when he had recovered from his amazement, acidly enquired why an arrangement which had been declared satisfactory to Germany a few days before had now become unacceptable. Hitler rather lamely replied that Mr. Chamberlain's proposals were no longer sufficient because in the meantime Hungary and Poland had tabled new claims on Czechoslovakia. Hungary and Poland, he added, were good friends and Germany would insist that their claims must be met. Mr. Chamberlain retorted that on Hitler's own showing the German claim was urgent on account of the disorders in the Sudetenland; this was the ground on which he had been peremptory in demanding an immediate solution. These considerations did not apply to Hungary and Poland; no Hungarian or Polish minority was involved, there was no

allegation of persecution or even of disorders and there was no urgency.
Surely the practical course was to get the German problem safely out
of the way and then to tackle the Hungarian and Polish demands. Hitler
declined to agree to his proposal, and repeated truculently that all the
claims on Czechoslovakia must be considered and met together.

We seemed to have reached a deadlock, but for internal reasons Hitler
did not want an early breakdown. So after a considerable period of ill-
tempered floundering on both sides he suggested that it might be well
to have a look at Mr. Chamberlain's proposals in regard to the ways and
means of meeting the German demands. Mr. Chamberlain had indicated
in his opening statement that he had proposals under this head and he
would perhaps say what they were. The conversation, which a moment
or two before had seemed a corpse, returned to life. Schmidt looked
relieved and hopefully picked up his pencil. Mr. Chamberlain, however, seemed far from reassured; he had not got over the initial jolt.
Nevertheless he replied that the Sudetenland should be ceded without
a plebiscite, and that it should be agreed that the territory to be transferred should be that with over 50 per cent of Sudeten inhabitants.
Difficulties would, of course, arise from the fact that some of the areas
in question were islands in Czech territory, but the drawing of the exact
frontiers and the transfer of populations would be entrusted to a mixed
commission, which would have to complete its task within a stated
period. In return, the powers would guarantee Czech integrity and
independence. Hitler listened to these proposals with increasing impatience and replied that he must decline to accept them on the ground
that they involved an intolerable delay. Whilst we were arguing, he said,
Germans were being killed by the Czechs and that was a state of affairs
for which he could not be responsible. At intervals little scraps of paper
were sent in to Hitler reporting fresh outrages against the Sudeten Germans. No, he shouted, the territory within the so-called language boundary must be ceded at once, without any delay, and occupied by German
troops. Mr. Chamberlain said that he could not accept an immediate
German military irruption. Let Hitler send in police if public order were
threatened, but British opinion would be outraged by a military occupation. Hitler must remember that Britain was not ruled by a dictator and
he should take into account the Prime Minister's situation before Parliament and the public. Hitler characteristically retorted that his rule depended on the suffrage of the German people and Mr. Chamberlain must
take into account the rising anger of the German nation at the Czech
maltreatment of Germans. The German people were looking to their
Führer to see that justice was done and done quickly. Moreover, what
was the use of deciding to cede territory to him, if he were not to be
allowed to send in troops? Finally, troops were essential to put an end
to civil war. The argument waxed hotly and Schmidt had a trying time.
As soon as he began to interpret for Mr. Chamberlain, Hitler interrupted
with a tirade. When that had been translated, provided that Hitler did

not again interrupt the reply, Schmidt would go back: "With your permission, my Führer, I shall now return to the point where Mr. Chamberlain's statement was broken off." Schmidt's agile brain was working to pour oil on the dispute. At one point Mr. Chamberlain said dryly: "You assume that every Sudeten wants to join the Reich. What do you propose to do if the Sudeten Social Democrats prefer to remain in Czechoslovakia?" Schmidt, foreseeing a further outburst, translated this question: "The Prime Minister asks a theoretical question. I repeat, my Führer, a purely theoretical hypothesis. Supposing there were some Social Democrats who did not want to join the Reich, how would you propose to deal with them?" Hitler made a noise, a sort of angry snort, and replied: "It's an impossible hypothesis. But if there were such men, I should not want them in the Reich." Both sides declined to give way, but both were reluctant to provoke a rupture. Mr. Chamberlain asked for information as to the language boundaries referred to by Hitler. Hitler said that he could indicate these on a map. So we trooped downstairs to a large room where maps were unrolled and laid out on a table.

Here we were joined by Henderson, Sir Horace Wilson, Ribbentrop, Weizsäcker and Obergruppenführer Lorenz, an S.S. officer who was nominally entrusted with the protection of the German minorities abroad. Hitler was, as usual, well briefed and showed us on fairly large-scale maps where he would draw the boundary. A good deal of rather desultory conversation followed, but it was clear that there was a fundamental divergence of views and Mr. Chamberlain decided to adjourn. We entered our cars and drove back to the hotel for dinner.

After dinner a telephone call came through from the Cabinet in London, who naturally wanted to know how things were going. When this had been disposed of without much satisfaction to the Cabinet Mr. Chamberlain, who had had a very long and exhausting day, went to bed. I withdrew to my office with a typist to write the record of the conversation with Hitler. This ran to well over ten thousand words and took me till 4 A.M. to complete. I then turned my mind to the problem of the military occupation of the Sudetenland with a view to seeing whether any compromise were possible. I must admit that on this point I did not feel very happy about our case. If we were prepared to agree to the cession of the territory, it seemed illogical to object to its military occupation and to insist on inflicting the Gestapo rather than the Army on the inhabitants. I tried my hand at a couple of drafts and showed them to Sir Horace Wilson in the morning. He replied that the Prime Minister was resolved not to give an inch on this particular issue and that it was hopeless to think of any compromise.

Indeed so strongly did the Prime Minister feel that he declined to resume the conversations. Instead he despatched a letter to Hitler saying that the German proposals, and in particular a military occupation, would be unacceptable to public opinion in England and indeed in the world. Meanwhile our cars were standing idle at the door and the crowd

of bewildered spectators were anxiously wondering why Achilles was still
sitting in his tent. The rumour spread that things were going badly. We
sat down to a rather grim lunch. Mr. Chamberlain discussed the theatre
and spoke of his early days in Birmingham. In the afternoon we received
Hitler's written reply maintaining his demand for the immediate military
occupation of the Sudetenland. There was some discussion as to the next
move. A rupture was considered. Eventually Mr. Chamberlain decided
to send Sir Horace Wilson and Henderson to give Ribbentrop a written
request that the full German proposals should be set forth in a document. Apart from keeping the door open the Prime Minister was rightly
anxious to have in the event of a breakdown an official statement of the
German demands, which hitherto had been made verbally and could
consequently have been modified or misrepresented later. We should not
have been surprised if Hitler had objected to complying and had replied
that he had already fully stated his demands. The Germans, however,
were still anxious on internal grounds that Mr. Chamberlain should not
be driven to break off the negotiations, and so Ribbentrop was instructed to reply that the German proposals would be embodied in a
memorandum which would be ready later in the day when Hitler would
be pleased to discuss it. He undertook to telephone as soon as the document was ready. The drafting must have given the Germans some difficulty, for the hours crept by and we received no word from the Hotel
Dreesen. We dined and waited. Eventually we received a message that
the thing would be ready at 10.30 P.M.

We drove down to the appointment. This time the hotel was more or
less empty. The Praetorian guard had disappeared and Hitler received
us in the hotel lounge where Hoffmann, the court photographer, took a
photograph. We were then led to a low round table; Hitler, Ribbentrop
and Schmidt, Mr. Chamberlain, Henderson and myself. Hitler was on his
best behaviour, making an obvious effort to be pleasant. He produced
his memorandum and handed it to Mr. Chamberlain, who ran through it
whilst Henderson translated the salient points. Whatever Hitler's manner,
the memorandum showed that the passage of time had not brought an
abatement of the German demands. On the contrary, they had as usual
increased and were couched in peremptory terms. The Czechs were required to begin the evacuation of certain Sudeten areas by 8 A.M. on
September 26th (it was now 10.30 P.M. on September 23rd) and the
German troops were to complete the occupation by the morning of
September 29th. This was Hitler's last word.

When he had finished reading the paper the Prime Minister threw it
on to the table with a look of disgust and said that the proposals were
nothing less than an ultimatum and Henderson interjected the word
"Diktat." For years Hitler had been inveighing against the so-called
"Diktat" of Versailles. But that was a settlement imposed on a defeated
enemy after a long, passionate and bloody war. In the present case the

Czechs were being asked and had agreed to cede territory to Germany. They had not been defeated in war; on the contrary, they had made enormous concessions already to avoid a conflict. It was difficult to see therefore how Hitler, in the light of his attitude over Versailles, could now justify the imposition of this "Diktat" on the Czechoslovak Government. Hitler looked pained. There was a pause. He then said firmly: "Mr. Chamberlain, you are grievously mistaken; this is not a 'Diktat.' If you will look at the document again, you will see that it is headed by the word 'Memorandum.' "

In the course of the discussion which followed the Prime Minister represented that, apart from the substance, the form of the proposals was wholly unacceptable. Hitler clutched at this suggestion. He produced a pair of spectacles (it was the first time I had ever seen him wear them), picked up a pencil and began to go through his memorandum. He agreed to modify his time-table in the sense that the territory would have to be handed over on October 1st. He also made a number of pencilled changes in the text with a view to rendering its form more palatable. When he had finished he fixed Mr. Chamberlain with a penetrating stare and said in a hoarse disgruntled voice: "You are the first man to whom I have ever made a concession."

The Prime Minister remained unmoved by this display of generosity. He said that whilst he felt unable to accept or recommend the proposals, he could not as an intermediary refuse to submit them to the Czechoslovak Government. The meeting broke up on this note at about 2 A.M. and we returned to the hotel. I sat up all night dictating the record of this conversation straight on to a typewriter. It amounted to forty foolscap sheets, and we finished shortly after 8 A.M., just in time to enable Mr. Chamberlain to take the document home to London with him. It was the morning of September 24th. I motored to the Cologne airport to see the Prime Minister leave. My companion was Walter Hewel, a member of Ribbentrop's staff and one of Hitler's favourites. He was at pains to persuade me that Mr. Chamberlain's visit had been worth while. It was an excellent thing, he said, that the two men should have become acquainted, and he could tell me that Hitler had acquired a high regard for Mr. Chamberlain. I knew this was bunkum and said so to Hewel. My reliable informants in the German camp had already made it clear to me that Hitler regarded the Prime Minister as an impertinent busybody who spoke the ridiculous jargon of an out-moded democracy. The umbrella, which to the ordinary German was the symbol of peace, was in Hitler's view only a subject of derision. Ribbentrop, who sat in the first car, was as amiable to the Prime Minister as Hewel had been to me. It was clear that the Germans still hoped to be left alone to deal with Czechoslovakia.

After the Prime Minister had gone the Germans faded away and Henderson and I were left to take a morning train from Cologne to Berlin. We filled in the time by paying a visit to the Cathedral. Henderson, who was depressed by our experiences at Godesberg, knelt in the nave and prayed for peace.

The next day, September 25th, the French Ministers arrived in London. The Czechoslovak Government had ordered general mobilisation on September 23rd and the French Government had mobilised 500,000 men. During the London conversations with the French a communication was received from the Czechoslovak Government declining to accept the Godesberg proposals. The French Ministers declared that in the event of German aggression France would support Czechoslovakia, and the British Ministers promised that in that event Great Britain would stand by France. On September 26th General Gamelin arrived in London for service talks.

With this background Sir Horace Wilson arrived in Berlin during the afternoon of September 26th bearing a personal letter from the Prime Minister to Hitler. In this letter Mr. Chamberlain said that the Godesberg proposals had been rejected by the Czechoslovak Government. The difference was one of form. He considered accordingly that a further effort should be made to reach agreement and he suggested a meeting with Czechoslovak representatives to consider ways and means of handing over the territory. After a brief consultation Sir Horace Wilson, Henderson and myself set out for the Chancellery where Hitler was to receive us at 5 P.M. Hitler was in one of his worst moods. He was only induced with much difficulty to listen to the Prime Minister's letter. At intervals he rose from his chair and drifted towards the door as if resolved to leave the room. I gazed at him in fascination. During one of his many tirades I was unable to take my eyes off him and my pencil remained poised above the paper. Sir Horace Wilson noticed this and whispered: "Are you getting everything down? It's frightfully important." I whispered back: "I'm not likely to forget a word." Nor did I. With only a sketchy note I was able later without the slightest difficulty to reconstruct the whole conversation. At times, particularly when Wilson spoke about the Prime Minister's desire for a peaceful solution, Hitler pushed back his chair and smote his thigh in a gesture of frustrated rage.

After a long and painful discussion Hitler agreed to the proposed meeting, but only on condition that the Czechoslovak Government accepted the Godesberg memorandum. Moreover, the meeting must terminate satisfactorily in two days. Otherwise the occupation might begin before October 1st. In a word, he agreed to a meeting provided it was understood that the Czechs would give way at every point. Wilson promised to report to the Prime Minister. As we were leaving, Hitler observed that the whole of Germany was behind him. He thought it would be an excellent thing if Wilson could verify this for himself and he accordingly invited him to be present that evening at the meeting in the Sportspalast where he was going to make a speech on the Czech question. Sir Horace Wilson, looking slightly embarrassed, said that he would be able to hear the speech on the radio. "That is not the same thing," retorted Hitler. "You must be present to sense the atmosphere."

We returned to the Embassy to dinner. Henderson and Wilson dined in the dining-room, whilst I ate off a tray in front of the radio set to hear as truculent a speech as Hitler ever made. We sat up all that night reporting our conversation with Hitler and his speech. In the early hours of the morning the Prime Minister telegraphed the text of a statement which he was issuing immediately. In it he offered to see that the Czech promises were carried out with reasonable promptitude provided the Germans agreed to a peaceful transfer of the territory. We also received instructions for a second interview with Hitler. By this time it was clear to me that Hitler was bent on having his little war. I felt that the interview could have little result and Hitler's behaviour was so offensive that I wanted never to see him again. He seemed to be enveloped in an aura of such ruthless wickedness that it was oppressive and almost nightmarish to sit in the same room. I therefore asked Wilson if I might be excused from attending. This was very pusillanimous since the interviews were certainly interesting and exciting enough for the most blasé of officials. I can only say that Hitler had inspired me with such a physical repugnance that I could not bring myself to go. Wilson replied that he was very sorry, but that he must ask me to attend. So I put on my hat and we went off once more to the Chancellery. The time for the interview was fixed for 12:15. The ante-room was full of high officials, all manifestly depressed by the turn of events. Bodenschatz, the liaison officer between Goering and Hitler, whispered to Henderson that we must be firm and he wished us well. We went in. Hitler looked as black as thunder. He told us several times, grinding his heel into the carpet, that he had had enough of the Czechs. "I will smash the Czechs," he shouted. One could sense that he was itching to drop a bomb on Prague, to see Benes in flight. Sir Horace Wilson asked if in the light of the Prime Minister's statement he could take back any message to London. Hitler retorted that there were only two courses open to the Czechs, acceptance or rejection of the German terms. From this attitude he savagely refused to budge.

Sir Horace Wilson, speaking very slowly and quietly, then said that he had a message to give from the Prime Minister. He would try to give it in the Prime Minister's words and manner. If, he continued, the Germans attacked Czechoslovakia and the French in pursuance of their treaty obligation became engaged in a conflict with Germany, then Britain would feel obliged to support France. Hitler replied angrily that he could only take note of this statement. If France felt obliged to attack Germany, then Britain also felt obliged to commit an act of aggression against Germany. Sir Horace Wilson retorted that Hitler had clearly misunderstood the purport of the message. He must therefore in the interest of history repeat it. Still speaking very slowly, Wilson then repeated the formula to a Hitler who was showing signs of rising exasperation, wriggling in his seat, slapping his knee, drumming on the floor with his heel. But quite unperturbed, Wilson slowly recited his piece to the end. Before the translation was complete Hitler bellowed furiously: "It's just what I said. If France attacks Germany, then England must attack Germany too." He added, "If France strikes and England strikes, I don't care a bit. I am prepared for every eventuality"; and Ribbentrop sagely nodded his agreement. Sir Horace Wilson, looking very pained, said that it was evident that the Chancellor still misunderstood the message and he must ask leave to repeat it. But this time Hitler was on his feet shouting that he understood the purport of the message only too well. It meant that in six days' time we should all be at war with one another. Thereupon we all coldly shook hands with the infuriated Führer and took our leave. As I grasped his podgy hand I felt an overwhelming sense of relief that war would come and that I should never have to see him again. In the Embassy the feeling was the same. There was general satisfaction that the die had been cast. One member of the staff drove to Wannsee to collect his golf clubs, and I had a long telephone conversation with my wife in England, for which I innocently thought I should never have to pay. After lunch I went to the Tempelhof aerodrome to see Sir Horace Wilson off. We took the opportunity of sending home a member of the staff who had to travel to England on duty. This excited the Gestapo enormously, for they noted that the aircraft was flying away with one more passenger than it had brought. They did not interfere, though they could not refrain from asking who the individual was who had been added to Sir Horace Wilson's suite.

The same evening the Prime Minister informed Dr. Benes that it seemed likely that German troops would cross the frontier almost at once unless the Czechoslovak Government accepted the German terms forthwith. In this situation the British Government felt unable to tender advice as to what Dr. Benes should do. Later a further effort was made to induce Hitler to come to terms, and at 11 P.M. a note was handed to the German State Secretary embodying a proposed time-table for the evacuation of the Sudeten territory. He replied that the plan was out of date and he did not believe that it could possibly be accepted. While all this was going on our work in the Chancery was disturbed by the rattle of an enormous motorised and armoured column which passed down the Wilhelmstrasse in an easterly direction. The column took over three hours to pass and represented the flower of the German Army. I went out for a moment or two to have a look at it and returned to my desk both impressed and depressed. The people of Berlin who were standing glumly on the pavement stared at the passing troops but showed no emotion whatever. My friends in the Reich Chancellery told me that Hitler, who was watching from a window, was disgusted with the crowd for their apathy.

On September 28th the British fleet was mobilised. Meanwhile there was much coming and going in Berlin. Mussolini, appalled at the prospect of a general war for which he was not ready, had urged Hitler to compromise. Similar advice was being tendered by Goering and the German generals. In consequence Hitler decided to draw in his horns. A mass meeting at which Goebbels was to have announced mobilisation was cancelled at the last moment and Hitler informed the Ambassador in the morning that at Mussolini's request he had consented to postpone mobilisation until 2 P.M. on September 29th. After more telephoning around Europe the project of a four-power meeting at Munich, to be held the following day, was put forward and accepted. That evening Henderson and I set forth for Munich.

The Munich Conference was in every way a sad affair. I can remember no redeeming feature. Even its organisation was faulty, for the Germans had been unable at a few hours' notice to make proper arrangements for so large a gathering. The burden thrown on the telephone system, for example, was so great that it was quicker to send a car with a message to our office in the hotel than to attempt to telephone. The final blow came at the moment of signature when it was discovered that the pompous inkstand contained no ink. The conference was held in the Führerbau, a large building in the modern Nazi style. Mr. Chamberlain arrived by air about noon, shortly after Daladier and the French party. Mussolini came by train and was accompanied by Hitler from the frontier. The conference began shortly after 1 P.M. I had some preliminary conversations with members of the Italian and French delegations, many of whom I had known in Rome and Paris. The Italians were clearly terrified of being landed by Hitler into a European war. The French, including Daladier, were resolved to reach agreement at any cost. They were a harried lot of men who showed no sign of shame at being parties to the dismemberment of their ally. In fact nerves were so on edge that from time to time they gave the impression that Czechoslovakia was to be blamed for having brought all this trouble upon us.

In this atmosphere Hitler had little difficulty in getting his way. It was clear from the outset that there would be no war and the time was spent discussing, drafting and typing the various articles of the protocol. We adjourned for lunch and again for dinner. I observed Hitler closely as he left the building with Goering. He was obviously in a black mood, furious with the whole business. After dinner the work went on and it was 2 A.M. by the time the protocol was ready for signature. Goering and Mussolini were jubilant, there was a watery smile on Himmler's fish-slab face, but Hitler continued to sulk and did not disguise the effort he was making to take part in the conventional courtesies which closed the proceedings.

In order to recapture the mood of the conference I do not think I can do better than reproduce the text of a broadcast which I made during the war:

> At the morning session Hitler controlled himself. His manner was courteous and his behaviour was normal. His first sign of temper was at the lunch interval. The delegations left the Führerbau for their various hotels. Hitler

accompanied Mussolini. I can see him now, walking along the gallery on the first floor. He is talking very fast to Mussolini. The Duce's face is impassive, but Hitler's is black as thunder and he is emphasising his remarks with short angry movements of his hands.

The second sign of temper was after lunch. The delegations are assembling. Chamberlain and Daladier are deep in conversation. Hitler arrives. He cannot wait until the conversation is over. After making gestures of impatience for some moments, his patience is exhausted. Angrily he sends Ribbentrop to summon the two statesmen to the table.

As the day wears on to the night, Hitler's irritation increases. In the closing stages Goering and other Nazi leaders come into the room. Goering is the centre of a conversation and there is some laughter. It is an atmosphere of relaxed tension. The danger of war has been averted. But Hitler sits moodily apart. He wriggles on the sofa, he crosses and uncrosses his legs, he folds his arms and glares around the room. At intervals with obvious effort he joins in a conversation, only to relapse into silence. At last the agreement is ready for signature. The four statesmen sign. Three look satisfied that they have done the right thing. But Hitler scratches his signature as if he were being asked to sign away his birthright.

When the documents had been signed and the conference was over we had one painful task to perform, namely, to communicate the result of the conference to the Czech delegation. We called on M. Mastny, the Czech Minister in Berlin, and found him on the verge of tears. But he showed great dignity and restraint in the face of the peremptory attitude of M. Daladier, who did not mince his words conveying that France expected Czechoslovakia to submit without further ado. Mr. Chamberlain, on the other hand, showed the greatest sympathy and understanding. I imagine that M. Daladier's apparent brutality sprang from a guilty conscience rather than from any inherent cruelty. After all, Czechoslovakia was France's ally, whilst we were in the same position as any other member of the League of Nations who had no specific treaty obligation to protect her. I had never met Daladier before and he gave me the impression of a weak, bewildered man. He was certainly not a war leader, and his demeanour at Munich strengthened Hitler in his belief that when the time came France could be pushed over without much difficulty. He had never had much regard for France, and always rejected with contempt the advice given him by the German Ambassador in Paris and others that France possessed the finest Army in the world. I remember hearing from a German who had been present that Hitler had discussed in the Wagner family circle in Bayreuth the relative military value of the different Europeans. The German soldier he rated highest. After him the Englishman and then the Pole; the Frenchman was not even mentioned.

After seeing the Czechs in the early hours of the morning we went to bed. After breakfast the Prime Minister paid a brief farewell visit to Hitler and returned with the famous paper which he triumphantly waved on arrival in England. I was never able to discover what passed through Mr. Chamberlain's mind in this fleeting negotiation which he conducted entirely alone without, so far as I am aware, warning anyone in advance. Did he believe in Hitler's sincerity? Or was he carried away by the emotion of relief that war had been averted? Or did he believe that the best chance with Hitler was to try to bind him by a public declaration and then to proclaim the belief that Hitler would keep his word? I am inclined to think that the last is the most likely hypothesis. One thing is certain. The subsequent seizure of Prague was a bitter blow to Mr. Chamberlain, which provoked a personal resentment against Hitler. I noticed that whenever Hitler's name was mentioned after March 17th, the Prime Minister looked as if he had swallowed a bad oyster.

Having seen Mr. Chamberlain off at Munich airport, we returned by train to Berlin to begin the melancholy task of tying up the loose threads of the Munich agreement. In accordance with its terms an international commission was established for the purpose, but the Germans made it painfully clear from the outset that they intended to have their way on every issue. When Hitler received the new Czech Minister of Foreign Affairs soon after Munich he told him that on any sign of Czech recalcitrance he would "make an end of Czechoslovakia in twenty-four, no, in eight hours." The Munich surrender had stunned the Czechs and the Germans had little difficulty in imposing their will.

So ended the Munich Conference, an event which will continue for many years to provoke controversy, arouse passions and provide the occasion for much ill-considered and superficial comment. History will regard it not as an isolated occurrence but as the almost inevitable culmination of a long chain of events which preceded it. From this point of view Britain will certainly come in for criticism for ever having allowed Hitler to put himself in a position to blackmail the world. We had ample warning, from *Mein Kampf* as well as from every manifestation of German policy, which proclaimed Hitler's intentions from the housetops. Our last chance of intervening cheaply was, I think, in 1936 when the Rhineland was occupied and militarised by German troops. At that time the Germany Army and Air Force were painfully thin, and a relatively small deployment of force would have been sufficient to bring the Nazi regime crashing to the ground. It is perhaps not surprising that the people preferred the comforting and comfortable assurances of the Government, who were supposed to know the facts, to the strident and inconvenient warnings of Mr. Winston Churchill, who was only a back number. History will wonder how it came about that any Government should have deliberately closed its eyes and those of the nation to so clear and imminent a peril. The magnitude of German preparations for war, the ruthless speed with which they were pushed ahead and the vast scope of German ambitions were all known, but they seemed to leave our Government unmoved. In consequence the ignorance of the public was complete, and as late as April 1939 quite well-informed people in this country were surprised and shocked to be told that war was almost certain to break out that year.

But to come back to Munich, whilst history will certainly show no indulgence to British policy over the years, it is also certain that there will be some divergence of opinion on the expediency or otherwise of this particular transaction. Or to put it another way, having allowed ourselves by a succession of inexcusable errors to be placed in this frightful predicament, should we have yielded at Munich or have resolutely accepted the consequences of refusing to do so? To answer this question honestly a number of factors have to be weighed. In the first place, the documents we have accumulated since the war show conclusively that there is no ground for the belief that Hitler was bluffing, and that firmness would have caused him to climb down. On the contrary, he was not only resolved on war but was actually looking foward to it. It is true that the remainder of the German Government and the General Staff were equally opposed to war, and it is a fact that Halder and a number of other generals were contemplating a *coup* which was designed to take place on the outbreak of war. But we could place no confidence in the resolution of the opposition or the ability of the generals to stage a successful revolt and the issue must be boiled down to a simple choice: to yield or to go to war.

If this be accepted, it must be admitted that there were a number of excellent reasons for yielding. We were not ready either militarily or psychologically, and time had to be bought to make good both deficiencies. Secondly, if we were to go to war it was important that the Dominions should come in with us. But they were not yet convinced of the reality of the German peril, their governments and peoples were even more unprepared than we were, and it seems doubtful whether we could have secured an immediate and general assent to war on the Munich issue. Thirdly, the French were in a deplorable state of mind and our Ambassador warned the Government that the French were against fighting and would not hesitate to take the first opportunity of blaming us for having dragged them into war. This diagnosis was later confirmed by the events of September 2nd, 1939, by the French refusal to allow offensive operations against Germany in 1939 and by the conduct of the majority of the French Cabinet in June 1940. If the French had been equally coy in 1938, nothing effective could have been done to prevent the Germans destroying Czechoslovakia in a few weeks, if not days. This was certainly the opinion of General von Reichenau, who was to have commanded an army on the southern flank of the projected drive into Czechoslovakia.

On the other side there are a number of very respectable grounds for claiming that we should have taken our courage in our hands and defied Hitler to do his worst. First, the General Staff might have revolted. In view of their subsequent performance I personally do not think this was likely, but it was a chance. Secondly, the Germans were not fully prepared for war. It is true that many of our service chiefs considered that the Germans would have done better in 1938 than 1939. However this may be, there will, I believe, be a considerable body of opinion which will hold that in 1938 the Germans were still so far behind in their preparations for war that it would have paid us to tackle them. They will reinforce their case by pointing out that if we sought to buy time at Munich, we used it very badly, whilst the Germans used it so well that they were able during the year to increase the gap between us and themselves. This argument is not, of course, conclusive, for it might be said that whilst we were so weak in 1938 that we could have been liquidated even by a relatively weak Germany, by 1939, despite our sins of omission, we were sufficiently strong to defend ourselves, particularly in the air, until we could deploy our strength. Finally, there is the moral question. Unless a nation is faithful to its principles its credit must be impaired and its citizens suffer moral damage. Hence, it may be said, no consideration of expediency should have been allowed to dictate a shameful surrender of principles. This is an argument with which I have much sympathy. If Hitler had not so quickly given us another chance over Poland, the moral effect of Munich might well have been grievous. It may be that our conduct in 1939 and 1940 will distract the eyes of history from the Munich settlement, but no voice will be raised to defend or excuse the successive sins of omission which led inexorably to that capitulation.

Hubert Ripka · (1895-1957), leading Czechoslovak
journalist, government figure, and close personal associate of President
Benes. He served for many years as editor of a leading Prague newspaper, and following the Munich conference fled to London, where he
became a member of the Czechoslovak Government in Exile. In addition to his book *Munich: Before and After* (1939), he also wrote
Czechoslovak Democracy at Work (1945), *Czechoslovakia Enslaved:
The Story of the Communist Coup d'état* (1950), and *Eastern Europe
in the Postwar World* (1961). His work on the history of the Munich
crisis—from which the following is taken—derives much of its importance not only from Ripka's close personal association with President Benes and other government leaders, but from his inclusion of a
number of previously unpublished documents on the crisis. His book
has taken its place as one of the leading accounts of the crisis, and one
of the outstanding Czechoslovak sources on the period.

This . . . is an attempt to tell the dramatic story of the European crisis
from September, 1938, to March, 1939. It is not only because the author
is a Czechoslovak that the fate of Czechoslovakia is the centre of this
history. This place is sufficiently justified by the fact that events in
Europe and in the world took a revolutionary turn the moment the
external, and subsequently the internal, independence of Czechoslovakia was destroyed. The geographical position of this country in the
very heart of Europe inexorably determines the unalterable fact that
the whole face of Europe changes according to the fate of the Czechoslovak people. This assertion does not mean that the Czechoslovak
nation determines the fate of Europe. To say so would be absurd and
extravagant. But it cannot be denied that the Czech nation was always—in the Middle Ages as well as in modern times—a very important
factor in European politics. Its importance has always been out of all
proportion to its numerical strength. This is due not only to its geographical situation at the crossroads of conflicting European interests,
tendencies and movements, but also to its creative genius, which drove
it to take its place in culture and politics beside the greatest nations of
Europe. As the fate of this nation was insolubly bound up with the
general development and state of Europe, so everything that happened
to it did not remain confined to its immediate vicinity, but has always
had a far-reaching influence on the course of European history as a

From *Munich—Before and After*, by Hubert Ripka. Reprinted by permission of
Victor Gollancz, Ltd., publishers.

whole. All attempts to neglect, or to ignore, its importance, not only for Central Europe, but the entire continent, will always entail the gravest consequences. . . .

It is really unbelievable, how insufficiently the importance of an independent Czechoslovakia in the interplay of European forces was understood and appreciated. Only the Nazi imperialists fully realised the difference which its destruction would make in the scales of Europe. They knew that the fundamental condition of their success was the destruction of a strong Czechoslovakia. As long as they had not removed this obstacle all their plans for expansion, whether they were directed to the east or to the west, remained very hazardous gambles, without substantial hope of success. The Nazis were more practical and more earnest than their opponents among the Great Powers: they studied the map of Europe and its history with characteristic thoroughness. From all such studies the European importance of Czechoslovakia emerged more and more clearly. Czechoslovakia held a strategic position of first-class importance. This position was the key to the whole Danube Basin, the first-line defence of the Balkans. Even after the invasion of Austria, Germany could not hope to dominate the Danube Basin and the Balkans, so long as an independent Czechoslovakia was in existence. Her destruction was a necessary condition of the success of a Pan-German *Mitteleuropa.* . . .

Thus the Pan-Germans fully realised what Czechoslovakia meant on the European chess-board. They were also well aware of the military potential of this state, which was out of all proportion to the number of its inhabitants. Of all Central European states Czechoslovakia alone had an army equipped with modern technical weapons, an army which in every respect, technical and moral, was on the same level as the armies of the European Great Powers. Her air force was two thirds the strength of the French. Furthermore, she was enormously strong in economic resources, both in industrial production and in agriculture. For her extensive armaments and metal industries she was called by the Germans the "Arsenal of Europe." Czechoslovakia was the most important and the strongest of the opponents of the Third Reich in the whole of Central Europe. It was for this reason that the Pan-Germans had to work for her destruction before they could embark on their long-term plan for the domination of Europe.

The tragedy of the Czechoslovak nation was the fact that this destructive work of the Third Reich found support among its own allies and friends. Czechoslovakia was the only state in Central Europe which had with unshakable consistency preserved her loyalty to the two Western democracies. The Czechoslovak Government had invariably resisted the policy of time-serving opportunism which was followed by Colonel Beck in Warsaw and M. Stojadinović in Belgrade. When, however, Nazi aggression centered on the Czechoslovak nation, its appeal for help went unheard by those in whom it had trusted and towards whom it had fulfilled all its obligations.

In September, 1938, Czechoslovakia yielded not so much to the pressure of the Third Reich, but, first and foremost to the pressure of France and Great Britain. This pressure took the form, not only of informing the Czechoslovak Government that failure to accept their terms would result in the complete international isolation of Czechoslovakia; but also the threat, in so many words, that Czechoslovakia would alone be responsible for the outbreak of war and would therefore have to take the consequences of refusing to yield to Germany. It is a unique occurrence in history that the Great Powers should deliberately prevent a small nation from defending itself, though it was ready to fight with all its forces. The threats and warlike preparations of the Germans were insufficient to break the readiness of the Czechoslovak people to defend themselves. That resistance was finally broken when they were not only deserted but ordered to conform to the German wishes by their former friends. . . .

The decisive turn in the tension which existed between Germany and Czechoslovakia in the autumn of 1938 came at the moment when Mr. Neville Chamberlain, the British Prime Minister, decided to fly to Berchtesgaden to seek an interview with the German Chancellor, Adolf Hitler.

News of this projected visit reached Prague on the night of September 14. It was just after 9 o'clock, I remember, when I received from the offices of my paper, the *Lidové Noviny,* a telephone message saying that a news agency had reported that Mr. Chamberlain was going to Berchtesgaden to see Herr Hitler. Several friends of mine, politicians of various parties and a few diplomats, had come in to see me that evening and were there when this message arrived. All of them, without exception, dismissed the story as a wild bit of sensational reporting, and we continued our discussion of the probability of a happy sequel to the collapse of Henlein's *Putsch*—for by that time his attempted revolt had already been virtually suppressed. A few minutes later, however, the report about Mr. Chamberlain was officially confirmed. Consternation is the only word which correctly describes our reaction to this shock. We rang up the Government departments concerned to find out what they thought about it, and from all quarters came replies that it was "very serious," "very bad," "extremely dangerous."

It should be explained, perhaps, for the benefit of the British reader why it was that the news of Mr. Chamberlain's visit to Herr Hitler should have caused us so much anxiety and alarm. It was because we realised at once, only too clearly, that such a gesture on the part of the Western Powers would encourage Hitler in his defiance, that he would interpret it as an indication of their weakness and become, therefore, more obstinate in his exaggerated demands and dangerous implacability. We rightly feared that we alone would have to foot the bill. When I write this, I am not being wise after the event, for I describe what was the feeling throughout Prague. Nor was this feeling confined to political circles; on the night of September 14, even the general public was alarmed. Heaven knows how many people there were—some of them strangers to me—who rang me up that night expressing excitement and fear lest we should be asked to concede everything that was demanded in order to satisfy Germany. Events justified their fears more even, alas, than we then imagined possible.

Mr. Chamberlain's decision to fly to Berchtesgaden was the explanation, in my opinion, of the sudden improvement in the situation for the Nazis which immediately ensued. We in Prague were at a loss to understand why it was that the further fulfillment of Germany's expansionist plans should thus be facilitated just at the moment when the complete collapse, within two or three days of its outbreak, of the Henleinist *Putsch*, which took place immediately after Herr Hitler's speech at Nuremberg on September 12, had radically transformed the situation with regard to the so-called Sudeten-German problem. It seemed to us that the far-reaching effects of that collapse were perhaps not fully recognised. Yet we knew that ample evidence was in the hands of the Prague authorities to prove beyond doubt that this *Putsch*, far from being a "spontaneous" revolt of the "oppressed Sudeten-Germans," had been deliberately prepared. As early as the morning of September 12—that is to say, before Hitler had made his Nuremberg speech—suspicious telephone conversations between Henleinist party officials and Germany had been intercepted; it was obvious from the fact that these officials had been reporting, "We are ready," that something was afoot. It is probable that it was this evidence which convinced even Lord Runciman that the revolt had been deliberately planned beforehand. In his Report of September 21 he stated that "incidents were provoked and instigated on the 11th September and, with greater effect, after Herr Hitler's speech on the 12th September."

The detailed story of the result falls outside the intended scope of this book, but I would stress the fact that the revolt was suppressed within two or three days by ordinary police measures, military aid being invoked only in a few exceptional instances. If the Czechoslovak Government had adopted more drastic measures, the revolt could have been suppressed within twenty-four hours. But this might have meant heavier civilian casualties, though the losses suffered by the Czech police in applying their milder methods would certainly have been fewer. I would underline, moreover, the fact that the revolt, although it was intended by its instigators to be a general one, was by no means universal throughout the Sudeten-German territory. A great part of the territory remained completely inactive, and in several places Henlein's extremist agitators were driven away by actual members of the Sudeten-German Party.

Two important facts must therefore be borne in mind: first, that the revolt was rapidly and comparatively easily suppressed, although the rebels were amply provided with arms, mostly of German origin, and secondly that it received no active support from the majority of the Sudeten Germans. This is surely proof—lamentable, because it led to the loss of seventy human lives, most of them Czechs who had been attacked—that the majority of the Sudeten Germans were not in sympathy with revolutionary National Socialism. It may be argued against this that Henlein's Sudeten-German Party received the majority of the German votes in the parliamentary elections of 1935 and even more in the municipal elections held in the spring of 1938, but the results on both occasions would certainly have been less favourable for Henlein if the Czechoslovak authorities had taken more effective measures against the physical and psychological terrorisation of the Sudeten-German masses which was exercised by Henlein's agitators, vigorously supported in every way by propaganda from Germany. The Czechoslovak authorities could, and should, have countered this, not only by enforcing the law against any kind of terrorisation, but also by widespread and effective support of the anti-Nazi elements, who always constituted at least one-third of the Sudeten-German population. Czechoslovak democracy deserves blame for having failed in the main to do these things. . . .

One cannot overstress the fact that the demand for union with the Reich was no spontaneous expression of the desire of the majority of the Sudeten-German people. This demand was imposed upon the Sudeten Germans by a minority of Pan-German extremists among them, who were working in close collaboration with and following the instructions of Hitler's political General Staff. This was revealed by the passivity of the greater part of the Sudeten Germans during the days of the revolt. As soon, moreover, as the revolt had been completely suppressed, it came in for criticism by important members of the Sudeten-German Party. These men disowned their radical leaders, who had meanwhile fled into Germany, and declared their loyalty to Czechoslovakia. A large proportion of Henlein's supporters were incredibly quick in ostentatiously discarding their membership cards and badges, while many of them even went so far as to ask German Socialists and Democrats to speak in their favour with the Czech authorities.

These developments did not surprise us particularly, since we had long been well aware of the situation among the Sudeten Germans. It was known that only a minority were active in the support of Pan-German National Socialism, while the majority, carried along with the stream, were merely being made use of in order to bring pressure to bear on the Czech authorities. When Henlein's revolt was so rapidly and easily suppressed, it was clear to us that, if only time could be gained, the whole movement would disintegrate and sane judgment would begin to predominate over passion among the Sudeten Germans. If this were to happen, it was absolutely necessary that decisive action by the Western Powers should hold up Hitler's expansionist plans. If the British and French had shown firmness at this point, we should have been able, on the basis of the "Fourth Plan," to come to a satisfactory settlement of the Sudeten-German problem—indeed of the whole problem of our minorities—without disrupting the integrity or the Constitution of Czechoslovakia. This is exactly what Mr. Chamberlain himself had advocated in his memorable declaration of March 24, which had been explicitly confirmed by Sir John Simon in his speech on August 27—scarcely two weeks previously.

But the possibility of this solution was exactly what was feared in Germany. The Nazis realised that as soon as Czechoslovakia settled the Sudeten-German problem, Nazi Germany would have lost a powerful instrument for the furtherance of her aggressive expansionism. The "liberation" of the Sudeten Germans was not an end in itself, but merely a means for the elimination of an independent Czechoslovakia, which the Nazis quite correctly—and, it must be admitted, with more foresight than the politicians and diplomats of Western Europe—regarded as the keystone of the balance of power in post-war Europe. It is unfortunate that what was really at stake at that time was not well understood, either in Britain or in France. Astute German propagandists used the great complexity of the Sudeten-German problem, which was naturally remote and strange to the majority of the English and French, to disguise its fundamental nature. The Nazis deliberately created the impression that it was a matter merely of a dispute between Czechs and Germans as to whether the Sudeten Germans should be granted the right of self-determination in a wider sense (union with the Reich) or in a narrower sense (autonomy within the Czechoslovak Republic). One can note the influence of this point of view in the British Prime Minister's speech of March 24.

The insufficient understanding in London and in Paris of the real significance of the Sudeten-German question proved fatal to us. We understood very well, and indeed shared, the desire of the allied Western Powers that this problem should be settled as quickly as possible and thus removed from the scene of international politics. If there was agreement, however, between London and Paris, on the one hand, and Prague, on the other, as to the end to be pursued, it was more difficult to come to such an agreement as regards ways and means of attaining it. The view which prevailed in London and Paris was that Hitler's aggressiveness should be toned down by "concessions," and it was considered that a "just" solution of the Sudeten-German problem on a basis of autonomy would satisfy Hitler. It was therefore thought wise—always with an eye on Hitler—to exert "friendly pressure" on Prague in order to make the Czechoslovak Government go "to the utmost limit" of concessions to the Sudeten Germans. Doubt prevailed in Prague whether this tactic of making "concessions" would serve to reduce the rapacity of the Nazis; it was feared, rather, that it would encourage them to put forward increasingly pressing and presumptuous demands. This fear was strengthened by the consciousness that Berlin was not concerned with the fate of the Sudeten Germans, but rather with the elimination of an independent Czechoslovakia which would be able to oppose successfully German expansion in Central Europe.

Konrad Henlein was a powerful agent of the Nazis in confusing in the British mind the real issues at stake. His moderate behaviour while he was in London created a good impression on the politicians he met. It inspired confidence and tended to refute the allegations that he was no more than the mere puppet of Berlin. We, in Prague, had no such confidence in him. The Czechoslovak Government realised that Henlein could not be considered as a leader who could come to decisions on his own, for he had neither the force nor the ability sufficient to make him independent of orders from Berlin. Furthermore, we had in our possession evidence to convince us that the policy of the Sudeten-German Party was controlled from Berlin. It was necessary only to read the Henlein Press to see that in everything, down to the very smallest details, it was following orders and instructions from the Nazi centres in the German Reich.

Under these circumstances, it is understandable that the Czechoslovak Government only made concessions reluctantly and often even with embarrassment to the "friendly advice" which came from London and Paris. There were often just grounds for criticism of this attitude, for there is no doubt that much time was wasted—to our cost—and many opportunities were missed. I myself consider, and many other Czech politicians have thought the same, that immediately after May 21, at the moment when our partial mobilisation and the firm decision of Britain and France had forced Hitler to retreat and when his prestige was considerably diminished even among the Sudeten Germans themselves, we should have proposed a broad-minded solution of our nationality problem. This solution should have been carried through quickly—by the end of July at the latest. It should have been carried through preferably in agreement with the Sudeten-German Party, but otherwise without it, and in any case, of course, in agreement with the loyal, democratic Sudeten Germans. It was undoubtedly a great mistake that we did not do this, for we gave the Nazis time to recover themselves and to become even more intransigent. By failing to take a firm and constructive line, we gave many people in the West, even those well-disposed towards us, the impression that we did not take seriously the settlement of our nationality problem. . . .

Every mistake of tactics or of principle which was committed by Prague or by the Western Powers in seeking a "just and reasonable" settlement of the Sudeten-German question was due to one and the same fundamental misconception: they were looking for reconciliation with a partner who desired, not reconciliation, but domination. London and Paris, and to a certain extent Prague also, though less consistently, hoped that it would be possible to come to an agreement with the Sudeten-German Party. This hope presupposed, of course, that such an agreement was within the bounds of possibility. Such a supposition implied, moreover, the assumption or hope that the Sudeten-German Party would be able to come to an independent decision, or that, even if it looked to Germany for guidance, which would be understandable, it would at least be free to adopt an attitude in accordance with the needs and interests of those whom it professed to represent. That would have meant, of course, that it would be prepared, if necessary, even to oppose the wishes of Berlin. Such ideas and hopes were, however, without foundation. There is no doubt that even within the Sudeten-German Party there were influential people who did not agree with the disastrous ideas of their extremists, and who followed with increasing alarm the development of the warlike, adventurous policy of German National Socialism. Influential groups of industrialists, having heard from their friends in Germany angry complaints against "Nazi Bolshevism," regarded with anxiety the State capitalist system of the National Socialists. The Austro-German *Anschluss* had intimidated the Sudeten-German Catholics and Agrarians into seeking safety by hastily merging into Henlein's party, but subsequent developments in Austria (with which country the Sudeten Germans had far more direct relations than with Germany), and especially the persecution of the Austrian Catholics, again alienated these new adherents of Henlein, as well as many of the older members of his party. The enthusiasm for the Nazi Reich was not increasing. The majority of Henlein's supporters were undoubtedly in favour of a larger degree of autonomy, but they scarcely desired union with Germany. In a party like the Sudeten-German Party, however, it is not the moderate elements, but rather the radicals and extremists, who decide policy, and with the latter no agreement was possible unless it granted the full 100 per cent of the Nazi demands.

Many misunderstandings, and consequently many grave political errors, are due to the fact the revolutionary character of National Socialism has not yet been widely appreciated. Hitler himself has always stressed the fact that his National Socialism is not a party, but a movement; and its character, aims and methods are all those of a revolutionary movement. It is true that he proclaims "order" as one of the highest laws, but he arrives at this "order" by upsetting and overriding the existing political, economic, social and international order. National Socialism, in no less a degree than Bolshevism, aims at a complete re-creation of all existing values (*"Umwertung aller Werte"*), revealing thereby its extremist and revolutionary character. Its more moderate elements necessarily fall more and more into the background, while the real leadership passes into the hands of the extreme radicals.

This process took place within the Sudeten-German Party: the radical elements always overpowered the more moderate, and whenever it has seemed possible that the latter might succeed in their policy, the extremists immediately provoked incidents which rendered further compromise impossible, just at the moment when such compromise seemed within reach. One of my friends, who belonged to the more moderate wings of Henlein's party, told me: "Whenever Kundt [who was the leading negotiator of the Sudeten-German Party in the summer of 1938] speaks reasonably at party meetings, he is met with ice-cold silence in his audience. What can he do, then, but adopt the tone of wild radicalism, even though that may be contrary to his original intention?" Only in this way could he win "unanimous and enthusiastic approval."[1]

In June and July, when the Nationalities Statute and certain administrative reforms which would grant increased local autonomy within the framework of the State were being drawn up, there were certain Henleinist politicians who considered this satisfactory, but dared not say so publicly for fear of their radicals. The sending of Lord Runciman to Prague as mediator at the beginning of August, 1938, stiffened the intransigence of the Henleinists, for they hoped from the very first that his mediation would help their cause. They manoeuvred in such a way as to convince the Runciman Mission of the "ill-will" of the Czechs and to persuade them that nothing short of the acceptance of the eight points of their Karlsbad Programme would constitute a satisfactory agreement. The mediation of the Runciman Mission was deliberately disturbed by the provocation of minor and major incidents, and it was no mere coincidence that such incidents should have become more numerous from the second half of August onwards. After August 20, when such important progress had been achieved in the negotiations that even the Henleinist politicians dared not fail to admit it, especially when they were in the presence of and under the control of the Runciman Mission, the leading extremist of the Sudeten-German Party, a deputy named Frank, took steps to counter it. On August 26 Henlein's paper, *Rundschau,* published a notice advising party members "to defend themselves" against "acts of aggression or provocation" by their opponents. This was nothing more nor less than an exhortation to individual acts of violence. Such action, of course, drastically prejudiced the success of further negotiation.

While all this was taking place in Czechoslovakia, Britain and France, alarmed by the increasing threat of a Germany already mobilised for war, urged Prague expressly to "go immediately and unconditionally to the utmost limit of concession." The British and French Ministers in Prague urged the concessions should be made before the National Socialist Congress opened at Nuremberg. It was thus that, on

[1] It should be noted in passing that Kundt, when he became leader of the Germans in the post-Munich Republic, adopted a tone which fully deserved the "unanimous and enthusiastic approval" of the Nazis.

September 5, the so-called "Fourth Plan"[2] was published. As has already been stated, this plan was considered by Lord Runciman to be a very favourable basis for renewed negotiation, since it satisfied nearly all the Karlsbad demands. A similar view was held by many of the leading men in Henlein's party, some of whom even went so far as to welcome the plan as a happy way out of a complicated situation. Certain Henlein leaders made no secret of their opinions to President Benes, with whom they had already been in confidential contact before the plan was published. I could without difficulty name the persons of whom I write, but, although they broke faith later on in order to secure posts for themselves under their new ruler, Hitler, I should not like to burden my conscience with responsibility for the consequences which they would probably suffer, if I were to write openly of their activities during those days. Suffice to say, then, that the "Fourth Plan" satisfied even the more prominent elements of the Sudeten-German Party, and that this itself was displeasing to the extremists. On September 7, the very day on which an affirmative answer to the Government's proposals (the "Fourth Plan") was expected from Henlein's negotiators, a violent disturbance was provoked in Moravskà Ostrava [Mährisch Ostrau] between Henleinist rioters and the local police. Although the incident was not of a grave character, the negotiators, evidently through fear of their extremists, announced that they could not continue discussions with the Government until the incident had been settled to their satisfaction. Satisfaction was granted them, though at no small sacrifice of authority by the Czechoslovak administration—a fact which naturally roused strong resentment among the Czech public. Nevertheless, the plot of the extremists was frustrated and on September 10 Henlein's negotiators said that they were willing to resume discussions. They insisted, however, that this should not be until September 13, i.e. only after Hitler had made his speech at Nuremberg, which was announced for the evening of September 12. The delay permitted the

[2] This was the name given the last—and most far-reaching—of the proposals put forth by the Czechoslovak Government. Submitted to the Nazi Sudeten negotiators on September 5, the Fourth Plan accepted nearly all the demands Henlein had made in his address at Karlsbad on April 24. The Plan provided for the utmost concessions to the Sudeten Germans and other nationalities, and if put into effect, would have resulted in the extreme decentralization of the Czechoslovak State. Indeed, it seems likely that the Fourth Plan would soon have led to the disintegration of the Republic, and this, of course, was the obvious intent of the German demands. Yet so far-reaching were the concessions contained in the Fourth Plan that, for a moment, even the Sudeten leaders seemed uncertain as to how to proceed to reject it. The manufactured "incident" at Mährisch-Ostrau, on September 7th, provided the Sudeten Nazis with the necessary "excuse" to break off all negotiations with the Czechoslovak Government. For the text of the Fourth Plan, see Monica Curtis (ed.), *Documents on International Affairs, 1938*, Volume II (London, 1943), pp. 178-184, and for a point-by-point comparison of the Fourth Plan and the Karlsbad demands, see R. G. D. Laffan, *The Crisis Over Czechoslovakia* (London, 1951), pp. 240-245. For Sudeten Nazi reaction to the plan, see *Documents on German Foreign Policy 1918-1945*, Series D, Volume II, no. 440, 441.—F. L. L.

extremists, acting on instructions from Germany, to renew their agitation, and immediately after Hitler's speech they provoked the attempt at widespread rebellion of which we have spoken above. The comparatively easy suppression of this attempt and the consequent discredit which it brought on the extremists, who immediately left the country, opened, it is true, the possibility of renewing negotiations in a more favourable atmosphere. However, it was just at that moment that the Western Great Powers intervened by Mr. Chamberlain's flight to Berchtesgaden. . . .

The policy of the British Government was clearly not dictated by an analysis of the Sudeten-German problem, but rather by the international outlook, political view-point and wider aims which the British Government envisaged for Europe. The essential miscalculation of the British was not understood until the following March. At the time Lord Runciman had come to the conclusion that those frontier districts which were inhabited by a mostly Sudeten-German population should at once be transferred to Germany. Yet he adds, in his Report of September 21: "The transfer of these frontier districts does not, however, dispose finally of the question how Germans and Czechs are to live together peacefully in the future. Even if all the areas where the Germans have a majority were transferred to Germany, there would remain in Czechoslovakia a large number of Germans, and in the areas transferred to Germany a certain number of Czechs. Economic connections are so close that an absolute separation is not only undesirable, but inconceivable; and I repeat my conviction that history has proved that in terms of peace the two peoples can live together on friendly terms."

He recommended, therefore, that an effort be made to find a basis for local autonomy on the modified lines of the "Fourth Plan" for those Sudeten Germans who would remain in Czechoslovakia even after the territorial cessions, but his Report continues: "As I have already said, there is always a danger that agreement reached in principle may lead to further divergencies in practice. But I think that in a more peaceful future this risk can be minimised."

The remarks which I have quoted do not, in my opinion, support Lord Runciman's principal point that the cession of the frontier districts was essential. Lord Runciman admitted that it would be impossible to draw a purely ethnographical frontier through the districts in which the nationalities are very mixed, that in any case there would always remain larger or smaller minorities of Germans in Czechoslovakia and of Czechs in Germany, and that there would always be numerous causes of friction and conflict so that minorities must be afforded a certain degree of autonomy. It may be mentioned, in passing, that Lord Runciman did not mention how to secure the interests of the Czech minority in Germany! Lord Runciman's Report will be an important record that even the man responsible for proposing the transfer of Sudeten-German territory was conscious that it did not represent a complete solution of the problem. Lord Runciman's solution did not do away with minorities; though it was dealing with the rights of the German minority in Czechoslovakia, it had to be admitted that "an absolute separation is not only undesirable, but inconceivable." Munich subsequently proved quite clearly that it was not a question of satisfying the German minority in Czechoslovakia, but of satisfying the Third Reich, which, bent on expansion, used the Sudeten Germans as a lever to disrupt Czechoslovakia and to smash the balance of power, not only in Central Europe, but throughout Europe. . . .

I should perhaps explain why we did not propose the "Fourth Plan" much sooner, instead of waiting till September. I have already made it clear that in my opinion we lost much by missing the favourable opportunity which presented itself after May 21, and I would stress the fact that this was not the fault of President Benes. It was our ponderous political system, based on a coalition of bureaucratic parties, which let us down. The advantage of this system was that it had considerable political and social stability; it prevented sudden and spasmodic political changes and subjected the parties and the whole of our political life to a strict discipline. Dr. Hodza defined Czechoslovak democracy as "an authoritative democracy based on voluntary self-discipline." But it also had grave drawbacks; it was clumsy and exceedingly slow at reaching a decision, which was, in any case only possible when all parties were in agreement. Furthermore, it automatically treated any new impulse, any original or daring proposal or idea, with grumbling suspicion. Finally, we must add to these drawbacks the deplorable fact that the leadership of every party, and thus of the State executive, was composed—with a few exceptions—of politicians who were worn out with old age or by long years of exhausting public activity. We had neither sufficient elasticity nor sufficient imagination to adapt ourselves to an age of rapid and revolutionary changes, which called for ready initiative and for quick and bold decisions. Many people were anxious for radical changes, and more especially for changes of the leading statesmen, which would lead, if not immediately to a new régime, at least to a new working procedure. President Benes could not do everything by himself, and had no constitutional authority to make vital decisions. But he was afraid that changes in leadership and working procedure might lead to serious crises in the political parties and in the State executive—crises which might have had unfortunate consequences when our State was the centre of grave international tension. This explanation, though not sufficient to excuse our having missed the favourable opportunity after May 21, may help the reader to understand what was happening in our country and why it happened.

It would, nevertheless, be wrong to suppose that it would have been possible to make such far-reaching proposals as those embodied in the "Fourth Plan" earlier than in September. Political and social ideas which will be acceptable tomorrow are generally unacceptable today.

Ideas need time to ripen in the public mind and there is always trouble if they are prematurely enforced. If the British and French Governments are compelled to pay attention to public opinion, the Czechoslovak Government could not afford to overlook it, and the Czechoslovak public only grudgingly accepted the making of concessions to the Sudeten Germans. One may justly reproach Czechoslovak politicians and journalists for having paid too little heed to the constant reproaches and reminders of Presidents Masaryk and Benes. Both men constantly spoke of the necessity for finding a completely satisfactory settlement of the nationalities question; their colleagues were to blame that they did not educate and prepare the public in time for this settlement. But, despite all the mistakes which we undoubtedly made in this respect, and even if I accept without challenge all the criticisms of our minority policy made by Lord Runciman in his Report—though it would be easy for me to add such limiting qualifications and comments on them as would reveal the real situation in a very different light—I maintain that the grossest errors on our part would not justify the injustice of our virtual subordination to Germany at Munich and the terrible consequences which it has entailed. I make this claim fully conscious of my responsibility, although—or, perhaps, rather because—from the very earliest post-war days I have repeatedly criticised, in the spirit of Masaryk's policy, the shortcomings and errors of our treatment of the minorities. Yet the fact remains that there was no nation in Europe which treated its minorities more justly and more liberally than we did. Switzerland has no minorities, being composed of three equal nationalities; Belgium is similarly composed of two equal nationalities. Whereas in Germany, Poland and Italy, or in any of the states which lie between us and the Aegean, the minorities are literally oppressed and are struggling against great difficulties to obtain the primitive right to their own language and culture, in Czechoslovakia—and I must underline the fact that it was only in Czechoslovakia—the minorities enjoyed not only the right to their own language and culture, but also full civic and political rights. The struggle of the Sudeten Germans was not for their nationality rights, but for political supremacy. For this reason it was not to be wondered at that Czechoslovak public opinion showed little enthusiasm in making concessions whereby the political position of the Sudeten Germans was gradually strengthened. It should not be forgotten that the Sudeten Germans themselves greeted each concession with fiercer and more insolent attacks on the State.

The Czechoslovak people as a whole are not chauvinistic nationalists, and their few chauvinists have never had great influence among them. From 1926 to the spring of 1938 the participation of German representatives in the Government was recognised by the vast majority of them as a natural and desirable phenomenon. But Czechs are profound patriots, and their uneasiness at the concessions which were being made sprang not from national ill-feeling or ill-will to the Germans, but from anxiety lest the Henleinists would abuse all concessions for the furtherance of the Pan-German Nazi aim of disrupting the Republic. The Czechs are, however, politically mature to a quite exceptional degree, even as compared with the peoples of much larger nations, and, despite their uneasiness—for which there was more than ample justification—they understood during the summer that it was in the interest of their State, for international reasons, to make concessions in the nationality question. I would not attempt, nevertheless, to pretend that our public received the "Fourth Plan" without unconcealed disapproval and misgiving. It would take me too long to analyse these sentiments in detail, but it must be obvious that if the Karlsbad Programme was considered very dangerous at the time of its publication, in April, 1938, a plan which would satisfy its main demands must seem no less dangerous five months later. We accepted the "Fourth Plan" because it was known that it had been extorted from our Government under urgent pressure from Britain and France, upon whose help we counted and whose wishes we therefore fulfilled, and because President Benes, in whom the people had absolute confidence, had endorsed it with the full weight of his authority. The Czechoslovak Government was obliged, however, to give an assurance that it was "final" and that, in the words of the Deputy Prime Minister, M. Bechyne, they would not go "one millimeter further" in their concessions. But this Government declaration, which was demanded by Czechoslovak public opinion, was not well received by the British and French diplomatic representatives in Prague, who expressed fears that it might "provoke" the Germans. There seemed to us a certain disproportion in their concern for the feelings of the Germans as compared with the absence of concern for the feelings of the Czechoslovak public. . . .

Germany, I repeat, wished to make use of the Sudeten Germans for the disruption of Czechoslovakia, and thus to open the road for her expansion into Central and Eastern Europe. That, as subsequent events have proved, was the only real reason for Germany's interest in the Sudeten-German problem, and the Western Powers undeniably assisted Germany in the achievement of the goal which she so ardently desired. The first open step in this direction was taken on September 14, when Mr. Chamberlain decided to visit the German Chancellor in his home at Berchtesgaden.

Paul Reynaud · (Born 1878) A moderate-liberal in French politics, he served in numerous Cabinet positions in the Third and Fourth Republic, and served as Minister of Justice at the time of the Munich crisis. He became French Prime Minister in March 1940, but was forced to resign on June 16, 1940, because of his opposition to an armistice with Nazi Germany. He has recorded his experiences in a number of volumes, including *La France à sauvé l'Europe* (2 vols., 1947), *Au coeur de la mêlée 1930-1945* (2 vols., 1951), translated as *In the Thick of the Fight* (1955)—from which the following account is taken—and *Mémoires* (2 vols., 1960-1963). A strong supporter of Western unity, he has also written *Unite or Perish: A Dynamic Program for a United Europe* (1951). Opposed to the betrayal of France's treaty obligations to Czechoslovakia, M. Reynaud's account is an important example of the anger—and impotence—felt by a leading Frenchman during the Munich crisis.

Six months after the Wehrmacht had entered Vienna came Munich. Hitler was striking whilst the iron was hot.

In the Europe created by Versailles, Czechoslovakia was one of the new-born States, and delicate like all the newly born. Victorious France was her ally. She had signed with France, as we have seen, the treaties of 1924 and 1925.

On Hitler's arrival to power, agitation began amongst the Germans who inhabited the mountainous Sudeten area in the north. Hitler, who controlled the movement, grouped these Germans into a single party, under the orders of a former teacher of gymnastics, Henlein. At the elections of 1935 Henlein gained forty-four seats in the Chamber, out of three hundred. He did not delay in demanding the return of the province to the Reich.

Menaced thus by Germany, whose claims Mussolini now openly supported, Czechoslovakia turned in her anxiety to Moscow in order to ask for help. Russia, as we have said, agreed to give this, but she only pledged herself to act according to how France herself discharged her own pledges towards Czechoslovakia.

In 1938, Nazi agitation amongst the Sudetens was becoming diabolical. The radio played upon the nerves enough to break them. On February 26, Delbos told the Chamber "France's pledges towards Czechoslovakia would, if necessary, be faithfully observed." "Empty words," thought Hitler again.

On March 4, Hodza, Prime Minister of Czechoslovakia, stated that his country, with the backing of France and Russia would defend her frontiers, which he considered sacrosanct, to the last.

On the 11th, Hitler, whilst preparing to enter Vienna, gave Czechoslovakia "his word of honour that the annexation of Austria was a family matter," and one which would in no wise influence relations between Berlin and Prague. Moreover, the Reich, he stated, had a keen desire to better these relations still further. Goering confirmed these assurances to the British Ambassador, and authorized the British Government to make them publicly known.

On May 22, came the first alert. Gamelin wrote:[1] "An attack by Germany on Czechoslovakia is thought to be imminent." European feeling was already resigned. Gamelin continued: "A very unfavourable note was struck by Belgium. The Foreign Minister, M. Bargeton, told our Ambassador: 'We have just carried out manœuvres on the French border to demonstrate that, if you enter Belgium to support the Czechs, you will run into the Belgian army.'"

Hitler's plan was ripening. On June 18, he came to a decision. He would attack Czechoslovakia. This was because he was convinced, he wrote on that day to Keitel, "that France *will not march* and that, as a result, Britain will not intervene any more than she did when the Rhineland was re-militarized or when the Wehrmacht invaded Austria."

On September 1, Hitler received Henlein at Berchtesgaden.

On the 9th, Prague announced measures in favour of the German minority in the Sudetenland. On the 10th, Benes said on the wireless "Nothing will be changed in the democratic structure of the State, nor in its policy. . . . Our country will come out of the present difficulties victorious."

On the 12th, Hitler proclaimed at the closure of the Nuremberg congress: "The Reich will not permit the oppression of three and a half million Germans to continue . . . If the democracies try to protect . . . those who attack Germans the consequences will be serious."

Tension was at breaking-point. On the 13th, Henlein, proclaiming that it was the will of the Sudeten people to be rejoined to the Reich, demanded a plebiscite. This was the worst solution of all, the one which Prague feared the most.

On the 15th, Chamberlain took the initiative in proposing an interview with Hitler. The latter accepted. Getting into an aeroplane for the first time in his life Chamberlain went to Berchtesgaden. The Führer asked for a plebiscite amongst the Sudetens to be held. This was also what Runciman asked, who had just made an inquiry on the spot on behalf of the British Government.

[1] Maurice Gamelin, *Servir* (Paris, 1946), Vol. II, p. 334.

On the 16th, Georges Bonnet[2] gave his instructions to M. de Lacroix, our Minister in Prague. He wrote: "It would be difficult, in any question of war with Germany, for the French Government to get the support of French public opinion, if, on one hand, France was not attacked, and if, on the other, France could not be sure of having Britain at her side in the event of war." The first of these two conditions resulted in the unilateral breaking of the alliance.

On the 18th, Daladier and Bonnet conferred in London with their British counterparts. We were at the decisive hour. Let us examine the state of mind of the chief actors in the drama. Recent revelations have enlightened us on the subject.

First of all let us hear what Benes has to say. His bitterness is well understandable:

France [he writes in his memoirs] was already shaping her course towards appeasement. The formation of the Daladier Cabinet, with Bonnet at the Ministry of Foreign Affairs, marked the critical moment. This Government gave a new orientation to French policy, which divorced it from its alliances in Central Europe. . . . Daladier . . . had never failed . . . to observe that he was not present . . . at Versailles . . . that it was necessary to adapt oneself to new situations, and that France could not indulge in the luxury of bothering about the crumbling states of Central Europe. He abounded in ironical criticisms, even scornful, about Poland and Roumania. . . . Bonnet had the reputation of being a gambler and a cynical intriguer, to whom any means were satisfactory, providing that they took him where he wanted to go. In his role as Minister he sent by telegram or letter, instructions tallying with the official declarations of the Government. At the same time he gave oral directives in a diametrically opposite sense.[3] He was *a priori* opposed to any military or diplomatic resistance to Hitler's policy of expansion. What he would have preferred above anything else was an armed struggle between Nazism and Bolshevism. Thus, it came about that Czechoslovakia and the Soviet Union were completely isolated in the camp of those, who, on principle, were openly and resolutely anti-Fascist and anti-Nazi. . . . Soviet

[2] This fact is mentioned by Jules Henry, at that time head of Bonnet's ministerial advisers, in the memoirs (unpublished) which he left.

[3] Jean Zay in his *Souvenirs et solitude* (pp. 83-4) addressed a similar reproach to Bonnet. He writes: "One cannot relive in memory this last year of peace . . . without making another observation, namely that amongst certain men, the desire to abandon Czechoslovakia and Poland, should war break out, that is to say, to repudiate pledges solemnly undertaken by all our Administrations from 1920, and the intention of allowing Germany an entirely free hand in the East and in Central Europe as she understood it, were formed well before the crises of September. It was the adoption of a principle previously and carefully deliberated, which found its principal interpreter, within the Daladier Cabinet, in the person of the Minister of Foreign Affairs himself, M. Georges Bonnet. One would not reproach the latter if he had openly proclaimed it. The Council of Ministers would have made its choice in the matter. But he followed this plan secretly whilst proclaiming an apparent fidelity to the official line of conduct pursued by the Government of which he was a member. The speech at Pointe-de-Grave was made, was it not, on September 6, 1938? 'France, in any case, will remain faithful to the pacts and treaties which she has concluded,' M. Georges Bonnet stated there. This was not his real intention; this was not his desire; this was not his personal policy."

diplomacy, on many occasions, made serious attempts to organize conferences at which views could have been exchanged on the common defence of Eastern and Western Europe against a Fascist attack. We were always prepared to join in such conferences. Yet, up to the end of September, 1938, the Soviet attempts encountered the negative attitude of the French and British. After the mobilization of 1938, I permitted the Chief of my General Staff, General Krejci, to establish direct contact with General Gamelin in order to draw up measures intended to co-ordinate the mobilization of France with that of Czechoslovakia. General Gamelin replied that he had received no instructions on the subject. We did not receive any other reply, and none of our general officers were invited to go to Paris. Therefore, some time before the Munich crisis, we came to the conclusion that the French did not wish, or were not able to enter into common preparations. In September, 1938, we were left alone with the Russians to put our heads together, to devise military steps to be taken in the case of a Nazi attack. At the time Europe was ready in every respect to accept without protest the *Diktat*[4] of Berchtesgaden. When Czechoslovakia energetically rejected the *Diktat*, she received, on September 18, from Great Britain and France a joint Note demanding that she should accept the terms of surrender which had been drawn up by Hitler and Chamberlain on the 15th at Berchtesgaden. When we refused, France and Britain sent us an ultimatum, which told us that, if we did not accept their plan, they would leave us to face the issue alone. . . .

. . . Official circles in Washington were seriously divided. . . . Certain individuals, beginning with Roosevelt, disapproved . . . of the policy of appeasement which was being followed by the majority of European countries. . . . Others . . . defended the policy of Munich, and some even went as far as actively supporting it. Joseph Kennedy, the American Ambassador in London, openly backed . . . the policy of Chamberlain, and the latter, on more than one occasion sought his help. Hugh Wilson, American Ambassador in Berlin, believed, in August, 1938, that a peaceful orientation of German policy was still possible. He . . . paid me a visit on August 6, 1938. I was surprised . . . at the naïve confidence which he had in the peaceful . . . intentions of Berlin. He repeated to me all through our conversation that Goering did not wish for war, and he was undoubtedly working for peace. The American Ambassador in Paris, William Bullitt, did not express his sympathies as openly as Kennedy, but, at the time of the crisis of September, 1938, his attitude to us was unfavourable. He did not hide it. Daladier indicated clearly on several occasions that his policy was in agreement with the views of the Ambassador of the United States, and as a result, with the officials of the State Department. Bullitt himself let it be understood, though feebly excusing himself for the position he took up, that he considered that the Prague Government had not shown itself sufficiently well disposed towards the German minorities, that . . . I [Benes] was anti-German to the point of being chauvinistic, and that my attitude was threatening the peace of Europe. Bullitt's policy at this time and later was governed by a personal antipathy against the Soviet Union, which he inherited from his term of office at Moscow. His part was later to take on a decisive importance, when, helped by Daladier and Bonnet,

---

[4] *Diktat*, dictation. The Germans, as is known, use this word to designate conditions imposed without discussion by the victor on the vanquished. It is in a pejorative sense that the word has been incorporated into international usage.

he succeeded in driving the Soviets out of the League of Nations, giving as a pretext the war which this power was waging against Finland. It was at this period, according to certain reports, that he sent to Washington his famous telegram which stated that he had at last obtained satisfaction, that is to say, that he considered himself avenged for all the misfortunes which he had suffered at Moscow. He followed out this policy right up to the defeat of France, and then later in the United States. It even seems that he then supported to a certain extent Pétain's régime against that of de Gaulle.

Neither do we lack insight into the London Conference of the 18th. Bonnet in his *Défense de la paix: I. De Washington au Quai d'Orsay* gives (pp. 234-42) a circumstantial account of it. The depositions of Léon Blum,[5] of Daladier[6] and of M. de Lacroix[7] before the Committee of Inquiry, have thrown light on certain controversial points. Let us hear what Léon Blum had to say: "I received . . . on the day before Daladier was to leave for London a visit from an emissary of Benes. This emissary . . . was a Social-Democrat member of the Czech Cabinet with whom I had very close relations, and who was called Netzas. . . . [He] came to tell me on behalf of Benes: 'Things have now been so arranged that Britain and France are going to ask concessions from us. I am sending you a map on which Daladier can see, by the very indication of our military works and fortifications, what is the most extreme line, at which, if it is overstepped, we would consider Czechoslovakia as surrendered and . . . ruined.' I was not able to see Daladier on the morning of the following day when he took off by air from London, but I sent Blumel to him who . . . handed him the document. . . . "

Alluding to this proposal and to the awkward situation in which it placed him, Daladier has stated: "Was it necessary to show it to Mr. Chamberlain and to try and establish there and then a position on which we could fall back? I made the decision to show it to him, but it proved a further argument in favour of the London thesis. . . . I completely opposed the idea of a plebiscite, because it was a plebiscite for all minorities. I informed Mr. Chamberlain in a private conversation of the proposals about Bohemian salients. . . . He said to me: 'You can see clearly that we cannot do anything. Prague recognizes this also.' I resigned myself to the idea of recommending the surrender of the Sudetenland, it being understood that it was a question of territories where there was a very clear majority of Germans wishing to become German nationals. I naturally reserved the decision of the French Government. The French Government met the next day, September 19, at the Elysée, and I did not hear one voice raised in opposition—not one. We all deplored what we called the 'sad necessity,' but no one in the Council of Ministers supported an opposite policy—no one. Therefore, this decision was taken unanimously . . . we gave to the Prague Government—associating ourselves with Britain—the advice which we had decided in London, to offer it."

[5] Sitting of July 30, 1947.   [6] Sitting of May 21, 1947.   [7] Sitting of March 16, 1948

Benes was not satisfied by merely warning Léon Blum. He had tackled the problem with M. de Lacroix. Bonnet relates this fact in the following words:[8] "On September 15, M. Benes had another and very confidential talk with M. de Lacroix. He raised . . . the consideration of a plan whose outlines had been sketched at the time of the discussions which preceded the Treaty of Versailles. M. Masaryk himself at the time had already thought of it. M. Benes suggested, therefore, to the French Minister in Prague the cession to Germany of three of the Sudeten territories, particularly important because they were inhabited by about nine hundred thousand Germans, and because they embraced an area of about eight thousand square kilometres. He had himself indicated in a precise manner what these territories were: one situated in the north-west angle of Bohemia, another in the north-east of the quadrilateral and the third at the border of the Silesian frontier and to the south of the salient of Glatz. M. de Lacroix had warmly thanked M. Benes. He sent us on the 17th at two o'clock a long telegram in which he informed us of the plan. This could, he said with reason, help us to find a conciliatory solution at the interviews which we would have in London with the British Ministers, and it would avoid the plebiscite so feared in Prague."

M. de Lacroix, in his deposition before the Committee of Inquiry, stated, on the contrary, that Benes had asked him "to beg the French Government not to depend upon" the past proposals which he had just recalled. Our Minister therefore recommended Bonnet to "keep the secret." But Daladier, as we have seen, revealed the proposal to Chamberlain. It is true that it had come to him also by another way and without being, in this case, modified by the reservation which M. de Lacroix stresses. The latter in any case has stated: "I have never forgiven my Government for this indiscretion. Moreover, I have noticed since, in examining the archives of the Ministry of Foreign Affairs, that my telegram had been so twisted that one might believe that the suggestions recalled by M. Benes were a solution which he was proposing."

The memorandum which, during the afternoon of the 19th, was to be submitted separately by the representatives of France and Britain to the Prague Government "without other comment," stresses Bonnet,[9] gave a verdict for the cession of those Sudeten districts, where more than fifty per cent of the population were of German stock. It was a "peremptory order," to quote the words of M. de Lacroix. The two Powers declared that, in their opinion, the maintenance of peace and the safeguarding of the vital interests of Czechoslovakia could only be ensured at this price. Britain, however, made a statement that she was ready to give her guarantee upon the new frontiers of Czechoslovakia, on condition that the guarantee was the result of a general pledge.

[8] *Défense de la paix: I. De Washington au Quai d'Orsay*, pp. 237-8.
[9] *Op. cit.*, p. 244.

In Prague, there was a surge of indignation; rather than resign itself to subscribe to the "complete mutilation" of the country, the Government preferred to recourse to the arbitration agreements laid down by the German-Czech treaty of October 26, 1925. But suddenly it changed its opinion. We were now on the evening of the 20th. M. de Lacroix stated: "I was in the act of drafting a telegram conveying the nature of this reply . . . when M. Hodza . . . summoned me. . . . I immediately interrupted my work to answer his invitation. M. Hodza asked me if I was certain that France would not honour her pledges, if there were a fight. I replied that I knew nothing about the possibility, and I proposed to him that I should telegraph immediately to Paris in order to obtain a definite reply. He objected that this step would take too long, and added: 'I admit, *a priori,* that France will not fight and, if you can get from your Government, tonight, a telegram confirming this, the President of the Republic will give way. It is the only way to save peace.' M. Hodza added, in reply to my questions, that he was acting in agreement with M. Benes and with the General Staff, which considered that, without the support of France, a war against Germany would be equivalent to committing suicide. I immediately informed my Government of this conversation. Now, in my examination of the archives of the Ministry of Foreign Affairs, I have noted that my telegram has had cut out of it the first question of M. Hodza and my own tentative reply. . . . I believe that this mutilation of my telegram is a grave act of guilt on the part of the French Government, for it seemed to imply that, without wishing to confess it, the Government was not resolved to keep its pledges."

Was this reproach uttered by M. de Lacroix known to Bonnet? The fact is that the latter, again in his *De Washington au Quai d'Orsay,* reproduces (p. 248) "this text of such supreme importance," stating that he "transcribes it entirely." Here is the document as Bonnet publishes it: "The President of the Council had just summoned me. In agreement, he told me, with the President of the Republic, he instructed me as follows. If I were to state that very night to M. Benes, that, in the case of war breaking out between Germany and Czechoslovakia over the Germans in the Sudetenland, France, because of her undertakings to Britain, would not fight, the President of the Republic would take note of this statement. The President of the Council would immediately summon the Cabinet, all of whose members were at the time in agreement with the President of the Republic and with himself in proposing to give way. . . .[10]

"The Czech rulers needed this assurance in order to accept the Franco-British proposal. They were sure of the Army, whose leaders declared that single combat with Germany would mean suicide. M. Hodza stated that the step which he was suggesting was the only means of saving peace. He wished to have the matter settled before

---

[10] The points of suspension are in the text as it is given by Bonnet.

midnight, if possible, or in any case, during the course of the night. The President of the Council conveyed the same communication to the British Minister."

Whatever be the truth, the move made by Hodza was examined in Paris. Bonnet relates[11] that he "insisted strongly to Daladier that the Council of Ministers should be summoned: the members of the Government apprised of the situation . . . could only approve our proposals, and we would thus avoid later criticisms. Daladier shared my opinion, but he observed to me that it was physically impossible to assemble the Council. The President of the Republic was at Rambouillet; several Ministers were out of Paris. How much time would be needed to call the others together? And, on the other hand, the reply had to be given very quickly, if possible before midnight. Now, it was after eleven o'clock. . . . After some discussion, we decided that it was necessary to send M. de Lacroix rather detailed instructions in order to guide him in the talks he was to have with M. Hodza. . . . However, before telephoning this message to Prague, the President of the Council and myself thought it necessary to warn the President of the Republic. I myself called M. Albert Lebrun at Rambouillet on a direct line. I insisted, despite the late hour, that the President himself should answer me. I explained the situation to him. . . . The President . . . gave his agreement, regretting at the same time like ourselves that we were obliged to take such hasty decisions." Half an hour after midnight the instructions were sent to Prague, whose Government, however, only gave way at 5 p.m. on the 21st, after having obtained from M. de Lacroix a written confirmation of the reply, which, in obedience to Bonnet's instructions, he had only given orally.[12] "Our friends," the communiqué of the Czech Government was to state shortly afterwards, "have advised us to pay for peace with our sacrifice. . . . We have found ourselves alone." The Minister for Propaganda, Vavreka, stated on the radio that the Government had been given no choice. "Our friends and allies," he said, "have forced us to accept conditions that one usually offers to a defeated opponent. We were not lacking in courage. . . . Do not let us judge those who have left us in the lurch at this hour of trial. Let us leave history the task of passing judgement on them."

On the 22nd Hodza resigned. Chamberlain again took an aeroplane to go immediately to meet Hitler, who this time received him at Godesberg-on-Rhine.

On the same day, Mandel, Champetier de Ribes and myself[13] considering that the statement of the Czech radio proved that, contrary to the decision taken in the Council of Ministers, the Government had not

---

[11] *Op. cit.*, pp. 249-50.

[12] Churchill writes (*op. cit.*, vol. 1, *The Gathering Storm*, p. 272, second edition): "The French Government at least was sufficiently ashamed of this communication to instruct its Minister only to make it verbally."

[13] Churchill writes (*ibid.*, p. 272, second edition): "At the height of the crisis (on September 20) I visited Paris for two days in order to see my friends in the French

left Prague free to accept or refuse the Franco-British proposals, sent
our resignations to Daladier, giving him, because of the gravity of the
circumstance, the freedom to choose the moment when he judged it
would be convenient to make them public.[14]

Daladier denied the allegation made by the Prague radio. Bonnet
ought, indeed, to have read to us, at the ensuing meeting of the Council the telegram by which M. de Lacroix had informed him of the step
of the Czech Government, made with the object of forcing his hand.

During the interview, Daladier added that the first measures for
mobilization were being taken, that war was coming, and that, under
such conditions, our resignations were equivalent to desertion. In the
face of these arguments we agreed to withdraw them.

On the 23rd, the crisis again grew acute. Hitler's demands had increased further. With the agreement of France and Britain, Prague
ordered a general mobilization. In France, mobilization was taking
place by stages.

On the 25th there was a new conference at London.

On the evening of the 26th the Foreign Office authorized the publication of the following statement: "If, in spite of the efforts of the Prime
Minister, Germany launched an attack on Czechoslovakia, France
would find herself forced to go to the assistance of her ally, and Great
Britain and Russia would take their places by the side of France. . . ."
Bonnet allowed certain papers . . . Le Jour, for example, to print, despite
the evidence, a statement that the communiqué was false.

Certainly Chamberlain's strongest wish was to prevent the outbreak
of war. He was never tired of saying so. But Britain had none the less
publicly assured us of her determination to come to our help if the
execution of our pledges dragged us into hostilities against Germany.
And Britain had notified Hitler of this determination.

The latter, moreover, took the precaution of reassuring Poland. At
the Berlin Sportspalast he declared on the 26th that Germany was
determined to keep up good neighbourly relations with Poland. Moreover, he said that Germany understood Poland's desire to gain access to
the sea, that the agreement reached with Pilsudski set aside any risk of
struggle between the two countries, and finally that it was only up to
both the rulers to improve still further German-Polish relations. In a
word, at the same time that he was executing Czechoslovakia, Hitler
was giving Poland the same promises that he had made to Czechoslovakia when he was executing Austria.

[14] Léon Blum, during his depositions of July 30, 1947, declared: "There were at
least two members of the Cabinet, whose resignations were only prevented with great
difficulty: Paul Reynaud and Georges Mandel."

Government, Reynaud and Mandel. Both these Ministers were in lively distress and
on the verge of resigning from the Daladier Cabinet. I was against this, as their
sacrifice could not alter the course of events, and would only leave the French Government weakened by the loss of its two most capable and resolute men. I ventured even
to speak to them in this sense."

We gain an insight into the attitude of the United States from *The Memoirs of Cordell Hull*. He writes:[15] "That same day [September 24] Bullitt telegraphed from Paris his belief that some effort should be made by us to maintain peace, even if it were unsuccessful. He suggested an appeal by the President to the British, French, Italian, German, and Polish chiefs of State to send representatives to The Hague to settle the crisis, and that we should indicate our willingness to be represented. . . .

"The President would be sent directly an appeal to this end by the heads of the interested States.

"On [the following day] the 25th . . . our Minister to Prague . . . telegraphed a plea from President Benes that President Roosevelt should urge the British and French not to desert Czechoslovakia."

The President adopted Bullitt's plan.

"On the night [of September 25] Bullitt telephoned the Department [and advised including in the appeals a 'further step'; namely, the suggestion made by Bonnet] that the President should offer to arbitrate. But neither the President nor I was willing to go that far. . . . Then at one o'clock on [the morning of September] 26 he sent [it in] identical messages direct to Hitler and Benes, and, through me to Chamberlain and Daladier. . . . 'I most earnestly appeal to you,' said the President, 'not to break off negotiations. . . .' [That same day, September] 26, Benes, Daladier, and Chamberlain stated their complete accord. . . . But Hitler's reply had not arrived. . . . Europe was mobilising. Kennedy telephoned me from London that the British Government had assured the French of its support in the event of war. . . . Bullitt cabled me that Daladier said he hoped the time would soon come when it would be possible to hold a conference to organize a genuine European peace; he thought the call for such a conference had to come from the President. . . . Hitler's reply arrived on the night of [September] 26. It was a long diatribe against the Czech Government, the Treaty of Versailles, and the League of Nations, and it concluded by placing the burden of peace or war upon Czechoslovakia, not Germany. . . . [During the morning of the 27th] Bullitt cabled a suggestion that a second telegram be sent by the President to Hitler requesting him to agree to send a representative to such a conference at The Hague [as Bullitt had previously suggested] Daladier, he said, was 'delighted' with the idea. . . . We also sent a telegram to Ambassador Phillips in Rome containing a personal and confidential message from the President to Mussolini asking Mussolini to 'help in the continuation of the efforts to arrive at an agreement of the questions at issue by negotiation or by other pacific means rather

[15] *The Memoirs of Cordell Hull*, London, 1948, vol. 1, pp. 590-3. Appointed Secretary of State on February 11, 1933, Cordell Hull held this post until November 27, 1944. Sumner Welles was himself Under-Secretary of State from May, 1937, to September, 1943. As is known, in the United States the *Secretary of State* and the *Under-Secretary of State* control respectively as chief and deputy chief the *Department of State,* that is to say, the Department of Foreign Affairs. Each of the other departments has at its head a *Secretary.*

than by resort to force.' [In the evening], President Roosevelt decided to send a further appeal, this time addressed to Hitler alone. . . . It suggested an immediate conference in some neutral spot in Europe, with all nations directly interested in the Czech controversy participating."

As for the attitude of Russia, it has raised a number of controversies. Moscow certainly did not think of getting out of its pledges to Czechoslovakia, but these pledges were linked, as we have seen, with parallel engagements which France had herself entered upon with Prague. It was natural that the Soviets should recall that any action by them could only be concomitant with that of France, and this concerted action remained in their opinion a natural *sine qua non*. Moreover, the implementation of pledges undertaken by Russia implied in practice, as we have also seen, a passage through Poland and Roumania. The Soviets rejected the idea of entering these countries by force, and only intended to do so if they were legitimately allowed, according to an agreement, that is to say, with Warsaw and Bucharest or, alternatively, and this came to the same thing, at the request of a combination of Powers or, at this juncture, by the Council of the League of Nations.

On September 26 Hitler declared that this time he had come to the end of his patience. He gave Benes six days to choose between peace and war: "We have," he proclaimed, "an armament so powerful that the world has never known its like. Once the question of the Sudetens has been settled, we shall have finished, in Europe, with the last territorial problem." Finished, yes, until the next time.

However, the French Government never grew tired of repeating to Hitler that, if he persisted in his intentions, war would be inevitable, that this would be madness, but that France would not be able to draw back. Suddenly there came the climax. During the afternoon of the 28th, M. François-Poncet telephoned from Berlin to Daladier that there was to be a meeting on the next day at Munich, to which he, Daladier, was invited.

We now know the reasons and the movements behind the scenes, which brought about this sudden change of policy. Both have been revealed by Ciano in his *Diary*.[16]

The initiative for Munich lay with Chamberlain personally, who consulted neither his own colleagues in the Cabinet nor the French Government, just as several days before he had refrained from informing them of the step he had taken in proposing to Hitler that he should go to Berchtesgaden in order to confer with him.

Whilst events rushed on at this giddy pace, disapproval in France was becoming more marked.

[16] Ciano's two notebooks which concern the years 1937 and 1938 were only made public in 1948, that is to say, two years after the publication of those which dealt with the years 1939-43. Moreover, the pages in the notebook of 1938, which dealt with Munich, had been taken out. They were finally discovered, and then published by *Le Figaro* in its editions of June 26 and 29, 1948.

On the 26th, Flandin published in *Le Temps* a letter in which he wrote: "For every kind of reason . . . I reject . . . the military intervention of France in the struggle between the Sudeten Germans and the Czechoslovak State . . . I do hope that France will not be faced by the *fait accompli* of a war which has been made inevitable, before the opinion of her legal representatives has been able to find expression in good time. Our British friends should in loyalty be told that the French Army will not be able to bear alone, or even with the support of a small contingent, the burden of land operations on three fronts . . ." So it was evidently only a matter of a difference between the Czechoslovak State and the Sudetens. . . .

On the 28th, Flandin went further. He had stuck up on the walls of Paris a placard whose text was, on the following day, reproduced by Doriot's *La Liberté*, a newspaper subsidized by the Reich. This read:

You are being deceived

People of France, you are being deceived. . . . A cunning trap has been laid for some weeks and months by secret elements in order to make war inevitable. . . .

What, on reading such a diatribe, could be the impression of young Frenchmen who were being mobilized? If they were the victims of a "cunning trap" created by diabolical men, would not their first reaction be not to risk raising the butts of their rifles off the ground?

The Government had the placard torn down and seized the issue of the paper. On the spot I sent to Flandin my resignation from the *Alliance Démocratique*,[17] of which he was the President, and with which I had for a long time avoided contact. Several of my friends, amongst whom were Rollin, Jacquinot and Laniel, followed suit.

The pacifist campaign gained both in strength and favour. The headlines appearing on the day of Munich in the Royalist paper *L'Action Française*—a patriotic paper during the First World War—show to what pitch feeling against war had risen in France. They consisted of a verse of the *Internationale* adapted as follows:

> *S'ils s'obstinent, ces cannibales,*
> *A faire de nous des héros*
> *Il faut que nos premières balles*
> *Soient pour Mandel, Blum et Reynaud.*[18]

[17] The *Alliance Démocratique* was a group of parties roughly representing the moderate Right and the Centre. In general it was Republican and Conservative, but differed from the extreme Right in being anti-Catholic and less opposed to the radical Left [Tr.].

[18] "If they persist, these cannibals,
To make of us the hero,
First we must reserve our shots
For Mandel, Blum and Reynaud."

However, the conference opened at Munich on the morning of the 29th. M. François-Poncet writes:[19]

The meeting began at 12:45 in an adjoining room. The ambassadors were not admitted. Two hours later, as the meeting adjourned, I was informed that the four participants exposed their points of view in turn in general terms. Hitler delivered a diatribe of extreme violence against Czechoslovakia. Thereupon Daladier clearly and vigorously posed the crucial question. Did the Conference wish Czechoslovakia to exist or not? Was the amputation intended to make her healthier and to give her better chances for life in the future? Or was it but a means to weaken her, a mutilation bound to bring about her death? If the point was to prepare the dismemberment and disappearance of Czechoslovakia, then he, Daladier, had no business in this place. He refused to be associated with such a crime and would take his leave. If, on the contrary, the point was to assure Czechoslovakia's future, then he was prepared to concur with the others in a spirit of reciprocal concession and collaboration. The French Premier spoke in accents of a determination and nobility that moved his hearers.

Mussolini declared that Hitler's idea had been misunderstood, and, like the Duce, all protested that they wished to consolidate and to respect the existence of the Czechoslovakian State.

At three o'clock luncheon was served.

There was a second session at the close of the afternoon. This time I entered by permission and sat behind Daladier. The delegates were grouped in a semicircle around a vast fireplace, the British on the left, the Italians and the Germans in the centre, the French on the right. Within the British group there was scant conversation; within the German and Italian groups there was much. Mussolini was deeply ensconced in his armchair. His extraordinarily mobile features were never at rest for a moment; his mouth would part for a wide smile or contract in a pout; his eyes, generally curious and amused in expression, would suddenly dart lightning.

Standing at his side, Hitler gazed intently upon him, subject to his charm and as though fascinated and hypnotized. Did the Duce laugh, the Führer laughed too; did Mussolini scowl, so scowled Hitler. Here was a study in mimicry. It was to leave me with the lasting and erroneous impression that Mussolini exercised a firmly established ascendancy over the Führer. At any rate that day he did.

No one presided at this session and there was no methodical agenda. For want of directive, the discussion proved difficult, confused, and interminably long. Hampered by the necessity of a double translation, it kept constantly changing its topic and ceased whenever a contradiction arose. The atmosphere grew thicker and heavier. At last toward evening the British produced a typewritten memorandum from their files. It had been drawn up by Horace Wilson with Strang's assistance. The debate, which had wavered, now concentrated upon this proposal for an agreement.

At half-past one in the morning the agreement was signed. The Ambassador continued:

[19] André François-Poncet, *The Fateful Years: Memoirs of a French Ambassador in Berlin, 1931-1938* (New York, 1949), pp. 270-3, *passim*.

We were bitterly aware of the cruelty of the event. Daladier shook his head, muttered, and cursed circumstances. He refused to take part in the congratulations exchanged by the other delegates. Worst, the most painful step had not yet been taken; we had now to break the news to the Czechoslovaks who were awaiting the outcome of the Conference at their hotel. Mastny, their minister in Berlin, broke into tears. I consoled him as best I could. "Believe me," I said, "all this is not final. It is but one moment in a story which has just begun and which will soon bring up the issue again."

Returning to our hotel at 2.30 a.m. I called Bonnet by telephone to inform him of what had happened, while Daladier, still cursing and lost in gloomy thought, weighed the difficulties he was likely to meet on his return to Paris. Bonnet swept aside my detailed explanations. "Peace is assured," he said. "That is the main thing. Everybody will be happy."

Whatever may be the truth about the meeting, Daladier was resigned to giving way. But in doing so he was the prey of extreme distress. Sadness showed on his face. Peace was saved, but he was well aware of the price of this surrender! We have a noteworthy account of his state of mind at Munich. Causoy, one of the journalists who went with the French delegation, quotes[20] the words uttered by Daladier at the *Quatre-Saisons* on the conference, ending: "And then, if we had not given way, there would still be a Czech problem; there would have always been Germans in Czechoslovakia."

As for Hitler, he was triumphant. He had secured complete victory. It seems to be a fact that, in order to carry out his manœuvres, he had to disregard all his advisers, and to ignore the opposition of Goering, Ribbentrop and the generals. The High Command, Brauchitsch and Keitel especially, feared a war, not believing that the Wehrmacht was sufficiently strong to win it. The eagerness of the Allies to "lick the boots of the Nazis," the ease with which Hitler got out of them much more than he himself dared to hope for, was to exert a tremendous influence on the course of events. Restraint, patience, conciliation were henceforth banned from the deliberations of the Führer. As on March 7, 1936, he had gambled and won. In the future, counsellors and favourites were to vie with each other in the audacity of their recommendations, and to bid for his goodwill by outbidding each other. The reproach which they were to fear above all others was that they possessed moderation or timidity. Because of Munich, Hitler conceived for those whom he had met in conference a feeling of scorn which burst out on occasions in foul expressions. His self-confidence, already tremendous, was to know no limits. He was no longer to have cause to find himself struggling with people who contradicted him. Henceforth, he was liable to be swayed by any mood of exaltation, by any extravagances, by any mania of omnipotence, whose outbursts nothing within him was capable of tempering.

Eva Braun, Hitler's mistress, notes in her *Journal Intime:* "October, 1938. Three of the *important* Four have left. The fourth, and without doubt the most important, has stayed. For nearly three hours he [Hit-

[20] *Le Populaire*, March 3, 1948.

ler] has talked of the negotiations. 'It is only now,' he said, 'that I know how weak the West is. . . . I shall wage the war which I need to impose my ideas on the world. Now, the difference between Mussolini and myself becomes more and more apparent. He aspires to peace; I, to war."

In any case Munich made Hitler the arbiter of Europe. Czechoslovakia was harshly punished for having wished to keep men of German blood under her thumb. The lesson, thought Berlin, would bear fruit. But the Führer had obtained another success, the certain pledge of new victories. He felt sure that he had broken the coalition which threatened, once again, to re-form itself against Germany: between Moscow and the Western Powers he had stirred up mistrust, discord and bad blood.

The Allies themselves laboured under a complete delusion.

Following his dream, whose secret he jealously kept to himself, Chamberlain stayed at Munich until the morning of the 30th. Just before leaving Hitler, he signed with him, without warning Daladier, a pact of friendship. When he got back to Croydon, he stated: "Peace has been won for a generation."

On the 30th also, Daladier got back to Le Bourget. He was expecting a hostile reception. Paris, which had just lived through days of anguish, experienced a slackening in nervous tension, and acclaimed Daladier, who crossed the town in an open car, with Bonnet beside him. Michel Clemenceau, son of the "Tiger," said to me: "The sight made me weep." He wrote an article in protest, which he hoped to publish in *L'Ordre*, but Petain, with whom at that time he was on good terms, advised him not to do so.

I was the only one, I think, of the members of the Government, who did not go to greet Daladier at Le Bourget. It was something which was beyond me. I went to see him at the Rue Saint-Dominique. At the top of the staircase I met Canon Polimann, deputy for the Meuse, who pretended not to see me. This was because the split between those who wished to resist Germany and their opponents, which had long been latent, occurred on the day of Munich. Daladier went with Gamelin and myself into his study. He found it full of baskets of flowers. He said to us: "It is my policy. It is the Four Power Pact," and he added: "It is possible to talk with those people. . . . Ah! If we had Ambassadors." I said to Gamelin: "You have now only got to find twenty-five divisions."

During the following two days, Champetier de Ribes, Mandel and myself talked over together the attitude which we ought to take. Here is the account which Francisque Varenne gives of this exchange of views in *Mon patron, Georges Mandel* (pp. 175-6):

> The day following the return of Daladier from Munich, at ten o'clock in the evening . . . Duff Cooper . . . warned Mandel that he had placed his resignation in the hands of Chamberlain, because he did not wish to be asso-

ciated with the policy of surrender, which had just been sanctioned at Munich. That very evening Mandel gave news of this to Paul Reynaud and to Champetier de Ribes. The three Ministers examined the problem as to what decision they themselves should take. . . . On the next day, there were several meetings at the Ritz of those Ministers who were opposed to a policy of appeasement. Finally it was decided that resignations would not be handed in. . . . An advocate . . . of resignation, he [Mandel] gave way before the reasons of his friends, and he acknowledged that those reasons were very strong ones. Public opinion, in overwhelming force, blinded by the more powerful newspapers and dominated by a fear of war, did not see in Munich the surrender of France and Britain to Germany. It only saw the dispelling of an agonizing nightmare. The resignation of the Ministers would have been badly received even in Parliament, and would have turned against them anger which would have been long in dying.

I have no recollection of this interview, which, in any case, could not have taken place at the Ritz. I only recall on the subject these words of Mandel at Portalet: "A resignation is justified when it is to accomplish something. Our own would have served no purpose."

On October 1 our friend Jules Julien, Minister of Post and Telegraph telephoned me:

"Flandin has just sent Hitler a telegram of congratulations."

"Impossible. Make certain about it."

He did make certain. The telegram[21] had indeed been sent. Here is its text:

> Please accept warm congratulations on keeping the peace, in the hope that out of this historic act will come a trusting and cordial collaboration between those four European Powers which met at Munich.

This "historic act" was not to be the last.

On October 2, Hitler thanked Flandin: "I am grateful for your efforts . . . on behalf of an understanding and complete collaboration between France and Germany. . . ."

On the next day, there were thanksgiving ceremonies at the Arc de Triomphe. In Prague, ex-soldiers threw their Legion of Honour and Croix de Guerre medals on the square in front of the French Legation.

On the 5th, Benes resigned the Presidency.

Polish troops occupied Teschen. I said to the Polish Ambassador in Paris, who did not hide his satisfaction: "You are satisfied because Hitler has put you in the refrigerator for his next meal."

Hitler spoke impatiently about British rearmament. He said on November 2: "The rearmament of others does not upset me. National Socialist Germany will never eat humble pie."

On November 20, Hacha succeeded Benes.

The amputated body of Czechoslovakia was stretched out on the operating table. But Hitler was not to summon the "butchers' club" again. In future he was to do the cutting up by himself.

---

[21] Flandin had also congratulated Daladier, Chamberlain and Mussolini.

Lord Strang · (Born 1893) Educated at the University of London, and at the Sorbonne. He entered the British Foreign Service in 1919, and following posts at Belgrade and Moscow, became Head of the Central European Department of the Foreign Office in 1937. He subsequently served as representative of the Foreign Office in the Anglo-French-Russian negotiations of July-August 1939, as British representative on the European Advisory Commission (1943-1945), and in 1949 became Permanent Under Secretary of State for Foreign Affairs, retiring in 1953. He has written a number of books, including a volume of memoirs *At Home and Abroad* (1953)—from which the following is taken—and a more general history, *Britain in World Affairs* (1957). One of the leading professional diplomats of his generation, Strang's account of the Munich crisis derives special importance from his position at the Foreign Office, and his close personal association with the development of British policy throughout this period.

Early in 1937, I became head of the Central Department of the Foreign Office on the lamented death of Ralph Wigram. I received the news of this appointment with misgiving. After three years of peripatetic duties as Adviser on League of Nations Affairs, following upon three years at the Embassy at Moscow, I had lost the habit of executive departmental work; and the thought of this new and arduous responsibility weighed heavily upon me. The department was well known to be the most hard-worked in the Office, handling, as it did, the problem of Germany in all its manifestations at a time when Hitler was launched upon his career of destruction. I was succeeding a colleague of unrivalled competence in this field, whose passionately-held opinions, powerfully presented and defended, aroused controversy. I was not that kind of person. Nor was I in entire sympathy with the uncompromising views which he had held about Germany. I confided my doubts to Sir Robert (later Lord) Vansittart, the Permanent Under-Secretary. He brushed them aside. If he had not thought me fit to bear the burden, he would not have proposed my appointment. . . .

In the middle 'thirties, many of those who are later to be the strongest opponents of what came to be known as appeasement thought that it was worth trying to reach a "general settlement" (as it was called) with Germany in co-operation with France. The League of Nations would be strengthened as an instrument against aggression. Some of

From *At Home and Abroad,* by Lord Strang. Reprinted by permission of André Deutsch Ltd., Publishers.

Germany's so-called grievances (demands would be a better word) would be met. Germany would come back to the League. This was the plan. No one was very hopeful that this programme would be achieved, if only because Germany would never be likely to renounce her aspirations in Central and South-Eastern Europe. Hitler's occupation of the Rhineland in the spring of 1936 knocked the bottom out of these schemes. The real question now was not whether a general settlement by negotiation was possible, but whether Germany's forceful acts should be resisted. As regards the Rhineland, I confess (and here I think I was wrong) that, although I was revolted by this flagrant breach of the public law, I leaned to the popular view that it would not be good policy to expel German troops by force from German territory. But, as Sir Robert Vansittart had foreseen, I came to different views once I had taken over the Central Department and had to deal with German problems at first hand. It became clear that the Nazis would stop at nothing; that sooner or later they would have to be resisted by armed force; that war was thus more than a probability; and that consequently—and this was vital—we should make all speed to rearm ourselves in order to be ready for the emergency when it came.

Among those who held this view there might still be some difference of appreciation as to which of the German grievances, if any, it would be prudent to remedy; and as to the point at which the risk of war should be taken in resisting Germany's drive to secure her objectives by force. As the events of 1938 and 1939 were to show, such differences could be important.

I remember a talk in my room in the Foreign Office with Ferdinand Kuhn, the gifted London representative of the *New York Times*, who questioned me sharply but in no hostile spirit about British policy in the current Czechoslovak crisis. I explained and defended the government's line. I was not very comfortable in having to do so, and yet I felt that there was much substance in it. Too many people were talking too glibly about standing up to Hitler even at the risk of war, and these were often the people who were opposing rearmament. Very few seemed to be conscious of the dangerous situation in the Far East, which the government had consistently to bear in mind. Nor did it lie in the mouths of Americans, given the United States policy of neutrality in face of the universal menace, to reproach us for our circumspection. Apart from the toll of human suffering which it brought, war would be a tremendous national hazard, and when the United Kingdom went to war, she, unlike some other countries, put her whole fortune to the touch. In what causes was a government justified in running that hazard? Was the future of the Sudeten Germans, or even the fate of Czechoslovakia herself, such a case? We had fallen into this position by not sufficiently pushing forward our preparations for defence and by failing to band together with our friends and with others who, though not friends, might yet be associates. But, since this was the melancholy situation we were in, would it not perhaps be best to avoid war this time, if we possibly could, and to make sure that by intensive rearmament we should be more nearly ready next time, since there would certainly be a next time? What I did not believe, and what I could not bring myself to say, was that (as some thought) a settlement of the Czechoslovak problem which could not fail to disrupt or truncate the Czechoslovak State would be a good thing in itself, morally and politically justified. I did not set the rights of minorities or the bare principle of self-determination so high in the scale of human values as did some others, and certainly not so high as to admit that they could rest as valid excuses for a contemptuous violation of the commonly accepted precepts of international law.

My years in the Central Department were the culminating years of "appeasement." This word has become a term of bitter reproach; but it has a respectable earlier history. In its French equivalent—*apaisement*—it was used by Briand to distinguish his policy towards Germany from that of Poincaré. It was in frequent use at the time of Locarno. Later on, in the 'thirties, it was chosen to describe their policy by those who thought that it was not beyond the power of diplomacy to improve relations between the democratic Powers and the dictators. It meant in their minds something like what we nowadays refer to as "relaxation of tension." It acquired its ill repute when too heavy a price began to be paid, a price which not only failed to bring permanent easement, but also carried with it impairment of national credit.

There had been three schools of thought. Some had wished to call a halt to Mussolini and meanwhile to try to come to terms with Hitler. Others, their minds filled by the menace from Germany, had wished to draw Italy into an anti-German combination. Others again, like Mr. Neville Chamberlain, thought that accommodation with both dictators was possible.

As Prime Minister, Mr. Neville Chamberlain took increasingly into his own hands the conduct of foreign policy, or rather of that branch of foreign policy which might involve issues of peace or war, namely relations with the two European dictatorships. This does not mean that he acted without consulting his Cabinet colleagues. He certainly made full use of the Foreign Policy Committee of the Cabinet, of which, as Prime Minister, he was Chairman; and, as the crisis developed, he tended to consult and carry with him an inner group of Cabinet Ministers composed of the Foreign Secretary, Lord Halifax, and two former holders of that office, Sir John Simon and Sir Samuel Hoare. But the policy was his; and so strong was his conviction and so powerful his drive that he was able to make it prevail.[1] As his agent and chief official adviser in these matters he called in Sir Horace Wilson,

[1] See Lord Templewood, *Nine Troubled Years*, Collins, London, 1954.

Chief Industrial Adviser to the Government, who had been seconded to the Treasury for service with the Prime Minister.

Foreign policy is most smoothly formulated and executed when the Foreign Secretary has the predominant voice in its formation and can rely on especial relations of confidence with the Prime Minister. This is not to say that the Prime Minister, as head of the Government and bearing general responsibility for its acts, should not intervene in foreign policy. It is his manifest right and duty to do so. In a passage which has often been quoted, and which has been called "the *locus classicus* on the constitutional relationship between the Prime Minister and the Foreign Office,"[2] Lord Granville stated his view on this problem in a letter to Mr. Gladstone on October 29, 1870, when he was Foreign Secretary in one of Mr. Gladstone's administrations: "I imagine that the Prime Minister has an undoubted right to communicate directly either with our representatives abroad or with Foreign Ministers in London. But I think that it is in his interest as much as in that of the Foreign Secretary that he should only appear as the *deus ex machina*." These words were written some while after Granville had emerged from a hard but successful tussle with his Prime Minister about the latter's desire to declare our objection to the transfer of French territory to Germany against the wish of the inhabitants, and more generally about "laying down general principles when nobody will attend to them."[3]

Mr. Chamberlain was a man of cool, calm mind, strong will and decisive purpose, wholly devoted to the public cause and with a firm confidence in his own judgment. These are rare and valuable qualities in a statesman. No civil servant who knows how grievous is the responsibility which lies upon Ministers of the Crown, and who has been present with them when they have passed through the agony of mind that can precede final commitment to a course of action, would judge lightly of their performance in the discharge of their high office. Of Mr. Chamberlain, it will be fair to say that his very qualities weighed in some measure against him in his operations in the field of foreign affairs. His mind was dominated by two thoughts. The first was a hatred of war so deep that he would think that heavy sacrifices would be justified in order to avoid it. The second was the belief that the German and Italian dictators were men whose word could be relied on; that it was possible to come to agreements with them which could transform the international situation for the better and give peace to Europe; and that by his personal influence with them he could hope to bring such agreements about. The first was in itself an entirely laudable sentiment, but it could be a hazardous guide to action in the jungle which Europe had now become. The second was a misjudgment, all the more serious

[2] *British Foreign Secretaries 1807-1916*, Algernon Cecil, Bell, London, 1927.
[3] *Life of Lord Granville*, Vol. II, Fitzmaurice, Longmans, London, 1905.

in that it continued to be entertained even in the face of strong evidence
to the contrary. It is unlikely that any Minister who had the whole
world within his purview and all the main problems of foreign affairs
upon his shoulders daily would so long have persisted in such an opinion: but Mr. Chamberlain was dealing with only one part of foreign
affairs, which must by their very nature be regarded as one whole. If he
had had to explain from day to day the progressive development and execution of his purposes to the French, United States, Soviet and other Ambassadors and to the Czechoslovak Minister, and had been obliged to
watch and respond to the impact of his actions upon governments and
peoples throughout the world, as a Foreign Secretary must do, he might
not indeed have modified his policy, but he might have seized its impli-
cations better than perhaps he did. It may be argued that, for all that,
his policy was justified in that it did save us from war. True, it saved us
from a probable war in 1938, but it did not save us from war. More will
be said on this point later. For the present it is sufficient to observe that
in 1938, with some loss of honour, we avoided a war which we might
not have won, and that in 1939 we had to face a war which we came
within an ace of losing but did in the end win.

The relationships between Mr. Chamberlain and the two Foreign
Secretaries who served in his administration have been discussed by
other writers and I do not touch on them here.

Sir Horace Wilson has been unjustly criticised. A civil servant, saving
personal honour and conscience, must do as he is bid. He may, indeed
should, put forward his views and he is entitled, up to a point, to press
his advice, but he must be ready to reconsider and in the end he must
comply. The orders which he receives are the responsibility of the
Minister. The civil servant must fulfill them to best of his capacity.
Sir Horace Wilson was a civil servant of the highest quality, well
skilled in negotiation. Though he was here operating in a field that was
unfamiliar to him, he performed his duties in a manner with which,
from the professional point of view, no serious fault can, I think, be found.
What, however, he was not in a position to do was to tender advice to
the Prime Minister on policy and procedure based on long years of
experience in the practice of diplomacy. It would have been proper for
him to represent to the Prime Minister that he was being asked to do
things which were outside his competence, and, for all I know, he may
have done so; but if the Prime Minister decided to use his services, that
was the Prime Minister's responsibility. What Sir Horace Wilson's personal views may have been on the policies which he was called upon to
carry out, it is not for me to say; I dare say that he agreed with them;
but I think that that question is irrelevant: whether we agree or not,
saving personal honour and conscience, we civil servants must act with
all our might. And if it be made a reproach to Sir Horace Wilson that
he did act with all his might, and indeed if it be suggested that he was
more zealous than as a civil servant he need have been, I would remark

that the work of a civil servant in putting public business through is not performed merely by writing words on pieces of paper. It means also seeing the right people at the right time and saying the right thing to them in the right way, a process which, if used for personal ends or to promote a personal policy, may justly be called intrigue, but which, if applied for the purposes of government as laid down by Ministers, is an essential skill in the professional repertory.

The story of the Czechoslovak crisis of 1938, from the occupation of Austria on March 12 to the signing of the Munich Agreement on September 30, is fully recorded in two volumes of the *Documents on British Foreign Policy 1919-1939*, Third Series, Volumes I and II.[4] The 1,231 documents and appendices contained in the two volumes fill nearly 1,350 pages. The course of these transactions as revealed in the *Documents* has been brilliantly analysed and illuminated by Sir Lewis Namier with the skill of a great historian, though with a severity of judgment which might perhaps not altogether commend itself to less rigorous spirits.[5] I can, I confess, add little beyond a few touches that will be of interest to the historian; while lack of expertise, no less than ex-official discretion, will deter me from attempting a dissection as thorough as that which the independent historian can perform: but as I handled these affairs in the Foreign Office under the instructions of Lord Halifax, and was of the party which accompanied Mr. Chamberlain on his successive visits to Hitler at Berchtesgaden, Godesberg and Munich, it may not be out of place if, on the strength of memories refreshed by a rereading of the documents, I offer some reflections and sidelights, together with enough of the sequence of events to make these observations intelligible.

One preliminary point is important. Though we had long been aware that, after the Rhineland, Hitler had designs on Austria and Czechoslovakia, we did not know in early 1938, as we know now from captured German documents and from the records of the Nuremberg trials, that on November 5, 1937, the die had been cast and that Hitler had definitely decided to proceed with the annexation of Austria and Czechoslovakia as the first objective in his programme of expansion in Eastern Europe in search of *Lebensraum,* and as a stepping-stone towards action against Poland and the Soviet Union. Nor did we know that Konrad Henlein, leader of the National Socialist Sudeten German Party in Czechoslovakia, in complicity with the German authorities who had been financing him since 1935, had engaged in an elaborate scheme of pretence to deceive the outside world as to the true objectives of his party. In a paper written in November, 1937, he says of his party that,

[4] H.M. Stationery Office, London.

[5] "The Road to Munich" in *Europe in Decay,* Macmillan, London, 1950; "The Makers of Munich" in *In the Nazi Era,* Macmillan, London, 1952.

while "at heart it desires nothing more ardently than the incorporation of Sudeten German territory, nay of the whole Bohemian Moravian and Silesian area within the Reich . . . outwardly it must stand for the preservation of Czechoslovakia and for the integrity of its frontiers . . ." Only by demanding "autonomy," and not separation, "was it possible to put the Czechs in the wrong before the world . . . but above all in the eyes of the British."[6] In this Henlein was successful. Members of the Runciman Mission, sent to Prague to act as independent mediators between the Czechoslovak Government and the Sudeten German Party early in August, 1938, were quite favourably impressed by him; and even Sir Robert Vansittart, whom Henlein visited in London in 1937 and 1938, did not plumb all the depths of his perfidy. I dare say that I should have been deceived by him too, had I met him. He was a plausible man: that was part of his value to Hitler.

The programme of demands for autonomy within the Czechoslovak State propounded by the Sudeten German Party, and the negotiations carried on between the Czechoslovak Government and the Sudeten leaders with the encouragement of the Runciman Mission, were thus from the German side a cynical farce and a highly successful one. By the time that Henlein threw off the mask in the first half of September, 1938, and openly declared for separation ("*Wir wollen heim ins Reich*"), the Czechs had been seriously and most unjustly discredited in the eyes of many good people in the world. The truth of the matter was, even on the evidence of despatches written towards the end of 1937 by Dr. Eisenlohr, German Minister in Prague, and found among the captured German documents, that the policy of Dr. Benes had been, in the interest of the maintenance of the Czechoslovak State, to work for a permanent good relationship with the German people outside and inside the borders of the State, and as a means to that end, to improve the position of the German minority, which, it should be noted, comprised substantial anti-Nazi elements outside Henlein's Sudeten Party.[7]

In the end, Hitler so contrived matters that at Munich (the ground having been prepared at Berchtesgaden and Godesberg) the British and French Governments, to save themselves from war, did his work for him and delivered the Sudeten areas to Germany with Czechoslovak consent, given under duress. It is not surprising, after this, that in our minds in the Foreign Office the conception of "peaceful change," like the conception of "peaceful co-existence" in our day, should have acquired a dubious connotation.

The problem which faced the British and French Governments in 1938 was in fact an insoluble problem, insoluble, that is to say, by agreement on any rational basis, since on the German side reason had been

[6] Quoted by Namier, *In the Nazi Era*.
[7] Namier, *op. cit.*

thrown overboard. The Czechoslovak problem was indeed solved in one sense in September, 1938 and March, 1939, and in other senses in 1945 and again in 1948. But the solution of 1938 and 1939 was not the kind of solution which British Ministers, at this stage at any rate, had in mind to secure. What they hoped for was a solution based on liberal principles by which the German minority would, as loyal citizens, live happily with full autonomy within the Czechoslovak frontiers. But such a system was not acceptable to Hitler or to the Sudeten population themselves; and as a matter of practical politics even the grant of autonomy would have been inconsistent with the integrity of the Czechoslovak State, since by autonomy the Sudeten Germans meant that they would be free to profess and to apply in their own area the principles of National Socialism on the German model.[8] This was clear enough from the eight points of the Karlsbad Programme announced by Henlein on April 24. And, for good measure, there was an additional demand, the effect of which was that Czechoslovakia should withdraw from her treaties with France and the Soviet Union and thus enter the German orbit.

When the Czechs and Slovaks and the peace-makers in Paris founded and confirmed the Czechoslovak State, they created a problem which, unless the Paris peace settlement was to be integrally maintained, would be well-nigh certain to plague its creators. Like the Empire from which it issued, Czechoslovakia was a composite, multi-racial state. A third of the population were minorities. But the peace settlement was not maintained. The victors lacked the unity and strength of will necessary to enforce it. Once Germany was again strong and predatory, and once the Allies had acquiesced in the seizure of the Rhineland and of Austria, a mortal threat to Czechoslovakia was certain to develop.

It may well be that, if wiser counsels had prevailed, the new State could have been organised on a federal basis, and some part of the areas of the German-speaking population allotted to Germany. But this would not have satisfied the Czech zealots, who wanted a centralised State in which the Czechs would be predominant and which would preserve the traditional frontiers. Masaryk and Benes would indeed have agreed to one appreciable frontier adjustment in favour of Ger-

[8] It is, alas, often the fate of policy makers to be driven to propound as a solution for an intractable international problem the achievement of two or more incompatible objectives. This is merely to translate the problem into other terms. To have thought that we could give autonomy to the Nazi Sudeten Germans without prejudice to the integrity of the democratic Czechoslovak State; or give Germany equality of rights without prejudicing the security of France (Disarmament Conference, 1932-3); or arrest Italian aggression against Ethiopia by League action without running the risk of hostilities; or make a mutual assistance treaty with the Soviet Union in 1939 without doing violence to the interests of Poland and the Baltic States; or satisfy the moral right of the Jews to nationhood without doing grave wrong to the Arabs—these are some examples. Too often in (as we think) solving one problem, we merely succeed in creating a greater one. There are some international problems which are not soluble except by erosion of time or by the stroke of force, and in such cases we have either to hold and wait, or to abide the stroke.

many, but the Peace Conference was opposed in principle to the cession of Austrian territory to Germany. The Conference found powerful reasons, economic, geographical, political and strategic, for holding that Bohemia-Moravia formed a "natural region" and was incapable of division. Those reasons were cogent enough. The whole of the region occupied by the Germans of Bohemia, it was argued, was industrially and economically dependent on Bohemia rather than on Germany. Bohemia formed a natural region, clearly defined by its fringe of mountains. Politically the Germans of Bohemia had always formed part of Bohemia. The chain of mountains which surrounded Bohemia constituted a line of defence for the country, and to deprive Bohemia of this would be to place her at the mercy of Germany.

These arguments were recalled by Mr. Newton, His Majesty's Minister at Prague, in a despatch addressed to Lord Halifax on May 16, 1938. He said that, broadly speaking, he believed the Peace Conference had been right in thinking that Bohemia formed a natural region. But he then turned the argument the other way round. At the Peace Conference, the question was whether the German fringe should or should not be included in Czechoslovakia. If, as might now be contemplated, the German fringe were to be joined to the Reich, the question in the near future might well be whether, on the same principle of the unity of a natural region, the Czech centre of Bohemia should or should not follow the German fringe into the Reich.[9] His conclusion was that any attempt to divide up the country would not provide a permanent settlement. In other words, the future Munich Agreement would be inevitably followed by the occupation of Prague.

In arguing, as they did argue, that if they went to war with Germany, whether to halt German aggression or to preserve the integrity of Czechoslovakia, the Sudeten areas would, even after a victorious war, have to be allotted to Germany, the British and French statesmen misjudged the harsh temper of their times. They were still thinking in terms of Wilsonian liberalism: they would correct a Wilsonian mistake by a reapplication of Wilsonian principles. But events had already shown, and were again to show later, that, given the requisite will and power, there were other ways of dealing with minorities than leaving them in their homes and transferring their homes from one allegiance to another. The Turks had swept the Greek population out of Anatolia, and had solved their remaining minority problems with the Greeks by an exchange of populations. In 1945, the "Succession States," Poland, Czechoslovakia and Hungary, themselves the creation of Wilsonian self-determination, were, in the wake of Allied victory over Germany, to drive their German minorities out of their territories and herd them into Germany, a process which the Potsdam Conference was fain to recognise and into which it tried, without great success, to bring some de-

---

[9] This was one of the arguments in favour of the traditional frontiers put by the Czechs themselves at the Peace Conference in Paris.

gree of order and humanity. When Konrad Henlein said in September, 1938: *"Wir wollen heim ins Reich,"* he was a better prophet than he knew. After Munich, he took his people and their territory together home into the Reich. But in 1945, after the arbitrament of war, the people and the territory were made to part company: the people alone went home. If we had gone to war in 1938 and if we had in the end won a decisive victory (a large assumption), the course of events might conceivably have been the same. The Czechs might simply have turned the Sudetens out, as they did in 1945, and re-established their original frontiers.

Faced with this predicament, the fruit of military weakness, the British Government tried to solve the insoluble political problem by diplomatic manœuvre, by making with mounting urgency representations of varying purport in Berlin, Prague and Paris.

In Berlin (where it was agreed with the French that we should act alone) what we said was that if there was a war in Europe over German action in Czechoslovakia in which France became involved under her treaty with Prague, the Germans should not assume that Great Britain would not also be involved: indeed it was most likely that she would have come in. Again and again during the months of the crisis, this warning, which carried no commitment, was repeatedly given, until at length, at a moment when the position seemed desperate, the British Government went a long step further and, in agreement with the French Government, informed Hitler on September 27 through Sir Horace Wilson that the French had definitely stated their intention of supporting Czechoslovakia by offensive measures if the latter were attacked, and that this would bring the United Kingdom in. This, it was said, would be the inevitable alternative to a peaceful solution. On the previous day, September 26, a press statement had been issued in London which said that "if in spite of all efforts made by the British Prime Minister a German attack is made upon Czechoslovakia the immediate result must be that France will be bound to come to her assistance, and Great Britain and Russia will certainly stand by France."[10]

[10] On page 318 of *Nine Troubled Years* (Collins, London, 1954), Lord Templewood says that there had been some trouble over a communiqué from the Press Department of the Foreign Office on September 26 stating that Russia was ready to join us and the French in resistance to an attack on Czechoslovakia, and that, as the British Government had not authority to speak for Russia, a repudiation of the statement was immediately issued.

As to this, there is the statement on page 550 of *Documents on British Foreign Policy 1919-39,* Third Series, Vol. II (H.M. Stationery Office, London) that the issue of the communiqué was authorised on the afternoon of September 26 by Lord Halifax himself.

For the genesis of this communiqué, see Churchill, *The Second World War,* Vol. I, p. 242 (Cassell, London, 1948). According to Sir Winston, the draft was written out in the Cabinet Room by a senior official of the Foreign Office as the result of an agreement there reached by him with Lord Halifax and (he had thought) Mr. Chamberlain.

In Prague, without committing ourselves to any specific proposals,[11] we continued more and more strongly to urge the Czechs to make generous concessions in order to reach without delay a compromise with the Sudeten representatives. This line was followed by Lord Runciman when he was sent to Prague in the first week of August as an independent mediator. He was a mediator, not an arbitrator; he was to try to promote an agreement, not to propose concrete solutions either on his own behalf or on behalf of the Government. The latter still wished not to have their responsibility engaged, though it was now pretty clear to everyone that by taking this step they had in fact engaged their responsibility. They could not now avoid, sooner or later, taking a direct hand in the negotiations and putting forward proposals of their own. However that might be, Lord Runciman was set an impossible task. As the situation deteriorated, he was preparing, as a final effort, to put forward proposals of his own, when, after Hitler's Nuremberg speech on September 12, tension rose to such a pitch that the Prime Minister decided to go to meet Hitler himself. The suggestion that it was possible to give satisfaction to the Sudeten minority within the Czechoslovak froniers while safeguarding the integrity of the State must have sounded very hollow in Czech ears; but our plea was made with ever-growing urgency as tension rose, with, on the one hand, increasing Sudeten demands and mounting violence, and on the other, anguished Czech attempts to satisfy the Sudetens under pressure from London and Paris.

In diplomacy, the word soon gets passed round; and the ambivalence of our policy of trying to deter the Germans from armed action by pointing to the probability of British intervention, and to discourage the Czechs from fighting by hinting at its improbability, was not long concealed.

In their dealings with Paris, British Ministers seem to have been genuinely apprehensive lest the French should imprudently involve themselves in war and thus face the British Government with a fateful decision. Their questions as to what the French would in fact do became increasingly pointed, their judgment as to the hazards of the military situation increasingly unfavourable, and their forecast as to the prospects of British intervention, and as to the scale of that intervention if it occurred, increasingly discouraging, until, in the throes of the September emergency, fear brought a new note of resolution. They were also most anxious that the French should consult them before coming to a definite decision.

The French were in an even more painful situation than we were. For them, with their clear obligation to Czechoslovakia, there was the point

[11] I find a revealing sidelight on one of the reasons for this cautious attitude in words which I used in Prague on May 28 when explaining the Government's view to Mr. Newton: "We did not," I said, "want to get into the position of endorsing Dr. Benes's plan (however good it might be) and then have to run away from it because the Germans rejected it and became violent again."

of honour. And unlike the British Government, the French Government were deeply divided, with Georges Mandel and his friends all for resistance and Georges Bonnet and his like all for surrender, and with Edouard Daladier, the President of the Council, torn between the two, leaning towards a robust policy but lacking the resolution to hold to it. The result was that, while the declared policy of France was to stand by her obligation, a very different impression was given by what French Ministers said behind the scenes, whether in social gatherings or to foreign representatives.

The British Government need not in fact have had any fears that the French Government would run ahead. The French Government in 1938 was already swayed by political and military conceptions whose exponents, occupying key positions, were to conduct the war with so little heart in 1939 and 1940 and in the end to collaborate with the invader. Vichy was not suddenly born in 1940. The British record up to 1939 was indeed not one to be very proud of: but it is understandable why, in the light of the French Government's record, the Foreign Office should have welcomed so whole-heartedly the reincarnation in 1940, in the person of General de Gaulle, of an older and truer French tradition.

The state of French opinion shortly before the Munich Conference was described by Sir Eric Phipps, British Ambassador in Paris, in a telegram dated September 24, from which I quote the following paragraphs:[12]

> Unless German aggression were so brutal, bloody and prolonged (through gallantry of Czechoslovak resistance) as to infuriate French public opinion to the extent of making it lose its reason, war would now be most unpopular in France.
>
> I think therefore that His Majesty's Government should realise extreme danger of even appearing to encourage small, but noisy and corrupt, war group here.
>
> All that is best in France is against war, *almost* at any price (hence the really deep and pathetic gratitude shown to our Prime Minister) . . .

In the Foreign Office, this telegram struck us with a sense of outrage. What shocked us was that the Ambassador should hold that those who thought like Georges Bonnet were the best of France and that those who thought like Georges Mandel were to be stigmatised as belonging to a corrupt war group. Challenged on this point, the Ambassador explained that by a corrupt war group he meant the Communists, who were paid by Moscow and had been working for war for months. Asked to ascertain and report the individual views of a range of French notabilities with honoured names, so that his judgment could be tested, he did so and, after noting a short-lived swing in opinion towards a

[12] *Documents on British Foreign Policy 1919-1939*, Third Series, Vol. II, H.M. Stationery Office, London, 1949.

robuster line, returned emphatically on September 28 to his original view.

In reporting that war would be unpopular in France and that there were many in positions of authority who were against war almost at any price, the Ambassador was probably not at fault in his judgment. Some of the dominant figures in governing circles in France had been deeply infected by the corroding spirit of the times which was to produce its full effects in June, 1940. Events were happily to prove that there were and are better Frenchmen than these. And if it should be supposed that in the late 'thirties the decay of resolution and paralysis of the will, then more characteristic of France, were not in some degree discernible on this side of the Channel also, a reading of the late Dr. Thomas Jones's *A Diary with Letters 1931-1950*[13] would supply a corrective.

With encouragement from Lord Runciman, negotiations between the Czechoslovak Government and representatives of the Sudeten German Party for some degree of home rule for Sudeten Germans within the Republic continued into early September on the basis of proposals put forward from the Sudeten side and of draft legislation (nationality statute, language bill and administrative reform bill) prepared by the Government. As late as September 4, Henlein was pretending to a member of the Runciman Mission that he had lately told Hitler that he still preferred autonomy to a plebiscite for transfer to the Reich. But after Hitler's speech at Nuremberg on September 12, there was a sharp deterioration. Hitler said in effect that failing the immediate grant of autonomy to the Sudetens he would march. That night there were Sudeten demonstrations at Eger and Karlsbad. The police opened fire and several demonstrators were killed, and the disturbances were suppressed. Lord Runciman now doubted whether any plan, however favourable, would be acceptable to the Sudeten Party. On September 14, Henlein broke off negotiations and said that autonomy would no longer suffice; there must be self-determination. The next day he declared that the Sudetens wished to go home to the Reich.

It was the growing danger of this situation that determined Mr. Chamberlain to try to find a peaceful way out at a meeting with Hitler himself.

Accompanied by Sir Horace Wilson and myself, he flew to Munich on September 15. During the flight—it was his first—he was, as always, aloof, reserved, imperturbable, unshakably self-reliant. From Munich, where he was met by Sir Nevile Henderson from Berlin, he travelled by special train to Berchtesgaden, made a brief stop at his hotel and then went straight up to Hitler's mountain home at Obersalzberg. There was a somewhat macabre tea-party at a round table in the room with the great window looking out towards Austria. The small-talk of statesmen

[13] Oxford University Press, 1954.

whose only point of contact is an international emergency cynically created by the one and stoically grappled with by the other is best left in oblivion. Mr. Chamberlain and Hitler then retired for their conference accompanied by the Führer's interpreter alone. It was at Mr. Chamberlain's own choice that the talks were held *tete-a-tete*. What passed at this talk is well known. From Mr. Chamberlain's record, Hitler seems to have led off with a couple of characteristic untruths, namely that three hundred Sudeten Germans had just been killed, and that he had made an agreement with Poland which finally settled territorial questions as far as Germany and Poland were concerned. Hitler said that he wanted the Sudeten majority areas to pass to Germany, and that he was prepared to risk a world-war rather than allow the present situation to drag on; but he agreed to hold his hand, if possible, while Mr. Chamberlain consulted his colleagues and the French Government on the principle of the separation of the Sudeten areas. After staying the night in Berchtesgaden, travelling by car with von Ribbentrop to Munich next morning and being entertained by him to a luncheon party there, Mr. Chamberlain flew home.

Hitler could hardly have been expected to require less than this. He had good reason to believe that Mr. Chamberlain had already for some time had it in mind that the cession of the Sudeten areas was the best policy; and *The Times* advocated this in a leading article on September 7. For his part, Mr. Chamberlain had no need to be discouraged by the interview. He still regarded Hitler as "a man who could be relied on when he had given his word." As he would see it, there was the basis here for a solution which might save Czechoslovakia from destruction and Europe from Armageddon.

On September 18, the British and French Ministers spent the whole day in London concerting the action to be taken in Prague. They came to a decision which was to seal the fate of Czechoslovakia. They agreed upon a message to President Benes, delivered to him in the early afternoon of September 19, which said that, for the sake of European peace and in Czechoslovakia's own vital interests, the areas mainly inhabited by the Sudeten Germans (perhaps over 50 per cent) should now be transferred to the Reich; that as a matter of principle direct transfer might be thought preferable to a plebiscite; that necessary frontier adjustments could be negotiated through an international body (which would include a Czech representative), which might also deal with possible exchanges of population; and that the British Government would join in an international guarantee of Czechoslovakia's new boundaries against unprovoked aggression, the independence of Czechoslovakia being safeguarded by the establishment of this guarantee in place of existing treaties involving reciprocal obligations of a military character (i.e. the Czechoslovak treaties with France and the Soviet Union). The earliest possible reply was asked for, since Mr. Chamberlain had to meet Hitler again within two days.

On the evening of September 20, the Czechoslovak Government urged all their objections to this Anglo-French plan, proposed arbitration and begged the two governments to reconsider their point of view. In response to this, President Benes was urged to withdraw his reply which, if maintained, would lead to an immediate German invasion, and Mr. Chamberlain would have to cancel his visit to Hitler. The Czechoslovak Government were begged to consider urgently and seriously before producing a situation for which the British Government could take no responsibility. Dr. Benes asked for, and was later given, this communication in writing. Under such pressure, President Benes felt constrained to accept the Anglo-French proposals, which he did on the afternoon of September 21; but he added the earnest hope that the British Government would undertake in writing to come to the assistance of Czechoslovakia if she were attacked by Germany.

Meanwhile, it was only at this stage, on September 21, that Lord Runciman, who had regarded his mediatory functions as having lapsed with the breakdown of negotiations engineered by Henlein, presented to Mr. Chamberlain and Dr. Benes a report on his mission, together with recommendations for a solution. This was by now, in practice, of little more than academic interest. His mission of mediation had been doomed to failure, as indeed he seems to have foreseen from the start. "You are setting me adrift," he said to Lord Halifax, "in a small boat in mid-Atlantic."

At Godesberg, the meetings were held in Hitler's favourite Hotel Dreesen. We were lavishly accommodated in the famous Petersberg Hotel on the hill-top across the Rhine. At his first meeting, on September 22, Mr. Chamberlain had Mr. Kirkpatrick[14] with him to interpret and take the record. At the second meeting during the night of September 23-24, he was also accompanied by Sir Horace Wilson and Sir Nevile Henderson. The meetings took place in an atmosphere of extreme tension and the outcome was in the highest degree unsatisfactory. The Anglo-French proposals, accepted by Dr. Benes, were too dilatory for Hitler. He demanded immediate evacuation by the Czechs and occupation by the Germans of a defined wide stretch of territory, the operation to start on September 26 and to be complete by September 28, and a plebiscite in other areas. For all his efforts, Mr. Chamberlain could not, apart from getting the dates changed to October 1, move Hitler from his main position. This, Hitler insisted, was his last word. His final requirements were expressed in a paper which Mr. Chamberlain characterised as an ultimatum rather than a memorandum. He could only say that he would communicate it to the Czechoslovak Government, without recommendation or advice. This he did, and they declared it to be absolutely unacceptable. The Czechs were now told that we could no longer advise them not to mobilize.

[14] Later Sir Ivone Kirkpatrick, G.C.B., G.C.M.G., Permanent Under-Secretary of State for Foreign Affairs.

I spent many tedious hours in the main hall of the hotel at Godesberg while the talks were going on. The hall was thronged with members of the Führer's *entourage,* prominent members of the National
Socialist Party, senior military officers and officials of the German in-
istry for Foreign Affairs, laughing and talking. Here at Godesberg, as
earlier at Obersalzberg and later at Munich, one thought—making the
necessary historical transposition to a more sordid and vulgar key—of
the domestic establishment of some great barbarian chieftain of Germanic heroic legend, Ermanaric, Theodoric, Gundahari or Alboin—
Goth, Burgundian or Lombard—attended by his companions, retainers
and housecarles; and the impression was heightened in each place by
the glimpse through an open door of a great table laid ready for a meal,
where the leader would sit down to eat and boast with his men. But
first he would assert his authority. When the Führer came out from the
conference room he advanced towards the company, halted and fixed
them with his eye. They rose to their feet and froze to immobility and
silence. The Führer then turned on his heel without a sign and moved
away.

One of the German Foreign Office legal advisers with whom I was
sitting told a characteristically malicious story about Dr. Hodza, the
Czechoslovak Prime Minister. He was, it was said, discussing affairs
one day with a foreign visitor who at one point remarked: "To a
Czechoslovak like yourself, Prime Minister . . ." "Oh! No!" said Hodza
interrupting, "I am not a Czechoslovak. I am a Slovak." "Well," said the
visitor, "what about Dr. Benes? Is he a Czechoslovak?" "No," was the
reply, "Benes is a Czech." "Who then is a Czechoslovak?" "Ah!" said
Hodza, "that is not so easy. But yes, I have it. Konrad Henlein. He is
a Czechoslovak."

The Anglo-French meetings held in London on September 25 and 26
to consider the results of the Godesberg talks were among the most
painful which it has ever been my misfortune to attend.

Mr. Chamberlain's hope that a personal meeting between himself
and Hitler might prove to be the opportunity for bringing about a
marked change for the better in the international situation had been
rudely dashed by the rough treatment which he had received from the
Führer. It was natural that he should have been deeply wounded and
profoundly disappointed; but he allowed his mortification to appear in
his attitude to M. Daladier. At the meetings he had with him Lord
Halifax (Foreign Secretary), Sir John Simon (Chancellor of the Exchequer) and Sir Samuel Hoare (Home Secretary). M. Daladier was
accompanied by M. Georges Bonnet (Minister for Foreign Affairs) and
M. Alexis Léger (Secretary-General of the Ministry).

After Mr. Chamberlain had outlined the course of the Godesberg
discussions, M. Daladier raised the strongest objection to Hitler's plan,
which would, he said, mean the dismemberment of Czechoslovakia and
German domination of Europe. Mr. Chamberlain asked what, then, he

proposed to do next. Daladier replied: "Return to the Anglo-French plan." Mr. Chamberlain asked what should be done if Hitler refused. Daladier said that in that case each of them would have to do his duty. Mr. Chamberlain said that they must get down to stern realities. If the Czechs refused Hitler's demands, Hitler would probably treat a return to the Anglo-French proposals as a rejection of his plan and decide to march. What would the French attitude be then? Daladier could only repeat that each would do what was incumbent on him. Mr. Chamberlain pressed him to say whether France would declare war. Daladier reaffirmed that France would fulfil her obligations: he had already asked a million Frenchmen to go to the frontier. Mr. Chamberlain asked whether the French General Staff had a plan and if so, what was it? Daladier said that it was not possible for France to send help directly to Czechoslovakia by land, but she could materially help by drawing the greater part of the German army against France.

Mr. Chamberlain then asked Sir John Simon to speak. Sir John took up the cold interrogation. He asked whether Germany would be invaded by land. Daladier suggested that General Gamelin should come to London to explain his plans. Not to be deterred, Sir John asked whether French troops would man the Maginot line without a declaration of war, or would the French Government declare war and take active measures with their land forces? Would the French Air Force be used over German territory? Daladier seemed disinclined to answer these questions and Sir John repeated them. Daladier, by now much irritated, said that it would be ridiculous to mobilise land and air forces and leave them idle. An offensive should be attempted by land. Military and industrial centres should be attacked from the air. But he was more interested at the moment in the moral issue than in strategy. The Anglo-French proposals had been bad enough, but where were we to stop? He could not agree to the Godesberg demand as it stood. Sir John Simon here persisted in asking whether, if that plan were rejected, the decision would be to fight Germany, and if so, how? At this point Daladier developed the idea that it might be possible to go some way to meet Hitler by speeding up the work of the international commission under the Anglo-French plan. Mr. Chamberlain then intervened to say that he was sure that Hitler would not accept this. The Germans might be in Prague within a few days. The British Government had to know what attitude the French would take up. He had had disturbing reports about the French Air Force and the capacity of French industry to supply it. Could France defend herself against air attack and make an effective reply? The French press did not give the impression that France was prepared for war. It would be a poor consolation if, in trying to help Czechoslovakia, she herself collapsed.

At this point, Daladier counter-attacked. Were the British Government ready to accept the Godesberg plan and apply the necessary pressure in Prague? The sentiment of France was not to be gathered from the newspapers. The moment had come to call a halt. France was perfectly capable of mobilising an air force and attacking Germany; and Russia could hold her own with Germany. He therefore put three questions: Would the British Government accept the Godesberg plan? Would they press Prague to accept it? Did they think that France should do nothing?

Mr. Chamberlain evaded all three questions. It was not for Great Britain or France but for Czechoslovakia to accept or reject Hitler's demand. The preliminary reply of the Czechs was an unqualified refusal, and we had no means to compel them to reverse it. As to action by France, this was for the French Government alone to decide, but the British Government had to know what the French decision would be.

After this grim bout of fencing, the meeting adjourned. As is so often the way in diplomacy, a decision was reached behind the scenes which seemed to bear little relation to what had been said round the conference table. Next morning, September 26, Mr. Chamberlain conferred alone with Daladier and General Gamelin. No full official British record of this talk appears to exist. When the conference resumed later in the morning, it received a report of full agreement between the two Prime Ministers. This was to the effect that Sir Horace Wilson was to carry to Hitler a letter from Mr. Chamberlain, with authority to deliver an oral warning if the response to the message was unfavourable. The terms of the letter and the warning were agreed between the two Prime Ministers. The letter, after reviewing the course of events, proposed a meeting between German and Czechoslovak (and if necessary British) representatives who would try to settle by agreement the way in which the territory was to be handed over. The warning was the one already described. It made a more definite statement of British intentions in the event of a German attack on Czechoslovakia than the British Government had hitherto been willing to make either to the French or to Hitler. And we now seemed to have taken the French at their word when they said that they would support Czechoslovakia by offensive measures if the latter were attacked.

But although the Anglo-French meeting ended in agreement, the French still had a shot in their locker which they discharged from Paris on their return. If, they asked, France became involved in war with Germany, would Great Britain mobilise at the same time as France, introduce conscription and pool the economic and financial resources of the two countries? Lord Halifax's reply was sent on September 28. In regard to mobilisation, it referred to the calling up of defensive units of the Auxiliary Air Force and the decision to mobilise the Fleet. On conscription it repeated what the French had already been told, namely, that assistance to France would be mainly by sea and in the air and that the most we could send to France by way of military force, if it were decided to send any at all, would be two divisions, perhaps incompletely equipped and short of effectives. As regards the pooling of resources, this proposal raised constitutional issues on which a decision could only be taken with the sanction of Parliament.

Meanwhile, the British Government had requested and obtained the agreement of the French Government that neither Government would take any offensive measures (including a declaration of war) without previous consultation and agreement.

I have recounted these exchanges at some length because, looking back on 1938 from the (in spite of all perils) more hopeful days of 1956, we can measure the extent to which governments and peoples on both sides of the Atlantic have learnt the lesson that the price of safety lies in timely and resolute preparation for collective defence. Behind the shield, inadequate though it may still be, of the North Atlantic Treaty Organisation and the Western European Union, we can now permit ourselves to ponder on the tragic insufficiency with which the two governments faced a mortal danger from a predatory Power which was pulling down their world before their eyes, and at the aloof, if self-righteously disapproving, unconcern with which this spectacle was observed from across the Atlantic.

In spite of the letter and the warning delivered by Sir Horace Wilson on September 26 and 27, respectively, Hitler was not to be moved from his Godesberg memorandum. It was thought right to warn Dr. Benes, though without offering him any advice, that it was clear to us that unless at 2 p.m. on September 28 he had accepted the German terms, German forces would almost immediately cross the frontier and Bohemia would be overrun. In an effort to stave off the apparently inevitable conflict, the Prime Minister put to the Germans a somewhat retarded time-table and, agreeing that the Godesberg plan was unacceptable, pressed the Czechs to accept it as an alternative. This had no chance of acceptance by the Germans; but before final reactions had been received, the Prime Minister had proposed on September 28, and Hitler had agreed to, an international conference to discuss arrangements for the transfer. Hitler had also, on an appeal from Mussolini, postponed mobilisation for twenty-four hours.

When the members of the House of Commons sprang to their feet and enthusiastically cheered the Prime Minister's announcement of his third visit to Hitler, as with a few notable exceptions they did, they were in effect (whatever they may have thought about it later) endorsing the sacrifice of Czechoslovakia, for at Munich there was to be no question of saving Czechoslovakia. The surrender had already been made between Berchtesgaden and Godesberg. It was now merely a question of getting Hitler to agree to establish a time-table for carrying out the German occupation of the Sudeten areas with rather less haste than he had at first required. The blame, if blame there is, for the steps that led to the surrender cannot justly be laid upon the shoulders of Mr. Chamberlain alone.

The Munich Conference was a hugger-mugger affair. Mr. Chamberlain was met at the airport by von Ribbentrop at noon on September 29, and was rushed straight to the Führer House. There he met Daladier. The conference opened immediately, Mr. Chamberlain being accompanied by Sir Horace Wilson, and Daladier by Léger. Unlike the British and French Prime Ministers, Hitler and Mussolini had their Foreign Ministers with them. Sir Nevile Henderson and Sir William Malkin, Legal Adviser of the Foreign Office, joined in the proceedings later in the day. Sir Horace Wilson, who made a short note of the proceedings, records that the negotiations were conducted without order or method and that the material arrangements were chaotic. There was an adjournment for a late lunch at 3.15 p.m. and another for a late dinner, and it was not till 2 a.m. on September 30 that the agreement could be signed. The British and French delegations lunched and dined at their respective hotels. The Duce, as a privileged guest, was entertained by the Führer. It was a German-Italian occasion.

While the conference was sitting, I spent the time with the Prime Minister's Private Secretary in the room allotted to our delegation. Through the open door we could watch the comings and goings. Field Marshal Goering in his white uniform walking to and fro in the upper gallery. Flocks of spruce young S.S. subalterns in their black uniforms, haughty and punctilious, as though life were a drill, acting as A.D.C.'s and orderly officers, one or other of whom would from time to time come to us, click his heels, and ask if we required anything. Down in the basement there was a kind of beer-hall where life was less intimidating.

During the discussion, Mr. Chamberlain raised the question of the representation of the Czechoslovak Government at the conference, but he had no success. It was decided that the four heads of governments should accept responsibility for their decisions. Sir Horace Wilson did make a point, during the dinner interval at the hotel, of reporting on the proceedings to M. Mastny, Czechoslovak Minister in Berlin, and M. Masarik, Private Secretary to the Czechoslovak Foreign Minister, Dr. Krofta; and it was to them that the text of the agreement was handed jointly by Mr. Chamberlain and M. Daladier at about 2.15 a.m. on September 30, with the suggestion that it was a considerable improvement on the Godesberg memorandum and had better be accepted. Daladier had declined Mr. Chamberlain's suggestion that he should take the agreement to Prague, and this duty was performed by a member of the Runciman Mission. In a broadcast on the evening of the same day, General Syrovy, the Czechoslovak Prime Minister, said that the Government had decided to accept the terms of the agreement as they had been given to understand that in the event of refusal they could expect no assistance.

The Munich Agreement, based on a draft presented to the conference by Mussolini, provided for the evacuation and occupation of the Sudeten areas to proceed by successive defined stages between October 1 and October 10. An international commission composed of representatives of the four Powers and of Czechoslovakia would lay down the conditions for the evacuation; determine the boundaries of the territory to be occupied; settle the areas to be subject to plebiscite and fix the conditions and date of the plebiscite; and finally determine the definitive frontier. The United Kingdom and France stood by their offer to guarantee the new boundaries of Czechoslovakia against unprovoked aggression; Germany and Italy would give a guarantee when the question of the Polish and Hungarian minorities had been settled. If this question was not settled within three months, another four-Power conference would be held to deal with it.

To the professional diplomatist accustomed to the decencies of international life, the Munich Conference was a distressing event. In international negotiations, surrenders may well be imposed, if the disposition of forces or the disparity of wills so determines. What was disturbing was that, at an international conference, four Powers should have discussed and taken decisions upon the cession to one of them of vital territory belonging to a fifth State, without giving a hearing to the government of that State. The decision, after it had been reached, was merely communicated at the dead of night to representatives of the government concerned by two of the participants in the conference, for immediate acceptance under brutal duress from the beneficiary. In the circumstances as they were, the Czechs might well have preferred not to participate, but that would not have affected the principle. Mr. Chamberlain, though his original proposal had been for a conference of the four Powers *and* Czechoslovakia, did not seem afterwards to have been much disturbed by this. His two prime objectives had been achieved: he had saved the peace and he had, as he thought, opened the way for that improvement in Anglo-German relations by which he set such store.

After a few hours' sleep that morning, I was awakened by a message from the Prime Minister saying that he had arranged to see Hitler before leaving for home and asking me to draft a short statement on the future of Anglo-German relations to which he might secure Hitler's agreement. While dressing and taking breakfast, I composed three paragraphs, and then took the draft in to the Prime Minister. Mr. Chamberlain rewrote the second paragraph and made some other minor changes. The statement, as it emerged from his hand, was as follows:

> We, the German Führer and Chancellor and the British Prime Minister, have had a further meeting today and are agreed in recognizing that the question of Anglo-German relations is of the first importance for the two countries and for Europe.
>
> We regard the agreement signed last night and the Anglo-German Naval Agreement as symbolic of the desire of our two peoples never to go to war with one another again.
>
> We are resolved that the method of consultation shall be the method adopted to deal with any other questions that may concern our two coun-

tries, and we are determined to continue our efforts to remove possible sources of difference and thus to contribute to assure the peace of Europe.

I said that the Anglo-German Naval Agreement, to which he had introduced a reference, was not a thing to be proud of. He replied that on the contrary it was the type of agreement which we should now try to reach with Germany.

I urged that he should inform M. Daladier, who was still in Munich and staying nearby, of his intention to seek this direct agreement with Hitler. He said that he saw no reason whatever for saying anything to the French.

As he was about to leave for his interview, he asked: "What is that noise?" I said: "The street is full of people. They want to see you." I suggested that he should step on to the balcony. He did so, and received an ovation astonishing in its warmth. As he went down the stairs and through the hall of the hotel, he had to press his way through a gay and radiant crowd, bronzed and still in their summer clothing.

Never was a diplomatic document so summarily agreed upon: "As these observations were translated to Herr Hitler." Mr. Chamberlain records,[15] "he ejaculated at intervals '*Ja! Ja!*' and when it was finished he said he would certainly agree to sign this document. When did the Prime Minister wish to do so? The Prime Minister: Immediately. Herr Hitler: Then let us sign.

"At this point, they both rose, went to a writing-table and, without any further words, appended their signatures to the documents. . . . "

On his return to the hotel, as he sat down to lunch, the Prime Minister complacently patted his breast-pocket and said: "I've got it!"

On the flight home, Sir Horace Wilson asked me to set out in summary form all the points on which the Munich Agreement was an improvement, from the Czech point of view, on the Godesberg memorandum. On paper, they made quite a sizeable list, more extensive than might have been expected, and I remember remarking on this. In substance and in fact, apart from delaying the transfer of part of the territory for a few days, they proved to be worthless. And our promised guarantee proved, alas, to be a sham.

It was clear from Daladier's demeanour at the London talks in September and at Munich that he felt deep shame at the course of action which he found himself constrained to follow; and he was much surprised, on his return to Paris from Munich, to be greeted by popular acclaim instead of by hostile demonstrations. It is doubtful whether Mr. Chamberlain shared these qualms. He was in any event less sensitive than Daladier would be to the international significance of the course which he had deliberately set himself to follow and which he pursued with undeviating resolution and unshaken self-confidence. It is true that in a moment of unguarded

[15] *Documents on British Foreign Policy 1919-1939*, Third Series, Vol. II, H.M. Stationery Office, London, 1949.

exuberance on his return to Downing Street he used words about "peace with honour" and "peace for our time" which he afterwards regretted. It is true also that, as did others of us, he brought one lesson back from Munich (and to me it was by far the greatest lesson) namely that there was a pressing need to make good the deficiencies in our preparations for defence; but he would not see any cause for misgivings in the Munich settlement itself. His course was in harmony and not in conflict with the spirit of the times. On his return he had received a national ovation. Congratulatory messages poured in from Commonwealth and foreign statesmen. He could look forward to further work for peace and concord. This was only a beginning. "I believe," he told the House of Commons on October 3, "that there is sincerity and goodwill on both sides."

It was left to Mr. Churchill to sound another and more sombre note. Speaking in the House of Commons on October 5, he said: "We have sustained a total and unmitigated defeat"; and again: "We are in the presence of a disaster of the first magnitude which has befallen Great Britain and France." That is an opinion which it is difficult to controvert.

It has been argued that if the Soviet Union, the ally of Czechoslovakia, had not been excluded from the Munich negotiations, and if France and Great Britain had agreed to discuss military co-operation with the Soviet Union when this had been offered, Czechoslovakia might have been saved without war. I have always regarded these arguments with some scepticism. Hitler himself and the German General Staff seem to have thought it quite likely that the Soviet Government would intervene in arms if Germany attacked Czechoslovakia; but they seem also to have thought that Soviet intervention, what with the recent great military purge and geographical difficulties, would not reach serious proportions and could be discounted. It was France they had their eye on. The prospect of Soviet action would not thus have been an effective deterrent. Hitler would not in any event have admitted a Soviet representative to the Munich conference; and the circumstances in which the decision to hold it were arrived at excluded any chance that either Mr. Chamberlain or M. Daladier would think it possible to press for this, even if they had wished to.

The Foreign Office communiqué of September 26, when it stated that France would be bound to come to Czechoslovakia's assistance and that Russia would certainly stand by France, was, if perhaps rather too sweeping, doing little more than repeat what the Russians themselves, in public statements, had been saying for months. When questioned by the French and British Governments about Soviet intentions, Litvinov was, naturally enough, rather more circumspect and kept more closely to the terms of the treaty. Sir Eric Phipps reported on September 6 that, according to Bonnet, Litvinov had replied that Russia would, according to the terms of the Russo-Czechoslovak Pact, wait until France had begun to fulfill the obligations incumbent on her according to her own Pact with the Czechs. Russia would then bring the matter before Geneva. (This is substantially what the Soviet-Czech Pact provided.) On September 23, Sir Eric Phipps reported further that, according to Bonnet, Litvinov had said that the Soviet Union would only come in after France had already come in, and that she would request the Council of the League to recommend Rumania to allow the passage of Soviet aircraft over Rumanian territory. Bonnet has given a more detailed account of these exchanges with Litvinov in Annexe IV of his book, *Fin d'une Europe.*[16] The upshot of his story is that at Geneva on September 11, he had suggested to Litvinov that the Soviet Union should take advantage of Rumania's willingness to shut her eyes to the passage of Soviet aircraft over her territory, in order to afford assistance to Czechoslovakia; but that Litvinov had declined and had insisted on a recommendation of the League of Nations and on formal consent from Bucharest to the passage of land and air forces.

On September 23, Lord Halifax instructed his Parliamentary Under-Secretary, Mr. R. A. Butler, who was then at Geneva, to seek from Litvinov a precise indication of what action the Soviet Government would take in the event of Czechoslovakia being involved in war with Germany, and at what point they would be prepared to take it. Litvinov replied that he could say no more than that if the French came to the assistance of the Czechs, the Russians would take action. Mr. Butler asked, did he intend to raise the matter at the League? And would he wait to take action while the League was still discussing the question? To this, Litvinov merely replied that the Soviet Government might desire to raise the matter in the League, but this would not alter the fact that the Pact would come into force. He added that the Soviet Government had informed the Polish Government that if Poland attacked Czechoslovakia in the Teschen area, the Soviet-Polish Non-Aggression Pact would lapse and Russia would take action. In addition, Litvinov proposed that representatives of Great Britain, France and the Soviet Union and e.g. Rumania, should meet in some place away from Geneva, say in Paris, to show the Germans that they meant business. At such a conference he would be ready to discuss military and air questions, on which he was not at present posted.

Litvinov was here reverting to a suggestion which he had made much earlier in different form. On March 17, after the occupation of Austria, he had publicly stated that the Soviet Government were ready to discuss with other governments inside or outside the League of Nations "practical measures called for by present circum-

[16] Bourquin, Geneva, 1948.

stances," that is to say, collective action to stop the further development of aggression, with special reference to Czechoslovakia. And about the same time he had also, more specifically, proposed conversations with the French and Czechoslovak Governments in order to seek a concrete formula for military assistance to be rendered by the Soviet Union to Czechoslovakia.[17]

It is tempting to think that such conferences might have been of some avail; but later experience suggests that such hopes might well have proved delusive. In the spring and summer of 1939, when Poland in turn was threatened, Great Britain and France negotiated for months in an attempt to reach an agreement with the Soviet Union for the building up of a peace-front in Eastern Europe. These negotiations broke down owing to a failure to agree upon the practical arrangements for joint military action, and in particular because of the refusal of Poland to agree to the passage of Soviet troops over Polish territory. And in the event, the Soviet Union joined with the aggressor to partition the victim. In any negotiations in 1938 for the organisation of military assistance for Czechoslovakia, the Soviet Union would probably have made the most of the facts that the operation of the Soviet-Czech Treaty was contingent upon that of the Franco-Czech Treaty; that the Soviet-Czech Treaty, like the Franco-Soviet Treaty upon which it was founded, provided in first instance for action through application of Articles 15 and 16 of the League Covenant; and that the provision of military assistance by the Soviet Union to Czechoslovakia would require the consent of Rumania or Poland to the transit of Soviet forces across their territory, consent which was unlikely to be forthcoming. It is also not irrelevant to note that there were elements in the Government in Prague who were far from anxious to see Soviet intervention in their country.

No one who has negotiated with the Soviet Government would be bold enough to think that it would have been an easy matter to settle the political and military conditions for co-operation in war against Germany in defence of Czechoslovakia, in the light of the difficulties experienced in 1939. It is true that the Soviet Union was the ally of Czechoslovakia, while her relations with Poland were unfriendly, and that therefore the Soviet Government might be expected to be less difficult in a negotiation for common action against Germany in 1938 than they were in 1939. But in this period of rapidly growing German power, Stalin, if not yet perhaps an "appeaser" in the least creditable sense of the term, as he was to show himself to be in 1939, was at any rate determined to avoid if he possibly could being landed in a position in which, in a European war, he would have to sustain without effective support the first formidable shock of a military attack by Germany. This could mean, at the least, a policy of extreme circumspection in regard to Ger-

[17] Namier, *In the Nazi Era.*

many and, at the most, a composition with Germany. And from this point of view, his dropping in May, 1939, of Litvinov, whose anti-German sentiments were notorious and who was genuinely in favour of collective security, was in its way not unlike the parting company of Mr. Chamberlain and Mr. Eden in 1938, ostensibly over Italy, but in reality owing to a deep divergence of outlook and approach. The Soviet decision to compound with Germany in 1939 was not a sudden improvisation. As a policy, it had been for months a possible alternative to an agreement with the Western Powers.

Although this policy had received an impulse from the Munich Agreement, its roots went further back. There was enough in the earlier post-war history of Soviet-German relations to provide a foundation for it; but if, on the other hand, the Soviet Union were to make an agreement with the Western Powers against Germany, she would need to be satisfied, beyond a peradventure, that the military contribution by her partners would be precisely defined and, if it came to war, adequate, prompt and effective. It is fair to ask ourselves how far these conditions would, from the Soviet point of view, have been likely to be satisfied in 1938; but, be this as it may, if the Western Powers did in 1939 think it desirable to try to come to an agreement for common action with the Soviet Union, it may fairly be urged that the grounds for doing so were, objectively considered, no less compelling in 1938; and that though the prospects of reaching such an agreement might not have looked very bright, yet it would have been much better to try, while there was still time. The obstacle was that the Western Powers thought in 1938 that it was a better and more hopeful policy to try to satisfy Germany than to call in the Soviet Union against her.

As early as May 17, 1938, Dr. Benes, with a flash of intuition, had remarked to Mr. Newton that an attempt to exclude Russia completely from Europe would, he believed, be disastrous and would only force her to make an agreement with Germany against the rest of Europe. And Sir Lewis Namier has drawn attention[18] to a conversation on October 4, 1938, about the Munich Agreement between Potemkin, the Soviet Deputy Commissar for Foreign Affairs, and Robert Coulondre, the French Ambassador, in which the former, for once breaking his reserve, exclaimed: "My poor friend, what have you done? For us I see now no other way out except a Fourth Partition of Poland."

The best that can be said for the Munich Agreement is that it was a tragic necessity; but the responsibility for this great reverse in our affairs is not to be laid at the door of one man or of one group of men. It is easy enough to say, and it is indeed true to say, that we ought never to have allowed ourselves to get into a position in which

[18] *In the Nazi Era.*

we laid ourselves open to so grievous a surrender; but the responsibility spreads very wide and reaches a good way back. Since the First World War, the British electorate had at times given themselves governments which, in the event, had not proved capable of coping very successfully with the international problems of the new post-war world. For this, our people themselves must be held responsible, though it was not apparent that at any given moment any more promising alternative government was, as a matter of practical politics, likely to be available. For the handling of international affairs, the qualities most to be desired are knowledge enough to understand the past, perception enough to judge the present, imagination enough to scan the future and, when action is needed, resolution enough to take courageous decisions and act on them. It is our good fortune as a people that in later times, men with more than a touch of these qualities have been found holding commanding positions in Governments of both parties.

In the later nineteenth century, the United Kingdom had a foreign policy suited to her position in the world and to the character of the world in which she lived. That policy was well described in Sir Eyre Crowe's famous memorandum of 1907: naval preponderance, exercised with moderation; respect for the independence of weaker nations; a balance of power in Europe; the maintenance of the freedom of commerce. After the turn of the century, that policy was increasingly supplemented by growing, if still ill-defined, foreign commitments. The United Kingdom has since 1945 evolved another foreign policy, very different from the old, but suited to our relative decline in terms of power; its main characteristic is the merging of our defences with those of like-minded governments in an intimate community of free peoples bound by mutual engagement. In the interwar years, on the other hand, no clear policy was framed. The new problems of a changed and changing world tended to be interpreted in terms of old conceptions. Our position in the world had altered for the worse and we did not seem to recognise this in our actions. We continued too long to believe that the horrors of the war of 1914-18 would have convinced all civilised Powers that they must not have another war. We behaved as though we could play an effective part in international affairs as a kind of mediator or umpire without providing ourselves with the necessary arms and without entering into firm commitments, whereas the truth was that, for lack of international solidarity in face of the common menace, we were in mortal peril. We were not alone in this. The position of the United States had also changed, and she, for her part, failed to rise (as she has happily since done) to the height of her new responsibilities. With the United States still in neutral isolation and the Soviet Union still held at arm's length, Great Britain and France, having inadequately maintained their defences and failed to concert their policies, could not hope to restrain the three predatory Powers in Europe and Asia who were bent on upsetting the existing order and had gathered strength to do so. It may well be that there was no good way out of this predicament.

And yet the depth of the malaise of the 'thirties should not be exaggerated. It took only a few months, with the experience of the bitter deceptions of the immediate post-Munich period and of the act of force in Prague, to bring our people to a new outlook so that, having committed themselves to a guarantee to Poland, they faced the probability of war with calm resolution, though still reluctant to bestir themselves to make adequate preparation for it. The people of 1938 and the people of 1940 were the same people; and if the defenders of the Munich Agreement can claim that those who made the agreement gained time for the British people to find themselves, whether or not this thought was in their minds when they made it, this is not an entirely vain or empty plea. In the war that followed, the aggressor was indeed destroyed, but only with the powerful and uncovenanted help of the United States, and after Germany by her own deliberate act had broken her strength on Russia. The award of Munich was reversed and, save for the Ruthene territory ceded in 1945 to the Russians, her self-styled liberators, Czechoslovakia was reinstated substantially within her original frontiers. When all the inscrutable possibilities have been guessed at—and they are legion—it is still difficult to assert with any confidence, nor equally can it be disproved, that these results would have been achieved if we had gone to war in 1938. What is certain is that the German problem would still have remained with us, then as now. Judged by the cold light of reason, and questions of honour apart, the arguments against going to war in 1938 would have been no less valid if they had been used in 1939. Poland was also a "far-away country"; the prospect of American assistance was as remote as ever; and the Soviet Union was now openly ranged on the side of Germany. Was Poland, any more than Czechoslovakia, worth a European war? Why die for Danzig? The difference was that such arguments would not in 1939 have carried weight. Our people had made up their minds and would not have heeded them.

The Crisis in

Historical Perspective

Hugh R. Trevor-Roper

A. J. P. Taylor

Iain Macleod

Sir Charles Webster

Hugh R. Trevor-Roper · (Born 1914) Regius

Professor of Modern History, Oxford University, and a leading British historian of modern Europe. He has written a number of important volumes, including *Archbishop Laud* (1940, 2nd ed., 1962), and *The Last Days of Hitler* (1947, 3rd ed., 1956), based on his work as British intelligence officer at the close of the Second World War. He has also edited *Hitler's Secret Conversations 1941-1944* (1953), and has written an important critical commentary on A. J. P. Taylor, *The Origins of the Second World War*, in *Encounter*, July 1961. The following essay on Munich, published on the occasion of the tenth anniversary of the crisis, appeared originally in *The New York Times Magazine*, on the tenth anniversary of the crisis. Published before the appearance of the official British documents on Munich, Professor Trevor-Roper's essay is based, in large part, on the important German documents made public at the Nuremberg War Crimes Trials, and on the revealing excerpts from Neville Chamberlain's private diary, published by Professor Keith Feiling in his authorized biography of the Prime Minister (1946).

Munich—Its Lessons Ten Years Later

It is now ten years since the Munich crisis—a crisis recognized both then and now as a turning point in modern history. At the time it aroused violent passions: Government, parties, societies, even families were divided against themselves. I know houses in England where fathers sent for champagne to toast Mr. Chamberlain and sons refused to drink. The defenders of Munich regarded it as the triumph of peace, its opponents as the beginning of disaster. Now it is less controversial; it has only few and timid defenders; but it remains important. Time and new facts have merely altered, not lessened, its significance.

But first, whence do these new facts come? The richest source is supplied by the German archives, captured wholesale. No Allied Government has published, or will publish, such complete evidence as conquered Germany has been forced to divulge.[1] The Allied Governments have issued only selective blue books and white books; but

[1] Since publication of this article, the British government in 1949 published two important volumes containing over 1200 documents on the history of the crisis, as part of its series *Documents on British Foreign Policy 1919-1939;* and in 1955 the Department of State published a large number of valuable American documents on the Munich crisis, as part of its continuing series *Foreign Relations of the United States.*—F.L.L.

From *The New York Times Magazine*, August 8, 1948. © 1948 by The New York Times Company. Reprinted by permission of the author and the publishers.

a great deal can be gleaned from a systematic study even of these selections. Then there are the memoirs of statesmen, including the private papers of Neville Chamberlain, which have been used by his biographer. Finally, there is a systematic study of Munich by J. W. Wheeler-Bennett, who has used not only these sources but also the Czechoslovak state archives, put at his disposal by the late liberal Government of the country which was both the cause and the victim of Munich.

For though Munich was a European tragedy, it was also a Czech tragedy. The essential history is simple. The German minority in Czechoslovakia, controlled by Hitler, made impossible demands on the Czech Government, even threatening action which, if treaties were observed, would have led to European war. After months of tension and vacillation, the British Prime Minister made a spectacular gesture. He flew to Germany to save peace by a personal interview with Hitler.

The unconventional action aroused both enthusiasm and dismay; the consequence caused hysterical hero-worship and bitter recrimination. After three visits to Hitler, Chamberlain sacrificed Czechoslovakia and believed that he had saved peace; he failed to see, what his critics saw and what six months were enough to prove, that peace means security and that security and Czechoslovakia were indivisible. Hitler realized this fact, and he was the victor of Munich: he destroyed at one blow both Czechoslovakia and the security of Europe.

How clearly he saw it we now know from the German archives. In November, 1937, when the reorganization of his army was nearly complete, he summoned his generals to the chancellery, and in a speech of terrible logic and lucidity delivered to them his "political testament." "The question for Germany," he said, "is where the greatest possible conquest can be made at lowest cost." The answer, already familiar from "Mein Kampf," was in the East. But, he went on, such a policy "must reckon with our two hateful enemies, England and France, to whom a strong German colossus in central Europe would be intolerable."

Only force could solve this problem; it was a question not of avoiding war but of reducing the risk of failure. Hitler explained that it was "his irrevocable decision" to solve the problem of *Lebensraum* not later than 1943-45. But in order to guarantee victory he intended first to conquer Austria and Czechoslovakia.

Czechoslovakia was the bastion erected against the revival of Germany by the victors of 1918. If possible it must be isolated from its allies; if possible, it must be conquered from within; but it must be conquered, and in certain circumstances it could be conquered "perhaps even as early as 1938." Within three months of delivering this speech Hitler had completed the reorganization of his army and conquered Austria from within; then he turned the heat on Czechoslovakia.

Hitler's policy was thus clear and systematic: it was a policy of aggression. How clearly was this appreciated in the West! His speech, of course, had been secret; but there was plenty of other evidence. The evidence of "Mein Kampf," the German armaments program, bulk-purchases and calling-up policy all pointed conclusively to a war of Eastern Conquest "not later than 1943-45" and "perhaps even as early as 1938."

How then did the intended victims prepare for defense? Czechoslovakia had a treaty of military alliance with France, and France had a similar treaty with Russia. The effect of these treaties was that if Czechoslovakia were attacked by Germany, France would come to its aid, and in that case Russia would come to the aid of France. Britain was uncommitted but, could hardly remain unconcerned.

Thus on paper Czechoslovakia seemed sure of support. But how strong were those treaties? Their operation depended entirely on France, and France seemed uncertain and divided. Responsible statesmen wished to implement the treaties, but they could only do so if they were sure of British support; others like Bonnet and Flandin, recognizing the weakness of France, wished to admit German supremacy without a fight, to jettison Central Europe, and to retire behind the mystic safety of the Maginot Line.

If British help seemed doubtful, these men would be strengthened and Czechoslovakia might find itself isolated after all. Thus the effectiveness of the system of defense against Nazi aggression depended ultimately on the firmness of British policy: and British policy was at this time, as seldom in history, a personal policy—the policy of Neville Chamberlain.

The passions that once raged about the personality of Neville Chamberlain are now still. They have been stilled by the facts. His letters and papers reveal him as he was: a man of limited intelligence, unlimited complacency and narrow obstinacy, with a genius for banality in solemn moments and a genuine, emotional, almost mystical love of peace. The problem is not now why he carried out his fatal policy but how such a second-rate man acquired the control of policy.

Brought up as a business man, successful in municipal politics, his outlook was entirely parochial. Educated conservative aristocrats like Churchill, Eden and Cranborne, whose families had long been used to political responsibility, had seen revolutions and revolutionary leaders before, in their own history, and understood them correctly; but the Chamberlains, who had run from radical imperialism to timid conservatism in a generation of life in Birmingham, had no such understanding of history or the world: to them the scope of human politics was limited by their own parochial horizons, and Neville Chamberlain simply could not believe that Hitler was fundamentally different from himself.

If Chamberlain wanted peace, so must Hitler; and if there were difficulties about the terms of agreement, they could be settled by a personal interview between the heads of the negotiating firms. Obstinate in this illusion, Chamberlain was determined from the moment he assumed power to follow a policy of direct negotiation with the dictators. If the evidence contradicted him, he ignored it; if Ministers resigned or opposed him, he was unmoved, for he had his own substitutes.

And so he gathered gradually around him those fatal associates in his policy: Sir Horace Wilson, the industrial bureaucrat who replaced his diplomatic adviser; Sir Nevile Henderson, the trivial snob whom he fetched from Montevideo and sent to Berlin; his own sister-in-law, who acted as unofficial ambassador to Mussolini; Lord Runciman, the northern shipowner whom he sent to Prague, and Lord Maugham, who as Lord Chancellor of England publicly declared that the opponents of appeasement ought to be hanged or shot.

For Neville Chamberlain was not like the Continental appeasers who accepted the policy as an unpleasant but necessary expedient; to him it was a positive faith, valued for its own sake. This faith both fortified him in his obstinate complacency and enabled him to draw disciples after him, not only the business men whose interests he represented but all those ordinary unthinking persons who, like him, hated war, and who, seeing that he believed in himself, were prepared to believe in him.

Such was the man on whom, after Hitler, the whole European situation depended in 1938. What did he do? Separated from its emotional content and virtuous intentions, his policy is the most discreditable episode in modern English history. For Chamberlain sought not to strengthen the coalition against Hitler but to dissolve it in order to clear the ground for purely personal diplomacy; and the fact that he did so out of arrogance and stupidity, not malevolence, is no excuse for a politician, in whom intelligence is more useful than virtue.

Chamberlain realized that action by Hitler would automatically precipitate a war if the Czechs appealed to the treaties; he saw that in fact Britain held a key position in determining the effectiveness of those treaties; and he sought to use this key position so to isolate Czechoslovakia that the treaties should never be invoked. To do this he had to deceive others and blind himself; he had to evade every issue that a politician ought to face; he had to pretend that Czechoslovakia was not the keystone of the defense of Europe but "a small far-off country" which was not worth a war. He had to persuade himself that Hitler sought not conquest but self-determination and that the Sudeten Germans were not a manipulated Fifth Column but a discontented minority; and he had to claim that any agreement was a victory, even though it was an agreement to capitulate.

A glance at the period between February and September reveals the working of this disreputable policy. At first the position of the Western Powers was strong. After the seizure of Austria, both France and Russia declared that they would fulfill their treaty obligations "instantly and effectively." And on May 22, when Hitler tried to force a crisis, the mobilization of the Czechs and the prompt assurances of France and Russia, cautiously supported by Britain, forced him to retreat.

But from that moment Chamberlain's policy began to bear fruit. Angered by his rebuff, Hitler stated his "unalterable decision to smash Czechoslovakia"; at the same time, Chamberlain, shocked by so narrow an escape from war, set out to weaken French morale by obscuring British policy, and to prevent the invocation of the treaties by a local surrender in Czechoslovakia. To do this he sent Lord Runciman as an "investigator and mediator" to Prague, and tried to take the control of Czech policy out of the far more skillful hands of Benes. The Czech Government protested bitterly at the Runciman mission, but Chamberlain insisted on sending it and afterward told the House of Commons that it had been sent "in response to a request from the Government of Czechoslovakia."

Lord Runciman spent his time staying with pro-German landlords who guarded their castles with Storm Troopers, and on his return advocated the policy of surrender. There is even evidence that his report, though antedated, was written after that policy had already been decided upon by Chamberlain, as a spurious justification of it. Meanwhile, Chamberlain had twice suggested solutions of "the Czech problem" which were more favorable to Hitler than any which Hitler himself had yet dared to demand.

In spite of this he had the effrontery to pose as the advocate of the Czechs, even telling Benes "not to hinder his decision" at Munich by making Czech conditions.

By the time Chamberlain flew to see Hitler, his policy had already achieved its result: the French Government, despairing of British support, had retreated from its former firmness, and France and England together had so isolated Czechoslovakia that no negotiation could avert its fate, or do more than find a formula for surrender.

Chamberlain's three visits to Germany were really never more than a theatrical gesture. Nevertheless, he was confident that by sacrificing Czechoslovakia he had secured a great personal triumph. After Munich, when informing the Czechs of their fate, he yawned unrestrainedly throughout the interview. He was very tired, but, as he said later "pleasantly tired."

When Daladier returned to Paris and saw the crowds at the airport, he thought they had come not to cheer but to lynch him; but such a thought was inconceivable to Chamberlain as he waved a worthless scrap of paper and boasted that he had secured "Peace in our time." Hitler had flattered his vanity by telling him that he was the only man to whom he had ever made a concession and Chamberlain believed him. When his colleagues reminded him of Hitler's broken promises, he replied, "This time it is different; this time he has made the promises to *me*." The German archives reveal what Hitler really thought of Chamberlain. "Our enemies are little worms," he said, on the outbreak of war. "I saw them at Munich."

Since the policy of Munich has been proved a fiasco, its defenders have fallen back on two separate lines of defense. First, it has been stated that Munich was an unfortunate but necessary expedient to gain time for rearmament. This argument was never used by Chamberlain; to him, as his papers clearly show, Munich was a positive triumph, a final settlement of Europe. And anyway it is factually wrong.

Munich, as Mr. Churchill has clearly demonstrated, lost more than it gained. It lost the equivalent of thirty-five army divisions and the greatest arsenal in Central Europe; it lost the alliance of Russia and the moral support of the world; it gave Hitler three and a half million new subjects; and the time which it gave was given also to him—for in the year after Munich German arms output was nearly three times that of Britain and France together.

Only in one respect did Britain gain relatively to Germany: in the year after Munich the Royal Air Force was equipped with the Hurricanes and Spitfires which won the Battle of Britain; but without Munich the Germans might never have conquered France and the Low Countries: then there would have been no Battle of Britain.

The second line of defense for Munich is that Chamberlain's hand was forced by the unwillingness of France to defend Czechoslovakia. This argument has been shown to be untrue. If the French Government collapsed at the end and left the responsibility of decision to Chamberlain, it collapsed because Chamberlain had succeeded in undermining it.

Nevertheless, although the Messianic complacency of Chamberlain gave a limelit outline to the Munich crisis simplifying the dilemma and dramatizing the defeat, in fact it is improper to isolate it, either in time or place. Like all great international crises, Munich was a consequence of preceding events and a convergence of different issues, and probably no Western statesman, inheriting such a problem, could really have triumphed over it.

For what were the alteratives? Hitler had posed them as peace

or war—a discreditable and disastrous peace, or a difficult and un-
wanted war. Chamberlain refused even to contemplate the choice;
firm in his illusions, he preferred to capitalize rather than correct
his country's unreadiness and to hypnotize it into surrender.

But did the Opposition face the facts with any greater responsibility? Appeasement was supported in fact even by those who opposed the theory, and the record of the Labor party in 1938 cannot
be excused by the inexpensive virtue of having opposed Chamberlain. In 1937, when Hitler was announcing the policy of conquest,
and Chamberlain the policy of appeasement, Sir Stafford Cripps
publicly exhorted armament workers to make use of "the most glor-
ious opportunity" they had ever had: "Refuse to make munitions!
Refuse to make armaments!"

The Labor party Executive voted against conscription even after
the occupation of Prague had finally shattered the complacency of
Chamberlain. If Chamberlain refused to face the prospect of war,
the Opposition refused to believe in its reality: they blamed Chamberlain not for yielding to force but for yielding to bluff which, as
we now know, was untrue.

For, in fact, nothing that any Western politician could suddenly
do could deprive Hitler of his initiative in 1938; that could only be
achieved by a change in Germany. Was there any hope of such a
change? We now know that at least there was a conspiracy. It is
established beyond doubt that a group of generals directed by General Beck, the Chief of the German General Staff, who had resigned
in protest against the policy of aggression, was preparing a military
coup to overthrow Hitler when the news of Chamberlain's surrender at Munich dashed the weapons from their hands. They had even
conveyed a message to the British Government, promising firmness,
in exchange for firmness, but their message had been ignored, and
after Munich Hitler's prestige in Germany made any repetition impossible.

This is a dramatic fact, and much has sometimes been made of it,
but I do not think that it is really significant. No responsible Government, facing the alternatives of peace and war, can afford to be influenced by a private message from a group of unknown conspirators.
The message might easily be a trick, and even if genuine, who could
guarantee that the conspiracy would have succeeded? The history of
German opposition to Hitler is now well known; it does not suggest
that the British Government should have gambled on its success.

Thus, as in all great tragedies, we find that study enlarges the
problem and reduces the responsibility of individual persons. A
tragedy consists in the predicament of a man challenged by a problem too large for his resources: a problem which he is expected to
solve but which he has not created. In this sense Munich was a
great tragedy.

Nothing can excuse Chamberlain's ungenerous shifts and obstinate self-deception; but, although his vanity led him to enlarge his own share in the drama, seeking a personal triumph and finding a personal disaster, in fact the crisis was the accumulated inheritance of time and neglect: he neither caused it nor solved it, and his crime before history consists not in his failure to solve an insoluble problem but in his refusal to face it or understand it.

Therein lies the lesson of Munich for us. We must be warned by Chamberlain's example. In world politics there are no short cuts, no personal triumphs, problems must be understood, not simplified, and mystical faith is no substitute for calculating reason. Above all, it is certain that an aggressor can never be appeased. Appeasement has never succeeded in history. If Chamberlain knew no history, at least he supplies us with further proof of that certainty. From the debris of his disaster we may extract some comfort only if we can be sure that Munich was the final end of appeasement.

A. J. P. Taylor · (Born 1906) Educated at Oriel

College, Oxford, he taught first at the University of Manchester, and has been for many years Fellow of Magdalen College, Oxford. A most prolific, and controversial, historian, he has written numerous books including *The Italian Problem in European Diplomacy 1847-49* (1934), *Germany's First Bid for Colonies 1884-5* (1938), *The Habsburg Monarchy* (1941, 2nd ed. 1948), *The Course of German History* (1945), *The Struggle for Mastery in Europe 1848-1918* (1954), *Bismarck* (1955), *The Troublemakers* (1957), and *The Origins of the Second World War* (1961). The following essay, which first appeared in the *Manchester Guardian Weekly*, anticipates some of the main themes of his work on the origins of the war, in which he, for instance, strongly defends the Munich settlement, and suggests that the coming of war in 1939 was, essentially, accidental.

MUNICH TWENTY YEARS AFTER

On a morning twenty years ago the Munich conference was breaking up. In the early hours a yawning and impatient Chamberlain had told the Czechs their inexorable fate. Now it only remained to sign the agreement formally. At the last moment Chamberlain proposed to Hitler that they should renounce war between their two countries for ever. Hitler replied with an ecstatic "Ja ! Ja !" adding that he hated the thought of women and children being killed by gas-bombs. Then Chamberlain flew off, to proclaim Peace with Honour; Daladier more gloomily to receive an enthusiastic welcome which surprised and humiliated him.

Nothing now remains of this gathering where the Great Powers of Europe occupied the centre of the stage for the last time. Chamberlain lived long enough to see the ruin of his policy. Hitler and Mussolini perished miserably, their names a byword of infamy for ever. Only Daladier ploughs on with an ox's stubbornness, still upholding democracy, still unsuccessful. The Sudeten Germans have indeed gone "home to the Reich," in a way most unwelcome to them. Czechoslovakia has again her pre-war frontiers. She has not recovered her independence. The rulers of Soviet Russia occupy the place left vacant by Hitler. The settlement of Munich was meant to bring peace to Europe. Instead it was the prelude to a fierce conflict which ended her centuries of world dominance.

How does it seem to us twenty years afterwards—this glittering affair, so trumpeted at the time, so soon discarded? Was it simply a

From the *Manchester Guardian Weekly*, September 30, 1958. Reprinted by permission of the author.

fraud—for Hitler merely a stage in his plan of world conquest, for the British a device to buy time while they completed their rearmament? None of these things. The leading actors at Munich were sincere—at any rate for the time being. They really thought that they had secured the peace of Europe, though, of course, their versions of this peace varied. Chamberlain supposed that Germany's last grievance was removed; Hitler that his mastery of East-Central Europe was recognised. Daladier and Mussolini only cared that their countries had escaped living up to their pretensions as Great Powers.

The Czech crisis was made in London not in Berlin. Hitler had indeed visions of world conquest, but no defined plan. The seizure of Austria earlier in the year had been improvised at the last moment. Thereafter he was content to wait while the Spanish civil war continued to distract the Western Powers. He began to push at the Czech door only when the British Government insisted that it was already opening. The British had been caught napping over Austria. They were determined not to be caught again. They would anticipate Hitler's next grievance instead of acquiescing in it. It was the British, not Hitler, who wrung concessions from Benes in a melancholy series; the British, in fact, who envisaged the conference at Munich from the beginning. Hence Chamberlain's jubilation at the end. In the most literal sense, he had beaten the gun.

Why did Chamberlain prefer concession to resistance? This is the central question of the Munich affair. Obviously, his temperament pulled him towards negotiation and away from war. More than this, war seemed ineffective for the purpose. Everyone exaggerated the strength of his defensive position—and of his opponent's. The French did not believe that they could break through the fortifications of the reoccupied Rhineland; yet themselves felt secure behind the Maginot Line. The British had virtually no expeditionary force, but limitless confidence in the Navy. Alone the Western Powers could not "stop" Hitler, or so they supposed. What of alliance with Soviet Russia? Here the decisive obstacle was undoubtedly political—profound suspicion on both sides. Even in June, 1939, George VI recorded of his conversation with President Roosevelt: "He was definitely anti-Russian. I told him so were we." Yet alliance was unrewarding even on a military basis. How could the Russians help Czechoslovakia effectively while Poland remained neutral or even, as she was, anti-Czech? The idea of sending Soviet forces through Rumania was futile, evidence only that the Russians had never contemplated the problem seriously.

But supposing that the Czechs had firmly rejected British promptings and stood to their defences? The Russians, we know, constantly urged them on this course. The Czech Army was certainly strong enough to hold its own against the Germans. But there are factors on the other side. The Czech frontier with Austria was unfortified; and the Czechs would have been hard pressed if they had been attacked also, as seemed likely, by Hungary and Poland. These speculations are in any case unrewarding. Benes never contemplated isolated resistance from first to last. He relied on treaties, not on armed strength, and could not change his nature at a moment's notice. Besides, in view of the Spanish war it was difficult to believe until June, 1940, that the British would resist Hitler seriously; and Benes shrank from fighting with only Soviet Russia as a doubtful ally. He played for time. Assuming rightly that Hitler would go on to new conquests, he hoped that Czechoslovakia would sit out the next round and thus survive unbroken, as in a sense she did.

There was another military factor of an opposite kind. While everyone exaggerated the strength of land defences, they also exaggerated the power of air bombardment. Munich was played out under the shadow of Guernica. Everyone supposed that London and Paris would be razed to the ground within the first few hours of war. The Russians even believed that their planes, operating from Czech airfields, would do the same for Berlin. In the event indiscriminate bombing turned out ineffective. I would even guess that it cost more in manpower and economic effort to the attacker than it did damage to the attacked. This has had a curious effect to the present day. Since bombing in the last war was a hundred times less effective than was expected, men now fail to realise that nuclear bombing in the next will be hundred times more devastating than anyone can foresee.

Essentially, however, the Munich crisis was determined by moral considerations, not by calculations of war. On the one side was collective security, loyalty to allies, and the sanctity of treaties; on the other the sacred claim to self-determination. The Czechs defended an "historic" frontier; the Bohemian Germans asserted their national character. How could a Chamberlain refuse to these Germans what had been granted to Ulster? Partition along the national line is now the accepted rule, in the Indian subcontinent and in Cyprus; and even the Czechs agreed that nationalities could not live side by side when they expelled the Sudeten Germans after the war. Liberals and Labour could talk of defending democratic Czechoslovakia; it was difficult to forget the many years when they had denounced her as an imperialist creation of Versailles.

Has the story a moral? An obvious one: no deal with Hitler was ever possible. But he was a human phenomenon who occurs once in a thousand years. Appeasement was a sensible course, even though it was tried with the wrong man; and it remains the noblest word in the diplomatist's vocabulary.

Iain Macleod · (Born 1913) Educated at Cambridge, he entered politics at the end of the Second World War, and since 1950 has been a Conservative Member of Parliament. He has served, successively, as head of the Home Research Department of the Conservative Party, Minister of Health, Minister of Labour and National Service, and Secretary of State for Colonies. From 1961 to 1963 he served as Co-Leader of the House of Commons and Chairman of the Conservative Party Organization, but resigned these positions upon the appointment of Sir Alec Douglas-Home as Prime Minister in 1963. His biography of Neville Chamberlain, published in 1961, attracted widespread attention on account of its authorship. Although not the work of a professional historian, Mr. Macleod's book merits serious consideration because it reflects, for instance, the work of numerous official historians on the contemporary state of British defenses, and because it re-emphasizes also the great public support, at home and abroad, that Mr. Chamberlain enjoyed at the time of Munich.

In Defense of Chamberlain

The arguments about Munich will continue, but it is possible now that the archives have been opened and so many private accounts published to judge them in perspective. Few people seriously claim now that a League of Nations with more than half the great powers outside it would have or could have stopped the Second World War. No-one seriously claims who has studied their speeches, particularly in the General Election of 1935, that the Labour Party would have pushed rearmament ahead faster, or indeed anything like so fast, as Chamberlain did in 1936 and 1937. In their television appearance together in the autumn of 1959, on the occasion of Mr. Eisenhower's visit to London, both Mr. Macmillan and Mr. Eisenhower agreed that the Second World War was inevitable because Hitler was determined on it, and the evidence that this was in fact so is now overwhelming.[1] Should then Britain have fought in October 1938 rather than September 1939? Was the year's respite a gain on balance to Great Britain or the Axis Powers? And here one of the most interesting witnesses is Mr. John F. Kennedy, the President of the United States. His father was at the time the American Ambassador at the Court of St. James, and felt deep despondency in 1940 about

---

[1] Though accepted by every other historian of authority, this view has been challenged—unconvincingly, I think—in *The Origins of the Second World War*, by A. J. P. Taylor (Hamish Hamilton, 1961) which was published whilst this biography was in proof.

Britain's chances of survival. His son did not share this view and (aged 23) put forward his own. This is his judgement:

[People] felt and many still do feel that Hitler in 1938 was merely bluffing . . . Many in England shared this belief even in August 1939. There, people felt Chamberlain was badly taken in, but I think a study of the position of the two countries will show that Chamberlain could not have fought even if he had wanted to. I do not claim that Munich was simply the result of British inability to fight as set forth by Baron von Neurath.[2] I believe that Chamberlain was sincere in thinking that a great step had been taken towards healing one of Europe's fever sores. I believe that English public opinion was not sufficiently aroused to back him in a war. Most people in England felt 'It's not worth a war to prevent the Sudeten Germans from going back to Germany.' They failed at that time to see the larger issue, involving the domination of Europe. But though all these factors played a part in the settlement of Munich, I feel that Munich was inevitable on the grounds of lack of armaments alone.[3]

It is not at Munich but at the locust years, 1934 and 1935, that the finger of criticism should be pointed. Too little was done, even though Chamberlain was the most valiant for rearmament in the Government—so much so that the contrast of his tough attitude with Baldwin's more pliant one brought stern condemnation from *The Economist* in October 1935:

It is certainly a regrettable departure from British tradition that the Chancellor of the Exchequer should himself be the foremost advocate of increased expenditure on armaments. And it certainly will not help to promote national agreement on foreign policy if collective security is to be used as an excuse for unilateral rearmament by Great Britain.

It is fair to add, as Mr. Kennedy does, that *The Economist* later changed its mind, but also, again following Mr. Kennedy, that rearmament policies cannot change as swiftly as editorial views.

We can now check Mr. Kennedy's assessment against the known facts and figures of military production at the time.

Eleven months separated the Munich Agreement from the outbreak of war. Diplomatically, the period falls into two equal and distinct parts, divided by the death blow which Hitler delivered to Czechoslovakia and to the policy of appeasement in March 1939. "A new epoch in the course of our foreign policy," to use Chamberlain's own description, opened after the occupation of Prague. The military turning point, however, antedated the diplomatic. "A new

[2] Mr. Kennedy quotes the former German Minister of Foreign Affairs to this effect: "Immediately after his return to London Mr. Chamberlain announced a huge programme of rearmament. At the same time the defects of Britain's military preparedness became plainly visible. It was then no longer possible to conceal the true reason for her 'peaceful' attitude at Munich. She had simply been unable to embark on a European war at that time."

[3] John F. Kennedy, *Why England Slept* (Hutchinson, 1940), pp. 195-196.

epoch in the history of rearmament," to quote the echoing phrase of the historian of British war production, "began in the autumn of 1938 and ended in the summer of 1940."[4] After Munich, that is to say, rearmament was "definitely geared to eventual military action," and the last strong hopes of peace were not allowed to hold back our accelerating preparations against war.

"One good thing, at any rate, has come out of this emergency through which we have passed," said Chamberlain at the end of the Munich debate in the House of Commons. "It has thrown a vivid light upon our preparations for defence, on their strength and on their weakness. I should not think we were doing our duty if we had not already ordered that a prompt and thorough inquiry should be made to cover the whole of our preparations, military and civil, in order to see, in the light of what has happened during these hectic days, what further steps may be necessary to make good our deficiencies in the shortest possible time."

The deficiency upon which public and Parliamentary attention chiefly and rightly focused was in our defence against air attack, including civil defence. The Munich crisis had found us still with barely 10 per cent. of the estimated "ideal" requirement of A.A. guns, and most of those we had were not the newer 3.7-and 4.5-inch guns but 3-inch conversions. Only 1,430 searchlights were available out of an approved programme of 4,128, only 140 barrage balloons out of 450, and, as Chamberlain told Baldwin in the last weeks of his life, only 60 fire pumps in the whole of London. Expert scepticism and official parsimony had had a particularly damping effect on the progress of civilian A.R.P. What is more, Hoare wrote to Chamberlain in October, "the burden of A.R.P. is too heavy for me with all my other work." At Hoare's suggestion, therefore, John Anderson was that month appointed Lord Privy Seal and took over the administration of the Air Raid Precautions Department at the Home Office together with the co-ordination of policy on all aspects of civil defence. Estimates of expenditure on A.R.P. now shot up from £9¼ million in the current year to £42 million in the financial year 1939-40, plus another £9 million aid for emergency fire-fighting purposes. A campaign for voluntary national service (which included the Regular Forces as well as the several branches of civil defence) was launched in a broadcast by the Prime Minister in January 1939, and a handbook on the subject was distributed to every household in the land. "Anderson" shelters were constructed to protect ten million people in their own homes and gardens. Walter Elliot's plans for evacuating school children and finding emergency beds in hospitals were perfected. All this took place in the

[4] M. M. Postan, *British War Production* (History of the Second World War: United Kingdom Civil Series, H.M.S.O. and Longmans, 1952), p. 53.

year after Munich. At the same time, the last Defence White Paper of the peace, published in February 1939, announced a substantial strengthening of our ground defences against air attack. By the time war broke out, the provision of A.A. guns had increased fourfold to 1,653, of which more than half were the larger guns, and balloon defence had been completed in London and extended outside. More important still, the chain of radar stations which during the Munich crisis had been in operation only in the Thames estuary now guarded Britain from the Orkneys to the Isle of Wight.

The year's breathing-space was also vital for the modernization and expansion of our air power. Here the Government was not so much taking fresh decisions as reaping the harvest of Swinton's brilliant tenure of the Air Ministry. This had come to an end in May 1938 for the straightforward political reason, confirmed in Chamberlain's papers, "that when a Department is under such continuous bombardment as the Air Ministry has been it is impossible to maintain its position with the head in 'another place'." "It's a cruel job" he wrote afterwards to Hilda, "to tell one's friend that he would do well to give up . . . I said to him that he would never have a fair chance while he remained at the Ministry but the moment he left people would begin to recognise the worth of what he had done." This was certainly how it turned out. Some two weeks before Swinton's resignation the Cabinet had given authority to a new programme, known as Scheme L, which for the first time and in accordance with the Prime Minister's personal view defined Air Force expansion not in terms of finance, but simply in terms of industrial capacity. Great additions to this capacity had been sponsored by Swinton and the 12,000 modern aircraft in two years which were now contemplated would be of types he and his Ministry colleagues had ordered off the drawing-board.[5] At the time of Munich, of course, Scheme L had just got under way. In September 1938, the R.A.F. had only one operational fighter squadron equipped with Spitfires and five in process of being equipped with Hurricanes; by the summer of 1939, however, it had 26 squadrons of modern eight-gun fighters, and a year later during the Battle of Britain it was to have on average 47. The new types of bombers, particularly the "heavies", took longer to reach the squadrons, though when they came they would be decisively better than the corresponding German machines. Meanwhile the resources of the aircraft industry, with output climbing from a monthly average of 240 in 1938 to 660 in 1939, were stretched to the peacetime limit, and at the turn of the

[5] Cf., "It would have been easy to produce large quantities of aircraft of the types then in production. Firms would have been only too happy to do so. We could have produced a fine balance sheet of numbers; and we should have lost the Battle of Britain. Few people realise (or did then) how heartbreaking are the delays in getting out a new type." Viscount Swinton, *I Remember* (Hutchinson, 1948), p. 110.

year the office of Director of Planning of War Production was set up to crystallize plans for expansion under wartime conditions.

Though the numerical increase in the total strength of the Luftwaffe during this period was at least as great as that of the R.A.F. the extent to which we caught up with the Germans in modernising the quality of our fighter force has been authoritatively described as "the most important achievement of rearmament between Munich and the outbreak of war."[6] This great gain was freely admitted by Churchill in *The Gathering Storm*. But Churchill went on to make a powerful argument that 1938 nevertheless presented us with a more favourable military situation than 1939, since the Germans would have found it less easy then to win bases in France and the Low Countries from which to raid Britain with decisive effect.[7] I doubt, however, if he gives sufficient weight to contemporary estimates of the vulnerability of London and other nerve centres in 1938. More important, the argument rests upon assumptions of Allied, or rather French, military superiority at that date which are, to say the least, controversial. The contrary considerations are economically deployed in an entry in Hore-Belisha's diary a few days before the Munich settlement: "The P.M. yesterday spoke to us of the horrors of war, of German bombers over London and of his horror in allowing our people to suffer all the miseries of war in our present state. No-one is more conscious than I am of our present deficiencies. Chiefs of Staff view—to take offensive against Germany now would be like 'a man attacking a tiger before he has loaded his gun'."[8]

It is true, and was frankly recognised after Munich, that with every month that passed the Reichswehr would become stronger and the challenge to the French Army correspondingly greater. For this reason, a radical change was made in the policy governing the role and size of the British Army. We have seen how, in February 1937, the War Office capitulated to Chamberlain's argument that, if only on grounds of manpower shortage, this country must "renounce all idea of a Continental Army on the scale of 1914-18 and continue to concentrate resources or building up the Air Force and Navy." In the November after Munich, Anglo-French conversations took place at the Quai d'Orsay during which Daladier impressed upon Chamberlain the need for a larger British contribution to land fighting. Hore-Belisha, supported by Halifax, now weighed in with a proposal that the fundamental doctrine of the Army's "limited liability" should be dropped, and in February 1939 the Prime Minister recommended this course to the Cabinet. In March, it was agreed in staff talks with the French to raise our Army to 32 divisions, and

---

[6] M. M. Postan, *op. cit.*, p. 108.
[7] *The Second World War* (Cassell, 1948), Vol. I, pp. 264-265.
[8] R. J. Minney, *The Private Papers of Hore-Belisha* (Collins, 1960), p. 146.

before the end of the month Chamberlain announced in the House of Commons that the Territorial Field Force would be brought up to war establishment and then doubled.

This break with past policy inevitably, and almost at once, led to two further developments against which the Prime Minister had hitherto set his face. First, in order to convince the French that we meant business and the Territorial volunteer that he was not being asked to make sacrifices that others were allowed to shirk, a measure of compulsory military service was introduced for the first time in Britain in a period of peace. Secondly, in order to cope with the vast administrative and industrial problems caused by the sudden expansion of the Army programme, steps were taken to set up a Ministry of Supply. Both these decisions were announced by Chamberlain in April, though the Ministry of Supply did not begin work until August, on the very eve of war.

Conscription was voted against by the Opposition in Parliament. ("Looking back," wrote Attlee long after the war, "I think that our attitude was a mistake."[9]) It was also denounced by the Trade Union leaders, Citrine and Bevin, at a stormy interview in Downing Street. This reaction had been clearly foreseen by the Prime Minister. Indeed, his reluctance to antagonise those upon whom the rearmament programme so largely depended for success was particularly noted by Hore-Belisha in the course of persuading him to change his mind. A similar thought had prompted Chamberlain's steady objection to appointing a Minister of Supply. "If you are really to produce any substantial result—and even then it could not come at once—you would have to arm such a Minister with compulsory powers," was the point he had made again and again in the House. "I am not satisfied that we cannot get what we want by voluntary co-operation of employers and trade unionists. When we find that we still cannot fill our requirements, then it will be time enough to talk about a Minister of Supply." Though the Opposition did not accept his argument against the Ministry, they and the T.U.C. certainly concurred in ruling out compulsion. In this period, and even beyond, it was simply not "on" politically to enforce transfers of skilled labour or to increase the supply by dilution or upgrading. These were among the handicaps to full economic mobilisation that must be kept in mind when assessing the progress that was made in the output of war-stores.

Where a peace-time industry could be drawn upon without much need for expansion or adaptation, the tasks of re-equipment were achieved with remarkable despatch. Lord Woolton, for example, was appointed Adviser on Army Clothing at the end of April 1939 and

---

[9] *As It Happened* (Heinemann, 1954), p. 103. "I agree with him," wrote Dalton in his memoirs, *The Fateful Years* (Frederick Muller, 1957), p. 250.

by the beginning of September he was able to write to Chamberlain: "I am glad you let me help in getting the Army clothed: it is ready." Even so, he described this, twenty years after, as the most difficult and worrying job of his life.[10] How much more difficult must it have been to accelerate the pace of weapon production by industries unused to the work and requiring additional capacity, tooling up, and (above all) experienced manpower. This does not mean that the extra year after Munich was not useful in terms of current production. "If in October 1938," says the official History of British war production, "this country was not able to put into the field more than two fully-armed divisions, it disposed in September 1939 of sufficient equipment for about five divisions more or less adequately equipped."[11] The rub, however, lies in the "words more or less adequately"; for assuredly, it was less rather than more. In the early war summer of 1940, Chamberlain was to write to his sisters: "We have plenty of man-power, but it is neither trained nor equipped. We are short of many weapons of offence and defence"; and, from Gort's dispatches to Montgomery's memoirs, this has been the general judgement. What Chamberlain's critics were not satisfied to allow, and he himself did not live to see confirmed, was that "not only was an ever-growing flow of munitions finding its way into the hands of the fighting men, but the country was also acquiring the industrial capacity, organisation and experience which a year or two later was to give forth a supply of war-stores more abundant than that at any point in the First World War."[12] The eleven months saved at Munich were eleven months in which this industrial momentum could pick up, and they brought the Army that much closer to the fuller flow of tanks, artillery, machine guns, rifles and ammunition which would reduce Hitler's superiority in the field.

So far as the Navy was concerned, there was never any question of inferiority to the Germans. Our effective strength, a quarter of which had been either newly built or brought up to date between 1935 and 1938, was overwhelming. "It would be unjust to the Chamberlain Administration and their Service advisers to suggest that the Navy had not been adequately prepared for a war with Germany, or with Germany and Italy," wrote Churchill in describing the situation when he took over the Admiralty in 1939. "The effective defence of Australasia and India in the face of a simultaneous attack by Japan raised more serious difficulties," he added, "but in this case—which was at the moment unlikely—such an assault might well have involved the United States. I therefore felt, when I entered upon my duties, that I had at my disposal   at was

---

[10] *The Memoirs of the Rt. Hon. The Earl of Woolton* (Cassell, 1959), p. 159.
[11] M. M. Poston, *op. cit.*, p. 109.
[12] *Ibid.*, p. 102.

undoubtedly the finest-tempered instrument of naval war in the
world, and I was sure that time would be granted to make good the
oversights of peace and to cope with the equally certain unpleasant
surprises of war."[13] In fact, a decision to plan for a "two-power
standard"—that is to say, the naval force needed to protect our
interests simultaneously against Japan in the Far East and Germany
in Europe—was taken before war broke out as a result of discussions following the Munich crisis. This decision was certainly not of
immediate importance; what was really urgent after Munich was to
make good the deficiency in destroyers and smaller vessels for
convoy-escort and anti-submarine duties. Accordingly, the naval
building programme for 1939 included two destroyer flotillas and
twenty fast escort vessels of a new type, as well as some other
smaller craft, and preparations were completed to take up many of
the largest trawlers and equip them with Asdics.

To sum up: by September 1939, Britain was still very far from
having completed her preparations for war, but in the preceding
year these preparations had greatly increased in scale and in urgency. We had improved our absolute strength in every respect, and
in air power we had improved our relative strength. The capital of
the Empire and the centres of armament production had had their
nakedness covered. Our civil defences had been put in order. Far
more fighter squadrons had been remounted on the modern aircraft
that were to win the Battle of Britain. At the Admiralty, pro-
grammes had been pressed ahead to encounter the menace of the
U-boat. A fundamental revision of Army policy had enabled a siz-
able British Expeditionary Force to be planned. Output of war-
stores had risen and at quickening rates and so had our industrial
potential for war.

All these gains are matters of historical fact. On the other hand,
many of the "losses" by which critics have supposed the gains to be
outweighed are highly conjectural. Thus it is said that between
1938 and 1939 we "lost" France's opportunity to strike at German
unpreparedness in the West, Czechoslovakia's 36 divisions and famous arsenal, and Russia's adhesion to the common cause. But to say
this is to assume that, had we gone to war in 1938, the French
would not have betrayed the Maginot mentality, the Czechs would
not have collapsed like the Poles, the Skoda works lying close to
their frontier would not have changed hands anyway, and the Russians would not have behaved as they did the following year with
characteristically cynical opportunism. These assumptions crumple
under analysis. The true argument to be met is Churchill's observation that munitions production on a nation-wide plan is a four
years' task—"The first year yields nothing; the second very little;

[13] *The Second World War*, Vol. 1, p. 322.

the third a lot, and the fourth a flood."[14] It follows that Germany, already in the third or fourth year of intense preparation, added more to her total armaments between 1938 and 1939 than we did ourselves. This is an important point, but it is by no means conclusive; for, unless Allied strength at the time of Munich was unquestionably sufficient to enable us at once to strike a fatal blow at Germany's industrial heart (and it was not), the logical conclusion of Churchill's argument cannot be that we should have fought Hitler in 1938. The logical conclusion must be, either that we should have fought him much earlier before his rearmament programme had got under way, or else that we should have avoided fighting him until much later when the full flood of our own rearmament programme had reduced the ratios of his superiority. Strategically 1938 was about two years too late and 1939 was about two years too soon.[15]

Military considerations, however, can only be part of the argument. Whatever view one may take of the military consequences of the "Munich year," of its effect on the will to fight of the country and the Empire there can be no doubt. In 1936, the year of the Rhineland crisis, when we might have stopped Hitler in his tracks, the representative British view was that the Germans were "only going into their own back garden." In 1938, a denial of self-determination to three million Germans living under alien rule was not considered either here or in the Empire to be something "that Britons should be asked to die for." In 1939, on the other hand, it had become plain beyond doubt that the ambitions of Nazism stretched far beyond the ethnic frontiers of Germany, that it had indeed "made up its mind to dominate the world by fear of its force."[16] Here, far more than in the precise stages to which German rearmament or our rearmament had advanced, we may discern what determined the date of our declaration of war. At the heart of Chamberlain's policy lay the fundamental proposition he expressed at the end of the Munich debate in a moving passage on the dread features of modern warfare. "You cannot ask people to accept a prospect of that kind, you cannot force them into a position that they have got to accept it," he declared, "unless you feel yourself, and can make them feel, that the cause for which they are going to fight is a vital cause—a cause that transcends all the human values, a cause to which you can point, if some day you win the victory, and

---

[14] *Ibid.*, p. 263.

[15] Cf., the similar conclusion of the military historian Cyril Falls, *Listener,* November 11th, 1948.

[16] From Chamberlain's broadcast on the eve of Munich, September 27th, 1938, to which he frequently harked back. The famous phrase about the Rhineland was Lord Lothian's, that about the Sudetenland is from a letter to Chamberlain by Lord Kennet, formerly Hilton Young.

say, 'That cause is safe'." This was certainly what the nation did
feel in the autumn of 1939 and did not feel at the time of Munich.
As Lord Halifax put it: " . . . when all has been said, one fact remains dominant and unchallengeable. When war did come a year
later it found a country and Commonwealth wholly united within
itself, convinced to the foundations of soul and conscience that
every conceivable effort had been made to find the way of sparing
Europe the ordeal of war, and that no alternative remained. And
that was the big thing that Chamberlain did."[17]

No one can dispute that the avoidance of war in 1938 was in
accord with the overwhelming sentiment of British opinion. Chamberlain returned from Germany to a hero's welcome. "Come
straight to Buckingham Palace," bade the King, "so that I can
express to you personally my most heartfelt congratulations on the
success of your visit to Munich." All the way from Heston airport to
the palace, the streets, as the Prime Minister described to his sisters, "were lined from one end to the other with people of every
class, shouting themselves hoarse, leaping on the running board,
banging on the windows, and thrusting their hands into the car to
be shaken." A tremendous ovation awaited him when he and Mrs.
Chamberlain appeared on the Palace balcony with the King and
Queen, and later under his windows in Downing Street densely
packed crowds sang "For he's a jolly good fellow." The week-end
Press, London and provincial, dailies and Sundays, broke into a
chorus of almost unanimous thankfulness.[18] "No conqueror returning
from a victory on the battlefield," thundered *The Times*, "has
come home adorned with nobler laurels." "The gratitude of millions
of mothers, wives, sweethearts, pours out to feed a flood which will
sweep Mr. Neville Chamberlain to a high pinnacle in history," forecast the *Sunday Dispatch*. From the *Birmingham Daily Gazette*
came a special tribute: "Birmingham is proud that the peace of
Europe, when all but lost, has been saved by a cool-brained and
determined Birmingham man." Newspapers such as the *Manchester Guardian*, which stressed the high price paid for peace, nevertheless admitted that this could not be measured "against the horrors that might have extinguished not only Czechoslovakia, but
the whole of Western civilization." Even the *Daily Herald* hesitated
to condemn outright: "Summing up, we must say that this plan is
open to grave criticism on a number of important points. Nevertheless Herr Hitler has had to abandon the most brutal of his Godesberg terms. For the first time he has had to realise that there are
forces in the world more powerful than the absolute will of a dictator."

[17] *Fulness of Days* (Collins 1957), p. 198.
[18] For a detailed survey, see W. W. Hadley, *Munich: Before and After* (Cassell,
1944), pp. 93-110.

The British Press was certainly reflecting the mood of the nation. Argument grew hotter as time went on but it has been very properly pointed out that in the Commons debate after Munich the Opposition virtually evaded the issue of peace and war: "Just as on September 28th, no one of them had interrupted Mr. Chamberlain's speech to protest against the acceptance of the Berchtesgaden terms, so now, with one exception—Mr. Duff Cooper—no Member of the House was sufficiently certain of himself to stand up in his place and say that the terms of the Munich Agreement should have been rejected at the price of war, because no Member of the House was sufficiently assured that the people of Britain would have endorsed such a rejection."[19] Nor would the people of the Dominions have endorsed such a rejection. "No-one who sat in this place, as I did during the autumn of '38, with almost daily visitations from eminent Canadians and Australians, could fail to realise that war with Germany at that time would have been misunderstood and resented from end to end of the Empire"—this was written by Geoffrey Dawson, editor of *The Times*, in a letter to Chamberlain which arrived the day after he died. Mackenzie King of Canada told Churchill during the war "that he very much doubted whether his country would have rallied to us at once."[20] Though the Australian Government considered that constitutionally it was not possible for Australia to be neutral in a British war, the Opposition were flatly against involvement in 1938. So far as South Africa was concerned, Hertzog and Smuts were agreed on a policy of non-belligerency.[21] The telegrams which Chamberlain received from the Dominion Prime Ministers after Munich really speak for themselves:

W. L. Mackenzie King to N. C. 30.9. 1938.

The heart of Canada is rejoicing tonight at the success which has crowned your unremitting efforts for peace. May I convey to you the warm congratulations of the Canadian people, and with them, an expression of their gratitude, which is felt from one end of the Dominion to the other. My colleagues in the Government join with me in unbounded admiration of the service you have rendered mankind.

J. A. Lyons to N. C. 30.9. 1938.

My colleagues and I desire to express our warmest congratulations at the outcome of the negotiations at Munich. Australians in common with all other peoples of the British Empire owe a deep debt of gratitude to you for your unceasing efforts to preserve peace.

General Hertzog to N. C. 30.9. 1938.

The news of the outcome of the Conference at Munich was received in the Union with immense relief. May I convey to you my most hearty congratulations on the success of your efforts and those of the other statesmen

[19] J. W. Wheeler-Bennett, *Munich: Prologue to Tragedy* (Macmillan, 1948), p. 184.
[20] *The Memoirs of Lord Ismay* (Heinemann, 1960), p. 92.
[21] J. W. Wheeler-Bennett, *King George VI* (Macmillan, 1958), pp. 408-409n.

who took part in it in saving Europe from a conflagration the consequences of which one shudders to contemplate.

Not only from all over Britain and the Dominions but from all over the world the tributes poured into Downing Street. Within three weeks of Munich he had received more than 40,000 letters and his wife another 12,000 and not until after Christmas did this tide show much abatement. Accompanying the messages came flowers, and some poems, and gifts galore—with a strong emphasis, as might be expected, on fishing rods and salmon flies. Four thousand tulips arrived from Holland, cases of Alsatian wines from France, and from Greece a request for a piece of his umbrella to make a relic in an icon. King Haakon of Norway cabled his congratulations and King Leopold of the Belgians wrote in his own hand. From countless Englishmen in public life we may take two quotations. "You have done a most wonderful piece of work and done it under the guidance and providence of God," declared George Lansbury who once had led the Labour Party; and the Archbishop of Canterbury wrote: "You have been enabled to do a great thing in a great way at a time of almost unexampled crisis. I thank God for it." More impressive still were the letters from humbler folk, from total strangers, from private soldiers of the First World War, from those who had been unemployed for years yet still managed to send him a present in gratitude. Most touching of all were the thoughts of the women with most to lose. From Hampshire: "I feel with God's help that you have given me back my boys, at one time it seemed as if we must lose all three of them"; from Northumberland: "I thank you a thousand times from the depth of my heart, the mother of five sons": from Paris: "Il n'y a pas une épouse, pas une maman de France qui, à l'heure présente, ne vous vénerè et prie pour vous et ceux que vous aimez"; and from Rome: "Mister Chamberlain! God may bless your white head! I am an Italian mother who wishes express you all her devotion."

This is what that great-hearted Socialist James Maxton meant when he said during the Munich debate that the Prime Minister had done "something that the mass of the common people in the world wanted done." From his very different standpoint, Anthony Eden meant the same thing when he counted among the influences that had averted war, "that genuine desire for peace among all peoples, German and Italian, as well as French and British." Wherever Chamberlain went in the months that followed the truth of these observations was underlined. In the towns and villages of South Wales—scarcely a Conservative stronghold—"I never heard a solitary boo"; on the contrary "the streets were lined with people cheering and shouting 'Good old Neville' and 'God bless you' with the most evident sincerity and heartiness." In Paris, in November, and still more in Rome, in January, the warmth of his reception was particularly remarkable.

Eden, during the Munich debate, had acknowledged the significance of the spontaneous ovations which Chamberlain had been accorded in Germany. "It was clearly a manifestation of the deep desire of the German people for peace," he said; and added, "the fact that it has at last found expression may be a real signpost on the road to peace." This was Chamberlain's thought too; and, if he erred, it was in holding to this thought too obsessively, too obstinately, hoping against hope, even when every other signpost began to point the other way. It is not true that he trusted too much in Hitler; what he trusted in too much were the many deterrent and persuasive forces that might have been expected to hold Hitler back.

He trusted in the gathering pace of British rearmament, and in February we find him writing that Hitler had "missed the bus" at the time of Munich, since "they could not make nearly such a mess of us now as they could have done then, while we could make much more of a mess of them." He trusted in the difficulties created by economic crisis in Germany, as revealed by experienced travellers and, indeed, Nazi leaders themselves. "They might take it," he told a City luncheon party in the House of Commons, "that when the German statesmen—he would not say the German people—reflected on the possible consequences of a conflict, if it ever arose, they would think not only of our armaments but of our great financial resources which in a war of long duration, might well prove to be a deciding factor."[22] He trusted in the deterrent influence of the United States, and cordially and publicly welcomed Roosevelt's strong speeches to Congress in January and to the Board of the Pan-American Union in April. He trusted in the persuasive influence of Mussolini. By far the most important single feature of his conversations in Rome was the warning he tried to give Hitler *via* his ally that "it would be a terrible tragedy if aggressive action were taken under a misapprehension as to what lengths the democracies might be prepared to go to." The Duce, however, had his own aggressive intentions towards Albania, and, Chamberlain noted, "made no direct reply to this remark."[23]

Even when the assurances given at Munich had been thrown to the winds by Hitler, and Prague occupied, Chamberlain still refused to accept the view that war was inevitable. He trusted rather in the deterrent effect of the guarantees now made to Poland, Roumania, Greece and Turkey. He trusted, as ever, in the restraints of more moderate opinion inside Germany. . . .

[22] As reported in *The Times,* December 16th, 1938. Chamberlain believed himself to be speaking "off the record."

[23] *Documents on British Foreign Policy 1919-1939* (H.M.S.O., 1950), Third Series, Vol. 3, p. 529.

Sir Charles Webster · (1886-1961) Outstanding British diplomatic historian, he taught for a number of years at the Universities of Liverpool and Wales (Aberystwyth), and at Harvard University, and from 1932 to 1953, served as Stevenson Professor of International History at the London School of Economics. He wrote numerous well-known books, including *The Congress of Vienna* (1919), *The Foreign Policy of Castlereagh 1815-1822* (1925), *The Foreign Policy of Castlereagh 1812-1815* (1931), and *The Foreign Policy of Palmerston 1830-1841* (2 vols., 1951). He served as President of the British Academy from 1950 to 1954, and with Noble Frankland he edited *The Strategic Air Offense Against Germany 1939-1945* (4 vols., 1961). The following essay—a thoughtful and important commentary on the Munich crisis, viewing it in its broad historical and political context—was originally delivered as the Stevenson Memorial Lecture, at Chatham House, in December 1960.

MUNICH RECONSIDERED: A SURVEY OF BRITISH POLICY

This lecture is given in memory of Sir Daniel Stevenson, a generous and original benefactor, who founded the two chairs of International History at Chatham House and the London School of Economics. I was the first holder of the chair at the London School of Economics and shortly after my appointment I had lunch with the founder. His gift was, he said, based on the belief that war was caused by ignorance and the deliberate distortion of the truth both of the past and the present. An impartial and scientific account of international history would help, therefore, to maintain peace by correcting misapprehensions and prejudices such as had caused the first World War. It would have pleased him that the most objective and scientific account of the controversial subject which I bring to your attention is contained in the three volumes of the *Survey* for 1938 which were largely written by the staff of Chatham House. If I do so, it is because the subject is discussed today much more in other countries than in Britain, which played the leading part in the event, and because new material has become available on some aspects of it during the last ten years.

One of the foremost diplomatic historians of the United States has stated that at Munich Britain "suffered a defeat comparable only to

From *International Affairs*, April, 1961. Reprinted by permission of The Royal Institute of International Affairs.

the loss of the American colonies"[1] and Lord Cecil said at the time that it was the greatest disaster which had occurred to us since Austerlitz. On the other hand, after Munich, Professor Temperley compared Mr. Chamberlain to Pitt as "the pilot that weathered the storm."

At any rate our candour about Munich has been exceptional. No other country has revealed its Foreign Office records so completely, while those of the Cabinet and the Services have been freely opened to the official historians. There are also a number of memoirs and biographies of British statesmen and officials, with two significant omissions. Lord Halifax refused to discuss the subject and Sir Horace Wilson has not uttered a word. The defeat of Germany enabled a prolonged examination to be made of the German records. Of the policy of other countries there is not such complete evidence, but still the papers and memoirs of the principal actors tell us a great deal. In Eastern Europe historians have written much about Munich. It is their great defence against the obvious fact that the Soviet Union entered into a close alliance with Hitler at the beginning of the war. Munich is one of the reasons why Czechoslovakia is now a Soviet satellite, and it has been used to show the hostility of the Western democracies towards the Soviet Union.

The situation which we sum up in the appellation Munich was, of course, largely due to the policy of earlier years. It was produced by the failure to stop Mussolini in Abyssinia and Hitler when he marched into the Rhineland, both actions well within our military competence, and the refusal of Britain and France to rearm with sufficient effort, a course for which both the British political parties were responsible. But that does not mean that in 1937-8 there were no alternative policies open. I propose to consider first the British attitude towards the case for the revision of the frontiers of Czechoslovakia, secondly the manner in which the revision was made, and thirdly the question whether the time gained by refusing to risk war in 1938 was a sufficient excuse for the course pursued.

The Treaty of Versailles was no sooner signed than fierce attacks were made on it not only in the defeated countries but in those of the victors. So far as its economic provisions were concerned this criticism, though exaggerated, was largely justified, and they were in fact never carried out. But the territorial settlement was a different matter. The minorities under alien rule had been reduced from over a hundred million to less than thirty million and for most of these there was some real protection in the minorities treaties. When it is remembered that new and viable States had to be erected after the destruction of four empires, whose nationalities had been intermin-

---

[1] Bernadotte E. Schmitt, "Munich," review article, in *Journal of Modern History*, Vol. XXV, No. 2, June, 1953, p. 180.

gled by centuries of history, it was inevitable that minorities should exist. In 1919 civilized peoples shrank from the remedy of expelling human beings from their homes. Though there were some obvious injustices, "the boundary network established at that time fitted the complicated patterns of speech, folk groupings and sense of nationality more closely than had ever been the case before in human history."[2] But this fact was obscured by ignorance and skillful propaganda.

Czechoslovakia was, however, accepted in the West as one of the most successful creations of the Paris Conference. There had been no hesitation in continuing the historic frontiers of Bohemia, while the Czechs and Slovaks, then closely bound by a common interest, had a preponderant majority in the new State. Some of the three million Germans intermingled with the Czechs in the frontier districts did express a desire to join the new Austria: but it was clear that if a viable State was to be made with reasonable communications and economic potentiality the frontiers of Bohemia must remain substantially intact. Less necessary and more debatable was the inclusion of so many Hungarians in the south of Slovakia, but the Hungarian treatment of minorities had been such that they received little sympathy. The award of Teschen to Czechoslovakia rather than to Poland was made after the most meticulous examination ever given to such a problem, and a garden of friendship was erected on the frontier between the two new States.

President Benes had always, however, been conscious of the vulnerable position of his country. By means of the Little Entente treaties he secured protection from the irreconcilable Hungarians and by the Locarno treaties an alliance with France and a treaty with Germany which provided for the arbitration of any dispute between them. When those were later reinforced by the treaties by which the Soviet Union promised to support France, though subject to an appeal to the Council of the League, Czechoslovakia seemed to be as safe as treaties could make her. All Hitler's attempts to undermine this situation by a treaty of non-aggression such as he had made with Pilsudski were rejected out of hand by Benes.

Not until the depression of the early 'thirties did the problem of the minorities make any very great impression on public opinion. It increased their discontent, and among them were the Sudeten Germans of Czechoslovakia. It is generally agreed that their grievances were neglected at Prague, that they were not given a fair share of the measures of alleviation, and that they had not a sufficient proportion of officials in the central and local administration to look after their interest.

[2] Isaiah Bowman, "The Strategy of Territorial Decisions," in *Foreign Affairs*, January, 1946.

The rise of Hitler brought the question of peaceful change into the forefront of politics. Each breach of the Treaty of Versailles was accompanied by fervent promises that he had no further claims, and after the entry into the Rhineland and the rebuilding of the German air force these peaceful professions were accompanied by threats to devastate the countries of those who opposed him. His threats might have been met by reorganizing and making effective a system of collective security such as had been under consideration in Europe ever since the war. This was the policy of the Soviet Union, which in 1934 joined the League of Nations for that purpose. But, since this policy was combined with Communist propaganda and penetration in the West, it was naturally regarded there with the greatest suspicion. Nor did either Britain or France rearm, except in a half-hearted manner. The Conservatives used the excuse that normal business and production must not be disturbed, while the Labour Party denied the necessity and insisted that they could not entrust increased armaments to a Tory Government.

It was in these circumstances that the policy of appeasement as an alternative to resistance became respectable in Britain. President Wilson's Fourteen Points were resuscitated without any of the qualifications which had accompanied them. Self-determination, to which the Germans had appealed in 1919, was exalted into a magic formula without any consideration of the consequences of its application. In spite of the conduct of the Germans to the minorities in their own country, the extension of their rule over Germans outside their frontiers was sympathetically discussed by many in positions of power and influence.

Thus by 1937 peaceful change was a commonplace of conversation. It was the subject of the International Studies Conference and a course of lectures at the London School of Economics. There can be no doubt that this result was mainly due to Hitler's promises and threats. It is not surprising, therefore, that in this climate of opinion it became the policy of the most important persons in the British Government, though it was not as yet given any public expression. British statesmen were now acutely conscious of the inferiority of their armaments to those of Germany, and the state of France was very disquieting. It is obvious that the policy of appeasement was adopted less for high principle than for fear of the consequences if any other policy was pursued.

So far as territorial change was concerned, there was little suggestion until a late date that it should be applied to Czechoslovakia, apart from Lord Rothermere's ceaseless propaganda on behalf of the Hungarians and the lucubrations of Dean Inge. It was Danzig and the Polish corridor which attracted most attention. Nor was the matter put forward by the Sudeten Germans themselves. Though

strong hints had been given in *The Times,* whose editor and assistant editor were fanatical supporters of the policy of conciliating
Germany, the first definite advocacy in an important national journal in this country seems to have been made in the *New Statesman*
of 27 August 1938. Nevertheless in the approaches which were begun
towards the end of 1937 the Government might claim that it had a
substantial movement of British opinion behind it.

Throughout the negotiations the initiative was invariably taken
by the British Government. Sir Winston Churchill has thrown on
France an even greater responsibility for the result because she had
a treaty with Czechoslovakia. In reply the two French Ambassadors,
M. Coulondre and M. François-Poncet, have pointed out that the
diplomacy leading up to Munich was dominated and controlled by
Britain. They add that if the situation had been reversed France
would never have behaved towards Britain as Britain behaved towards France. However that may be, it is true that the main responsibility for the manner in which the diplomacy was conducted rests on
British statesmen and officials.

The Prime Minister himself directed the process. His confidence in
his own ability to do so was, perhaps, largely due to the fact that he
had had no experience of international diplomacy. He took as his
principal advisers in the Cabinet, Sir Samuel Hoare and Sir John
Simon, the two most unsuccessful British Foreign Ministers of the
twentieth century. Lord Halifax was in full agreement, though at
times he attempted to show a firmer attitude towards Germany. Mr.
Butler, his Under-Secretary, had little influence, but so far as it
went it reinforced the policy of appeasement. The Prime Minister's
principal official agent was Sir Horace Wilson, who also had had no
experience of international diplomacy. Whatever his own convictions,
he well represented his master in accepting the German point of view.

The Foreign Office officials had, of course, to carry out the orders
of their political chiefs. But the Germans recognized that there was
considerable resistance in the Foreign Office to the official policy,
and there are a number of indications in the records that some of
the most important officials did not at any rate agree with the manner in which the policy was being pursued. The principal Ambassadors compare very unfavourably with their predecessors in the
period before the first World War. Sir Nevile Henderson has revealed his own incompetence, and his book is amply confirmed by
the records. He went to his post with a self-imposed mission to
secure peace at almost any price. He allowed himself to be treated
by Hitler and Ribbentrop in a manner unworthy of his position.
His hostility to the Czechs, and especially to Benes, was freely revealed
not only to his own Government but to the Germans. Sir Eric Phipps
on his transfer to Paris took with him all the fears aroused by his experi-

ence at Berlin. He did his best to counteract any French tendency to resist. He had to be sternly rebuked by the Foreign Office for describing those statesmen who desired France to be faithful to her treaty as a "noisy corrupt war group." At Rome the Earl of Perth, who, as Sir Eric Drummond, had been Secretary-General of the League of Nations, never alluded to its principles or obligations. Mr. Newton at Prague was the only head of a mission directly concerned who showed any sympathy with the Czechs in the prosecution of a policy whose necessity, however, he admitted.

There was also in the 'thirties a spate of amateur British diplomatists, of whom the most important was Lord Lothian, because of his influence at the centre; Mr. Chamberlain was especially pleased when he reported Hitler as saying that Britain and Germany were the two pillars on which European order rested. Mr. Tom Jones used his influence with Mr. Baldwin in the same way. When in 1936 Professor Toynbee, after an interview, expressed his conviction of Hitler's sincerity in desiring peace in Europe, this judgment was sent by Mr. Tom Jones post haste to Mr. Baldwin and Mr. Eden, in an effort to persuade them to take no action against the reoccupation of the Rhineland which had just taken place. But perhaps the most important amateur was Colonel Lindbergh, who, with little knowledge of military aviation and strategy, accepted everything that the Germans told him about their air force and spread panic estimates of the probable result of war in high civilian circles in London and Paris.

To attain its purpose British diplomacy had to take into account the two protagonists, Germany and Czechoslovakia, its ally France, Italy, the ally of Germany, and the Soviet Union. One method might have been a conference of the great European Powers and Czechoslovakia on the classical model of the nineteenth century, and this was at times considered, though the Soviet Union was to be left out. But before this could be arranged the different parties had first to be subjected to persuasion or pressure to produce a more favourable situation. When the conference finally did take place at Munich neither the Soviet Union nor Czechoslovakia were admitted to the conference room and the issues had been already settled before the conference met.

The policy of appeasing Germany in order to prevent her using force to obtain her ends first became active in Lord Halifax's visit to Hitler on 19 November 1937. On 5 November Hitler had told a select few in great secrecy that he intended to attack Austria and Czechoslovakia when the political situation was ripe. But he now replied to Lord Halifax's suggestions for a comprehensive settlement of points of dispute, including disarmament, with his usual distorted history, complaints of unfair treatment, and professions of

peaceful intentions and readiness to negotiate a reasonable settlement. Lord Halifax was satisfied that progress had been made, but
it is perhaps not surprising that what made the greatest impression
at Berlin was the fact that Lord Halifax agreed that alterations
must take place in the political order of Europe, specifically men-
tioning Danzig, Austria, and Czechoslovakia, that the Soviet Union
was to be excluded from the negotiations, and that no reference was
made to the treaties protecting the independence of Austria and
Czechoslovakia.

Though there was little response to this overture, the policy persisted of persuading Germany to state her demands with a view to
finding a settlement. It was twice interrupted; first by the seizure
of Austria, which could hardly be said to have avoided the use of
armed force but was accompanied by renewed promises that there
was no intention of attacking Czechoslovakia; and secondly by the
supposed German mobilization in May which caused alarm all over
Europe. Lord Halifax said some strong things to Ribbentrop about
Austria and Mr. Chamberlain himself gave public warnings, later
repeated by Sir John Simon, that in certain circumstances Britain
might be drawn into war, while both the British and French Ambassadors made significant inquiries at Berlin. These warnings
were, however, so phrased that they could be and were interpreted
in different ways by German officials and diplomatists, all the more
so as they were receiving assurances from many sources, some
closely connected with the Prime Minister, that Britain was pro-
pared to force great concessions in order to preserve the peace. The
incident in May caused Hitler to determine that he must act by the
autumn of the year, and plans were then secretly prepared for that
purpose to be carried out without any official mobilization. Though
his generals were dismayed at the prospect, Hitler was sure that he
could attain his end by 1 October. The propaganda against the
Czechs was steadily increased and every incident in the Sudetenland
was magnified into a new example of their brutality.

Meanwhile the British Government continued to inquire what
Germany really wanted to be done in Czechoslovakia. The answer
always was that this was a question to be settled by the Sudetens
themselves. Anything that satisfied them would be accepted by Germany. We know now that the Sudeten leaders, Henlein and Frank,
were acting under the orders of Hitler on no account to come to an
agreement with the Czechs. If their terms seemed likely to be accepted they were at once to raise them. Thus the negotiation was to
continue until the German preparations for attack were ready at the
end of September, when the final rupture might take place.

There is no sign that this situation was appreciated by the British
Government and its advisers until August was well advanced. Then

they did begin to realize that only by direct contact with Berlin could any agreement be obtained. On 1 September Dirksen, the German Ambassador, reported that Sir Horace Wilson had told Kordt, his Counsellor of Embassy, that if Britain and Germany came to an agreement they could brush aside any Czech and French resistance. Since Ribbentrop's hostility after his failure as an ambassador was well known, it was considered necessary to establish direct contact with Hitler himself. When dealing with a dictator only a meeting at the summit could produce the necessary action. Mr. Chamberlain thought it his duty to make an attempt to negotiate a deal with Hitler himself.

Meanwhile for four months, while Germany was being conciliated, immense pressure had been exerted at Prague to change the whole structure of the Czechoslovak State in order to satisfy the demands of the Sudeten leaders. Here again the initiative was taken by the British Government, though France was constantly exhorted to take the same line. After seeing Hitler, Henlein had raised his demands and on 24 April formulated them in the Carlsbad programme, which would have given the Sudeten area more autonomy than a Swiss Canton. The British diplomatists pressed for large concessions and, when these were of course not enough, demanded more. Henlein proved to be an ideal instrument of Hitler's policy. His visits to Britain impressed those whom he met with his moderation and sincere desire for a settlement, and these people included Sir Robert Vansittart and Mr. Winston Churchill. Hitler himself was encouraged in his plans by the first visit and sent Henlein a second time, though he was, of course, to pretend that the initiative was entirely his own. At Prague, therefore, the insinuation was constantly made that if Benes and Hodza, the Premier, refused to give way to the justifiable claims of the Sudetens, Czechoslovakia would be left alone to face Germany, though France never said so explicitly. During the whole process the greatest care was taken by British diplomatists to ensure that no obligation was incurred to defend Czechoslovakia, however sweeping were the concessions made.

The process of transforming a unitary State into a union of nationalities in a democratic country with a coalition Cabinet was bound to be difficult and to take time. When it appeared to go too slowly, in view of German threats and armaments, the Runciman mission was forced on Czechoslovakia. Benes tried to refuse it but was compelled to accept and even made to appear to have asked for it by the threat of publishing his refusal. The device of an independent mediator was used in order that the British Government might have no responsibility for defending the result, whatever it might be, but it was in fact mainly conducted by foreign service officials who reported its progress to London. Its head had no qualifications for the task except a certain economic expertise which had no influence in the negotiations. After immense pressure Benes finally put forward his fourth plan which virtually satisfied all the demands of the Carlsbad programme, as Lord Runciman himself admitted. Some of the Sudeten leaders wished to accept it, but of course Henlein and Frank could not do so and proceeded to stir up their extreme followers and use the incidents as a pretext to refuse negotiation. These eventually resulted in a sort of rising and Henlein fled to Germany, demanding from Hitler the annexation of the Sudeten districts to Germany in time for the latter to present it as an ultimatum to Mr. Chamberlain at Berchtesgaden on 15 September.

A week before, on 7 September, *The Times* had suggested the same thing in its famous leader which prepared the way for this demand. Throughout Europe it was regarded as a declaration of official policy and a *démenti* immediately issued by the Foreign Office was not everywhere believed. It is true that the leader was written by the Editor himself without consulting anyone, but he was in close touch with Lord Halifax and Mr. Chamberlain and knew that he was expressing a solution that had long been in their minds. "The Foreign Office went up through the roof," wrote Mr. Geoffrey Dawson on 7 September. "Not so, however, the Foreign Secretary who came and lunched with me at the Travellers' and had a long talk."[3]

Lord Runciman then drew up a report which recommended cession but, no doubt influenced by the expertise of his advisers, he suggested that it should be applied only in areas where there was a preponderant majority of Germans. Nevertheless the report was so couched that he seemed to consider that Czechoslovakia would in the future be wholly under the dominance of Germany. This report did not reach Mr. Chamberlain before his meeting with Hitler. It exercised no influence on the negotiations with Germany, but Lord Runciman's judgment was a useful instrument to obtain the agreement of the Cabinet and the French.

Throughout these negotiations it had been made clear to France that, if she fulfilled her obligation to defend Czechoslovakia, the British treaty to defend her from unprovoked attack by Germany was not involved. If Germany did attack France herself Britain would implement her treaty, but the British Government would enter into no specific discussions as to how this would be done. Though at last in 1937 the British Chiefs of Staff recognized that military aid must be given to France in such a case, the British Government refused to allow official staff conversations. When the crisis came in 1938 and it was thought for a time that war was certain, Britain and France had no common plan or even any gen-

[3] Sir Evelyn Wrench, *Geoffrey Dawson and our Times* (London, Hutchinson, 1955), pp. 371-2.

eral knowledge of the other's strategic conceptions or the tactics necessary to carry them out.

The Soviet Union, though it had asked for consultation as to joint actions, was kept by the British Government entirely outside the negotiations. The reasons given were that the military purges had made it impotent and that Germany would be irrevocably antagonized. In this course the British Government undoubtedly followed the wishes of the majority of its Conservative supporters. The Right in France was even more hostile, while M. Bonnet succeeded in preventing the military convention which France's able Ambassador, M. Coulondre, came home, with the consent of the Soviet Government, to negotiate.

This was the situation when Mr. Chamberlain determined to play his lone hand against Hitler. He got the permission of the Cabinet but did not consult the French before the decision. M. Daladier, who had tentatively thought of a joint mission, was taken aback, but the French Government had no alternative but to approve a step already decided.

It was by his own choice that Mr. Chamberlain at Berchtesgaden went alone to the meeting with Hitler without even his own interpreter to take note of what he said. He does not seem to have had any specific proposals in his mind. He later told the French that he had intended to discuss Anglo-German relations but that Hitler insisted on discussing Czechoslovakia. When Hitler used Henlein's demands and a fantastic account of the situation in the Sudetenland to demand its absorption by Germany through self-determination and plebiscite, Mr. Chamberlain indicated his own agreement, though he could not of course commit the British and French Governments. He also agreed that the process should be applied to all areas where the Germans constituted 51 per cent of the inhabitants. He made no reservations or stipulations as to the method to be employed except that force must not be used. The threat of an immediate use of armed force, unless all German demands were granted, seems to have been regarded by him as legitimate. He thought that if these were admitted in principle an orderly process of transfer would be gladly accepted by Hitler. Though before he went he had called Hitler a madman he came away from the meeting with the impression that he was a man to be trusted to keep his word. He seems to have forgotten how many times it had already been broken.

As for Hitler, he was astonished and overjoyed at the ease with which he had obtained his demands. His generals became much more courageous and were ready to contemplate using the concessions already made to obtain complete control of Czechoslovakia. The Polish and Hungarian Governments, hitherto resistant to German invitations to participate, now prepared to take part in the kill.

Public opinion in Britain had enthusiastically welcomed Mr. Chamberlain's visit, and the result, so far as it was known, was also approved by the majority, though some bitter criticisms were made. It was generally expected, however, that the transfer would be made by some such method as had been used in the Saar.

When the French were consulted at a meeting in London, they were perturbed at the idea of a plebiscite which would lead to similar demands from Poland and Hungary. It was agreed, therefore, to propose a direct transfer of Sudeten territory. They also demurred to the 51 per cent majority plan but gave way when Mr. Chamberlain told them that Hitler would accept nothing else. They salved their conscience by demanding that Britain should join in a guarantee of the truncated State, and Mr. Chamberlain, after consulting his Cabinet, agreed to do so and this was included in the communication to the Czech Government. Subsequent developments made it clear, however, that he never intended that this guarantee should operate, though much play was made with it in the debates in the House of Commons.

All this was done in desperate haste under the threat of attack from Hitler, unless his demands were accepted within a few days. The same instant agreement was demanded of Czechoslovakia. After being warned not to mobilize for fear of provoking Hitler, Benes was asked to agree immediately to all that had been decided. When he resisted and suggested various compromises and conditions, Britain and France forced his consent by an ultimatum presented in the middle of the night, with the indication that if he refused he would be left alone to fight Germany.

When, therefore, Mr. Chamberlain returned, again without the French, to meet Hitler at Godesberg he expected to be received with warm praise and a readiness to accept an orderly and scientific international control of the transfer now conceded. This time he took with him to the meeting Sir Ivone Kirkpatrick, who has given us a vivid account of the scene. When Hitler made his new demands for German occupation of most of the area by 28 September, before the plebiscite on which he still insisted could take place, Mr. Chamberlain realized something of the nature of the negotiation. After an exchange of letters there was a second interview next day when Hitler produced a map of the areas in which a 51 per cent majority was claimed, based on the pre-war statistics which all experts knew were biased in favour of the Germans.

This time Mr. Chamberlain reacted strongly and protested vigorously against what he called a *Diktat*. Hitler made one or two minor concessions and eventually consented to delay the march of his troops till 1 October, the date which he had always fixed for that operation. While Mr. Chamberlain agreed to convey the new proposals to his allies, he intimated that they would not be accepted. Nevertheless he told Hitler on parting that a relation of confidence had grown up between them. While Hitler himself still remained confident, his generals and almost all his ministers except Ribbentrop were greatly alarmed at the situation, and in this they reflected almost the whole of German public opinion.

The effect on the British people was immediate when the nature of the transaction, though still imperfectly known, was at last realized. The advocates of peace at almost any price were reduced to virtually complete silence. Even *The Times* urged resistance, while *The Observer* was positively bellicose. The French Government, confident that Britain would now support it, determined to fight, in spite of the opposition of the Right which was vehemently expressed by important politicians. When, however, M. Daladier suggested resistance at the conference in London he was subjected to merciless criticism of the weakness of French armaments from Sir John Simon and Mr. Chamberlain. Nevertheless, after a private interview between the two Premiers, the two Governments moved closer together. The French agreed that further appeals should be made to Hitler, and Britain now promised to support France if they proved to be of no avail. The Foreign Office, apparently without the Prime Minister's cognizance, publicly announced that France, Britain, and the Soviet Union would come to the assistance of Czechoslovakia if Germany attacked her.

The situation was also transformed in Czechoslovakia herself. The mobilization that she was now permitted to put into force was smoothly carried out and the disorder in the Sudeten area was easily put down.

I need not dwell on the final stages which led to the Munich meeting. Hitler, after rejecting all concessions until the last moment in spite of urgent appeals from Britain and France, was finally persuaded by the attitude of the German people and the intervention of Mussolini, at the instance of Britain, to postpone the attack until another meeting took place. In the dramatic scene in the House of Commons only one person, Mr. Gallacher, the Communist, protested audibly; but it must be remembered that it was still expected that a reasonable method of procedure would be adopted.

At the Munich meeting the surrender was almost complete and was made without any discussion with the country most concerned. Hitler and Mussolini had agreed on a draft which in all its essentials was accepted by Britain and France. The short delay to which Hitler consented before his troops moved into the areas definitely ceded was of little importance. There was no plebiscite in the disputed areas and the British Legion, which had fondly hoped to act as an international police force, was politely told that it was not required. Instead a committee of the British, French, and Italian Ambassadors at Berlin with Ribbentrop and a representative of the new Czech Government was given the task of deciding the new frontiers. M. François-Poncet made an effort to reduce the area claimed by Germany, but Sir Nevile Henderson thought that a better result would be obtained if the Czechs were left to argue their own case. They could, of course, do nothing with the triumphant Germans.

Czechoslovakia was thus left, as Hitler intended, not only defenceless but without self-contained communications or economic viability. Her cessions to Poland and Hungary were decided by the Axis Powers without reference to Britain and France as had been agreed at Munich. Though the negotiations concerning the guarantee continued for a long time the British Government would undertake no commitment to defend the new Czechoslovakia against Germany. In these circumstances its disintegration and complete occupation by Germany was an easy task.

Mr. Chamberlain's reward was the agreement by Hitler that there would be consultation with Britain in all future international difficulties which, to his later regret, he emphasized during his enthusiastic welcome on his return. He told the French that this had not been premeditated but in the course of his last private conversation with Hitler he took the draft already prepared out of his pocket. The French were considerably disturbed by being thus ignored, while in the U.S.S.R. the agreement was regarded as a promise of benevolent neutrality if Germany attacked them.

The main defence for this conduct is the assumption that the delay of a year before war came saved Britain and all the Western world from irretrievable defeat. This argument, as his confidant, Sir Samuel Hoare, and his biographer, Sir Keith Feiling, attest, was not however the main cause of Mr. Chamberlain's decisions. He believed that what he had done was in itself right and the preliminary to further negotiations with Hitler to produce a peaceful world. Apologists for Munich have, however, stressed this argument, and Sir Winston Churchill admits that, if it were valid, it would be sufficient. But he denies its validity. Both sides are discussing an hypothesis, but the problem is one which everyone must consider before passing judgment on Munich.

In the first place there is the assertion by many high-ranking German soldiers and officials that if a firmer attitude had been taken towards Hitler he would not have risked a war. Nearly all foreign observers however take a contrary view, and Hitler's own words and conduct support this opinion. But Hitler was throughout acting a part and it was impossible for him later to admit that he had not meant what he said. Much depends on how early a firmer policy might have been adopted. But it does not seem likely that in the later stages Hitler would have accepted without war any solution which left Czechoslovakia substantially intact, whatever changes had been made in her internal structure.

It is also claimed by many Germans that if Hitler had been resisted, he would have been overthrown by a military plot. It is clearly proved that one existed in which some of the most important generals were involved. Sir John Wheeler-Bennett, in his meticulous examination of the evidence,[4] pours scorn on their claims. He does not however, to my mind, clearly establish that nothing would have been done if resistance had come at an earlier stage. But, even if he is right, the effect on the morale of the generals would have been immense. The war would have been begun in a very different mood from that of 1939.

The generals had good reason to be alarmed. The Czechoslovak army had been rearmed during the previous four years and had received much new material from France and Russia. It was able to mobilize immediately twenty-four to twenty-five divisions and could, perhaps, have added ten more in a comparatively short time. The men were well trained and their morale high and, even if a few politicians were defeatist, the soldiers and citizens showed themselves ready for an all-out resistance. Owing to the occupation of Austria their fortified line had been outflanked and there were some vulnerable frontiers. But the German generals thought that an attack in the South would be very difficult because of the terrain and bad communications. The Czech Government relied on its allies to keep Poland and Hungary in check. In such case the Czechs were confident of making a prolonged resistance. Their main weakness was in the air though Russia had sent some aircraft and it was hoped that more would soon come. It may well be that they would have suffered great damage and much loss of life by the attack of the German air force, and the argument that we had saved them from this ordeal was much used in Britain. But surely it was for the Czechs themselves to make this crucial decision.

On the other hand, the German army, though immediately somewhat superior in numbers and with an immensely larger population behind it, was as yet lacking in trained officers, non-commissioned officers, and reserves. Its three Panzer divisions were armed only with Marks I and II and would have been difficult to employ. The German generals considered the force hardly sufficient to overcome Czechoslovakia, and if they were attacked by the French army, much stronger in both numbers and training, they did not believe that the West Wall, still imperfectly organized, would enable them to resist it. Only a few weak divisions and some scattered forces

[4] *Munich: Prologue to Tragedy* (London, Macmillan, 1948).

were available in the West. Plans had been made to transfer divisions there, but even then they would be insufficient, and meanwhile what would become of the attack on Czechoslovakia?

France was able to mobilize a million men in 1938. But, if war had come, would she have attacked as the Germans feared? General Gamelin, both at the time and since, sometimes implied that he would have done so; but there were always qualifications and reservations. He had an exaggerated view of the strength of the German forces and the West Wall. He thought that the Czech army could only hold out for a long period by abandoning Prague and retiring into Moravia. The inability of the British to provide more than two divisions and 120 aeroplanes was not encouraging. In 1939 the French showed no disposition to attack, but if the Czechs had been fighting and the Soviet Union had also been in the war, the prospect of success would have been much greater in 1938.

It is often asserted that the Soviet Union would not have declared war in 1938 even if France and Britain had done so. It had been treated as an uninterested party until a very late date, but the repeated declarations of Litvinov and Potemkin at Moscow, Geneva, and Prague would have made such a course almost impossible, though it is true that Stalin himself had said nothing. The reports of the British and French diplomats, which threw doubt on the Soviet attitude, are not convincing.

More justified was the belief that the Soviet Union would not intervene effectively. The Soviets probably did not know themselves what they could do. Even if Rumania had allowed them, they could have sent few land forces by that route. But their air force was effective and some of it could, and almost certainly would, have been sent to the assistance of the Czechs. They had already put pressure on Poland to remain neutral and it seems certain that if they had entered the war neither Poland nor Hungary would have moved. It is, of course, impossible to say how this situation would have worked out, but that it would have been more favourable than that of 1939 does not admit of much doubt. Communist writers have even tried to show, in order to discredit the Czech bourgeois Government, that the Soviet Union would, if it had been asked, have gone to war even when France and Britain had refused. But if there was convincing evidence of this we should have had it long ago.

The attitude of Italy is more doubtful. In a sense Mussolini had committed himself after Berchtesgaden. But he was greatly alarmed later on. He had been convinced that Britain would not go to war, an opinion confirmed by Mr. Chamberlain's visit to Hitler. As late as 27 September he mobilized only sufficiently for an armed neutrality. On the whole, one is inclined to believe Mr. Chamberlain, who told General Gamelin that if Britain went to war Italy would stay out.

By 1939 this position had deteriorated in every respect except one. The threat from Czechoslovakia on the flank had been removed and her considerable armament industry set to work for Germany. The German army was more numerous, better armed, trained, and staffed, and possessed larger trained reserves. The Soviet Union was an ally instead of an enemy, and the Danubian countries, intimidated by what had been done, lay open to German pressure.

Britain and France had also increased their armaments but at a much slower pace. In the year before the war 35 per cent of German production was devoted to armaments, in Britain only 7 per cent, and in France even less. Britain and France had perhaps kept pace in naval armaments, but the Germans had more ocean-going U-boats in commission or nearly ready and the two great battleships were a year nearer completion.

But, though all this is accepted, it is claimed that German preponderance in the air was so great that the war could have been won in 1938 by a devastating attack on British and French cities. There is no doubt that this was one of the main reasons why Britain refused to risk war then. It is now clear however that the Germans had neither the intention nor the ability to make a strategic air attack on Britain in 1938. Their air force was organized and trained for co-operation with their armies. Though their Heinkel IIIs and Dornier 17s could have reached South-East England and London from Germany, they never imagined that an attack could be successfully carried out from German bases without fighter protection in daylight or under cover of darkness. The British defence was, it is true, pitifully weak. The British Government only realized in 1938 that its bomber deterrent was practically useless. Only five squadrons of Hurricanes were in existence and those were not fully equipped; only one hundred inadequate anti-aircraft guns deefnded Lodon. The radar warning system was already in existence but less dense and efficient than in 1939.

It is, however, surprising that the situation was so misjudged. It was thought that the Germans could inflict enormous casualties in a few weeks and, as is well known, 250,000 hospital beds had been provided to receive them. Even more mistaken was the view of the Cabinet and officials that the British people would be so shaken and intimidated by the bombing that order would be maintained in the cities only by the use of the armed forces.

The Germans could have inflicted heavier casualties in France, but they had no intention of doing so unless France attacked, and then their air force would have had many other tasks to perform. It is unlikely that in any circumstances they would have made a strategic attack on Britain sooner than they actually did in 1940.

Finally, there are the arguments concerning the attitude of the peoples of Britain, the Commonwealth, and the United States. It is suggested that while the British entered the war in 1939 as a united people, in 1938 they would have been divided, irresolute, and unconvinced of the justice of their cause. It is true that the Government, and especially the Prime Minister, had presented the issues as remote from their own interests. They were also deceived as to the manner in which the negotiations were being conducted. But, as I have already noted, when this was to some extent revealed after Godesberg there was a complete change in public opinion. Nor, in spite of the belief that aerial attack was likely to be immediate and devastating, was there any panic even when war seemed practically certain. The King's speech later justly remarked: "I was proud to observe the calmness and determination of all my people."

No doubt it would have been more difficult to convince the Governments and peoples of the Commonwealth of the necessity for action. No attempt had been made to enlighten them as to what really was at stake. Mr. Mackenzie King would not even allow Britain to train her airmen in Canada before war broke out. But if war had come in 1938, it is hard to believe that, apart from emotional ties, they would not have realized, as they did in 1939, that their interests were bound up with those of Britain.

The conduct of the United States in the crisis had been ambivalent. President Roosevelt had made little impression on their policy of isolation and pacifism. Only war could do that. His constant adjurations to keep the peace and his persistent refusal of any material aid if war came reinforced the policy of appeasement. His own relief was shown by the praise which he gave to Mr. Chamberlain after Munich. But the bitterest critics of Munich were in the United States. Isolation was in fact reinforced by it. There can be little doubt that if war had come Britain would have had as much help as she obtained at a later date.

When all these considerations are taken into account there can of course be no certain conclusion. But to my mind there is sufficient evidence to show that rather than gaining by the year's delay Britain would have been better off if she had fought for the issues so clearly revealed in 1938.

Some of the lessons of Munich are obvious enough. It shows the folly of unilateralism and neutralism, the necessity of close co-operation between threatened States, the penalty of deserting faithful allies, the dangers of discussions at the highest level without careful preparation and adequate advice, and the special danger of negotiating under the threat of immediate war.

Some may, perhaps, find in it even wider applications such as that employed by Mr. Somerset Maugham in an aphorism which he adapted from a reflection by Thucydides on the Peloponnesian War. "If a nation values anything more than freedom," he wrote, "it will lose its freedom and the irony of it is that, if it is comfort and money that it values more, it will lose that too."

A GUIDE TO FURTHER READING

There is a vast literature on the Munich crisis, and the American reader is especially fortunate because so much of this literature—important contemporary accounts, documents, memoirs, and historical studies—is available in English.

The best general accounts of the whole crisis remain Sir John W. Wheeler-Bennett, *Munich—Prologue to Tragedy** (2nd ed. 1963), and R. G. D. Laffan, *The Crisis over Czechoslovakia,* published as Volume II of the Royal Institute of International Affairs' *Survey of International Affairs, 1938* (1951), to which may be added the pertinent chapter of Radomir Luza, *The Transfer of the Sudeten Germans: A Study of Czech-German Relations 1933-1962* (1964). Keith Eubank, *Munich* (1963) is a competent narrative, not invariably sound in matters of interpretation and detail. Andrew Rothstein, *The Munich Conspiracy* (1958) is the work of a British Marxist with a strong anti-Western bias.

There are also two important German works—Boris Celovsky, *Das Münchener Abkommen von 1938* (1958), and Helmut K. G. Rönneforth, *Die Sudetenkrise in der Internationalen Politik* (2 vols. 1961).

There is no complete bibliography on the crisis, but there are detailed listings in the works of Wheeler-Bennett, Celovsky, Rönneforth, Luza and Eubank.

Historical Background

The historical origins of the Munich crisis date back many generations, and there are a number of valuable books on the history of the Czech people and the development of German-Czech relations. These include L. B. Namier, *The Czecho-Slovaks: An Oppressed Nationality* (1917), Elizabeth Wiskemann, *Czechs and Germans* (1938), R. W. Seton-Watson, *A History of the Czechs and Slovaks* (1943), Robert J. Kerner (ed.), *Czechoslovakia* (1945), S. Harrison Thomson, *Czechoslovakia in European History* (2nd ed. 1953), to which may be added William L. Langer, "When German Dreams Come True," *Yale Review* (Summer 1938), and S. Harrison Thomson, "Czech and German: Action, Reaction, Interaction," *Journal of Central European Affairs,* I (1940).

These accounts, generally favorable to the Czechoslovak view, may be compared with Wenzel Jaksch and Kurt Glazer, *Europe's Road to Potsdam* (New York, 1963), the revised memoirs of a leading Sudeten German Social Democrat. There is also a considerable literature on this subject by German historians and Sudeten German nationalists. Most of this literature is propagandistic in tone, but provides a good insight into the German point of view, and the bitterness of the German-Czech conflict. See, for instance, Alfons Dopsch, *Die historische Stellung der Deutschen in Böhmen* (1919), Gustav Pirchan and others (eds.), *Das Sudetendeutschtum* (2nd ed. 1939), and the voluminous writings of Paul Molisch, Josef Pfitzner, and Eugen Lemberg.

* Asterisked books are available in paperback.

For post-1945 accounts, showing that the events of the Nazi era (and of the Second World War) did nothing to reduce the dislike of Czechoslovakia by nationalist Sudeten Germans, see Wilhelm K. Turnwald, *Renascence or Decline of Central Europe? The German-Czech Problem* (1954), and Emil Franzel, *Sudetendeutsche Geschichte* (2nd ed. 1963), by a well-known Sudeten historian now living in West Germany.

The origins of the Czechoslovak Republic are discussed at length in the important new work of Dagmar Perman, *The Shaping of the Czechoslovak State* (1962), which may be compared with the earlier accounts of Harold Nicolson, *Peacemaking 1919* (1933) and Charles Seymour, "Czechoslovak Frontiers," *Yale Review* (Winter 1939).

J. W. Bruegel, "German Diplomacy and the Sudeten Question before 1938," International Affairs, XXXVII (1961), is a useful survey of German policy toward Czechoslovakia, from Versailles to the mid-30s, based on documents of the German Foreign Office.

The increasingly troubled relations between Czechs and Germans in the years immediately preceding the Munich crisis may be followed in Emil Sabota, "Czechs and Germans: A Czechoslovak View," *Slavonic Review*, XIV (1936); Frank L. Hayes, "Hitler and Central Europe," *Yale Review* (Spring 1938); Hubert Ripka, "Czechoslovakia: The Key to the Danube Basin," *Slavonic Review*, XVII (1938); and R. W. Seton-Watson, "The German Minority in Czechoslovakia," *Foreign Affairs*, XV (1938); and in a number of Sudeten German accounts, including "The German Minority in Czechoslovakia," *Slavonic Review*, XIV (1936), by an anonymous Nazi Sudeten leader; Konrad Henlein, "The German Minority in Czechoslovakia," *International Affairs*, XV (1936); and F. W. Essler (pseud.), *Twenty Years of Sudeten German Losses* (1938).

German views of Czechoslovakia, past and present, may also be followed in the extensive literature on *Mitteleuropa,* the intellectual companion of Pan-German political agitation. For important analyses of this literature, see the discerning studies of Paul R. Sweet, "Recent Literature on Mitteleuropa," *Journal of Central European Affairs,* III (1943), Felix Gilbert, "Mitteleuropa— The Last Stage, *ibid.,* VII (1947), and the more recent study of Henry Cord Meyer, *Mitteleuropa in German Thought and Action* (1955).

For postwar German views on this subject, see, for instance, Hans Rothfels, "Grundsätzliches zum Problem der Nationalitat," *Historische Zeitschrift,* CLXXIV (1952); Werner Conze, "Tschechen und Deutsche in Mitteleuropa aus Sicht der Sudetenkrise von 1938," *Aussenpolitik,* IV (1953); and, most interestingly, Joachim Leuschner, *Volk und Raum. Zum Stil der National-sozialistischen Aussenpolitik* (1958).

Contemporary Accounts

Because the Munich crisis was so protracted, and so much of it was played out in public, there is much valuable information and commentary to be found in contemporary books, journals, and newspapers. *The New York Times* and *The New York Herald Tribune* both had excellent coverage of the crisis, and so did *The Manchester Guardian. The* [London] *Times* is more important for its editorials and correspondence columns. The official *History of "The Times,"* Volume IV/2 (1952) is of great interest for the inner history of *The Times* and British policy in the Munich era.

Important contemporary books on the Munich Crisis include Hamilton Fish Armstrong, *When There is No Peace*; R. W. Seton-Watson, *Munich to Danzig*; Frederick L. Schuman, *Europe on the Eve*; G. E. R. Gedye, *Betrayal in Central Europe*; Alexander Werth, *France and Munich*; Hubert Ripka, *Munich: Before and After;* and Peter Buk, *La tragédie tchécoslovaque*, which includes a number of revealing documents. Winston Churchill's contemporary views are set forth in *While England Slept* (1938); and see also the thoughtful account and analysis of the crisis in John F. Kennedy, *Why England Slept** (1940, 2nd ed. 1961).

The Columbia Broadcasting System provided some of the most exciting accounts of the crisis; the texts of some of these broadcasts are included in *Crisis: A Report from the Columbia Broadcasting System* (1938). See also H. V. Kaltenborn, *I Broadcast the Crisis* (1938), by one of the outstanding commentators of the day; and William L. Shirer, *Berlin Diary** (1941), a classic of the period, by one of the leading American correspondents in Europe. Among American political commentary on the crisis Dorothy Thompson's articles in *The New York Herald Tribune* (and other newspapers) are outstanding.

Documents

The Munich crisis produced an enormous number of documents. The British Government published a few of its documents at the time of the crisis, but the full story became known only after the war when most of the records of the German Foreign Office fell into Allied hands, and the British and American Government published their own important records.

Some of the most important German documents were first made public at the Nuremberg War Crimes trials, and are included in the multi-volume series *Nazi Conspiracy and Aggression* (1946), *The Trials of the Major War Criminals before the International Military Tribunal* (1947-1949), and in the proceedings of other trials, notably *The United States of America vs. Ernst von Weizsäcker* (1951).

These collections must now be supplemented by the authoritative *Documents on German Foreign Policy 1918-1945,* based on the captured files of the German Foreign Office. See, especially, Series D, Volume II, *Germany and Czechoslovakia, 1937-1938* (1949), but also Series C, Volumes I-IV (1957-1962), on the relations of Germany and Czechoslovakia from January 1933 to March 1936. The documents for the period from March 1936 to October 1937 are still to appear.

The British and American Governments have also published impressive collections of their own documents. The former are included in E. L. Woodward and Rohan Butler (eds.), *Documents on British Foreign Policy 1919-1939,* Third Series, Volumes I-II (1949); the latter in *Foreign Relations of the United States, 1938,* Volume I (1955). For the development of British and American policy toward Germany after 1933, and for further light also on German-Czech relations, see the *Documents on British Foreign Policy 1919-1939,* Second Series, Volumes IV-VI (1950-1957), and the pertinent volumes in the documentary series *Foreign Relations of the United States* (1950-1954), which, again, include some of the most interesting and important accounts of these troubled years.

The French Government has just begun to publish its diplomatic docu-

ments on the interwar years and none of its documents on Munich have yet
appeared. There is, however, some interesting material in the records of the
Riom trial of 1943 and the postwar investigation of the French Parliament.
See Pierre Mazé and Roger Genebrier, *La Grand Journees du Proces de Riom*
(1945), and *Le evénéments survenus en France de 1933 à 1945* (1947-1951).

There are a few Czechoslovak and Russian documents. The Czechoslovak
Government hoped to publish some of its documents after Munich, but the
plan had to be given up. Some of these documents are included, however, in
the works of Ripka and Buk, cited above (p. 193), and in the important
account of B. Bílek, *Fifth Column at Work* (1945). In 1958 the Czech and
Russian Governments published *New Documents on the History of Munich*.
Some of these documents are important and revealing, but there is also some
reason to believe that the selection of documents is a tendentious one, designed
to discredit both the Western democracies and the "bourgeois" government
of President Benes, as well as to emphasize both the Soviet Union's readiness
to resist German aggression, and the strength of "progressive" elements in
Czechoslovakia at the time. For a critical discussion of these documents and
a fuller account of the Czechoslovak archives, by one of the few Western
scholars permitted to use them, see William V. Wallace, "New Documents
on the History of Munich," *International Affairs*, XXXV (1959).

See also F. Vnuk, "Munich and the Soviet Union," *Journal of Central
European Affairs*, XXI (1961); and Kurt Rabl, "Neue Dokumente zur Sudetenkrise," *Bohemia*, I (1960), for excerpts and critical comments on other Czech
government records.

Finally, Monica Curtis (ed.), *Documents on International Affairs, 1938*,
Volume II (1943), contains an excellent selection of important contemporary
statements by various statesmen and governments, including a number of im-
portant Russian pronouncements, and the full text of the important Fourth
Plan that President Benes submitted to the Nazi Sudeten negotiators on
September 5, 1938.

Memoirs and Biographies

Not surprisingly, there exist a large number of memoirs on the period,
and British political leaders have been most prolific in giving their versions of
events. There are also a number of important biographies of political leaders
of this period.

The classic account of the Munich era remains Sir Winston Churchill,
*The Gathering Storm** (1948). Chamberlain wrote no memoirs, but he left
a copious diary and numerous personal letters, and these have been used by
Sir Keith Feiling, his authorized biographer (1946). The recent biography
by Iain Macleod (1961) adds some new material, and also makes good use
of the recent official British histories of the Second World War, but remains,
in effect, a work of apology.

A number of Chamberlain's associates have written their story. The most
important of these—all more or less favorable to Chamberlain and the Munich
agreement—are by Viscount Maugham, *The Truth About the Munich Crisis*
(1944), Viscount Simon, *Retrospect* (1952), Sir Samuel Hoare, *Nine Troubled
Years* (1954), and Lord Halifax, *Fulness of Days* (1957). Alfred Duff Cooper,
who resigned as First Lord of the Admiralty over the Munich agreement, has

written an important critical account, *Old Men Forget* (1954). R. J. Minney has edited *The Personal Papers of Hore-Belisha* (1960). Eden's published memoirs have only reached his resignation as Foreign Secretary in February 1938, but a volume covering the Munich era is expected. On the twenty-fifth anniversary of the Munich Conference, he issued a lengthy statement highly critical of British policy.

Several British diplomats have written important memoirs of the crisis. These include Sir Nevile Henderson, who told his depressing story twice— first in *Failure of a Mission* (1940), and in a posthumously published volume *Water Under the Bridges* (1945). Lord Strang, then head of the Central Department of the Foreign Office, has written a revealing account in *At Home and Abroad* (1956). Sir Ivone Kirkpatrick, First Secretary in the British Embassy in Berlin, has recorded his impressions in *The Inner Circle* (1959), a work that conveys very well the frightening atmosphere under which the decisive agreements were reached.

In 1948 the British Broadcasting Company undertook a series of talks on Munich by leading contemporaries. They included talks, some of them very impressive, by Lord Vansittart, Sir Samuel Hoare, Agnes Headlam-Morley, Harold Nicolson, Cyril Falls, F. T. Ashton-Gwatkin, and Sir Lewis Namier. They are printed in *The Listener* (1948).

There are also some impressive memoirs by others close to the center of things. These include Leo Amery, *The Unforgiving Years, 1929-1940* (1955); Hugh Dalton, *The Fateful Years, 1931-1945* (1957); and Thomas Jones, *A Diary With Letters, 1931-1950* (1954), by a leading appeaser. There are important details on British military preparedness in the memoirs of Sir John Slessor, *The Central Blue* (1957), and in Roderick McLeod and Denis Kelly (eds.), *The Ironside Diaries, 1937-1940* (1961), based on the personal papers of the Chief of the British Imperial General Staff.

There are a number of interesting biographies, among them John Bowle, *Viscount Samuel* (1957), which includes a lengthy defense of Munich written by Samuel himself in 1955; Sir James Butler, *Lord Lothian* (1960), about the appeaser who redeemed himself as wartime ambassador to the United States; and Evelyn Wrench, *Geoffrey Dawson and our Times* (1955), on the influential editor of *The Times*.

No one should miss A. L. Rowse, *Appeasement—A Study in Political Decline 1933-1939** (1961), part history, part memoir—one of the great books on the period.

Continental statesmen have been more reticent. Daladier wrote no memoirs. Georges Bonnet's *Défense de la paix* [Volume I, *De Washington au Quai d'Orsay*] (1946), is better than its reputation. Paul Reynaud, Minister of Justice at the time of Munich, has written several books on the period, most notably *In the Thick of the Fight, 1930-1945* (1955). There are two important diplomatic memoirs—André François-Poncet, *The Fateful Years* (1949) and Robert Coulondre, *De Staline à Hitler* (1950), by the French ambassadors in Berlin and Moscow, respectively.

The record of Czechoslovak statesmen is equally sparse. Benes wrote two accounts—the first, a brief summary of the crisis, its origins, course, and consequences, appeared in his *From Munich to New War and Victory* (1954); the second, a more detailed account, *Mnichovské dny* (1955) remains untranslated, but for a critical summary see Otakar Odlozilik, "Eduard Benes on

Munich Days," *Journal of Central European Affairs,* XVI (1957). Hubert Ripka, a close associate of Benes, wrote *Munich: Before and After* (1939), a work of great importance.

Benes' former Private Secretary, Edward Taborsky, has written a number of thoughtful articles based, in part, on his personal experiences. These include "Benes and the Soviets," *Foreign Affairs,* XXIII (1949), "The Triumph and Disaster of Edward Benes," *ibid.,* XXXVI (1958), and "Benes and Stalin— Moscow 1943 and 1945," *Journal of Central European Affairs,* XIII (1953). See also the important articles of Otakar Odlozilik, one of Czechoslovakia's outstanding historians, now Professor at the University of Pennsylvania— "Eduard Benes' Memoirs," *Journal of Central European Affairs,* VIII (1949), "Concerning Munich and the Ideas of March," *ibid.,* IX (1950), and his essay on Benes' *Mnichovské dny,* cited above.

There are some interesting details also in *Count Ciano's Hidden Diary 1938-1939* (1953) and Jozef Beck, *Final Report* (1957).

The memoirs of Lord Massey, *What's Past is Prologue* (1964), reveal not only Chamberlain's lack of interest in mobilizing the energies of the Empire and Commonwealth in 1938 but also the widespread apathy, indifference, and spirit of appeasement that prevailed at that time.

The memoirs of Ivan Maisky, the Soviet Ambassador in London, *Who Helped Hitler?* (1964), contain the expected. Other Soviet leaders have written nothing.

American thinking and policy on the crisis can be followed more easily. On the background, see William E. Dodd, Jr., and Martha Dodd (eds.), *Ambassador Dodd's Diary 1933-1938* (1941), the perceptive American historian-diplomat cordially disliked by the German Government and some members of his own. Dodd's successor in Berlin, Hugh R. Wilson, was a mediocre man, inclined to agree with Sir Nevile Henderson, as is revealed in some diary extracts and personal letters published by his son, Hugh R. Wilson, Jr. (1961). Wilbur J. Carr, the American Minister to Czechoslovakia, was also a minor figure; see Katherine Crane, *Mr. Carr of State* (1960), based on his personal papers.

American policy, such as it was, was made in Washington. For the background of American diplomacy, see William E. Leuchtenburg, *Franklin D. Roosevelt and the New Deal 1932-1940** (1963), a superb book, which emphasizes Roosevelt's "non-interventionism"; and James MacGregor Burns, *Roosevelt: The Lion and the Fox** (1956), which contains a good account of Roosevelt's foreign policy during the Munich era.

The most farsighted official in the Department of State was Assistant Secretary of State George S. Messersmith. He left no memoirs. *The Memoirs of Cordell Hull* (2 vols. 1948) contain an elaborate defense of American policy. *The Secret Diary of Harold Ickes* (Volume II, 1954) contains a troubled account of American policy. Nancy H. Hooker (ed.), *The Moffat Papers* (1956) contains a smug account of American policy. John Morton Blum, *From the Morgenthau Diaries: Years of Crisis 1928-1938* (1959) adds further details about the confusion prevailing in Washington.

William L. Langer and S. Everett Gleason, *The Challenge to Isolation, 1937-1940** (1952) is a superb introduction to American foreign policy in the Munich era.

The record on Hitler and the other Nazi leaders, and their diplomatic representatives, is enormous. Hitler himself was the "new diplomat" *par excellence.* Certain that the democracies would not believe him, he broadcast his views (and plans) ahead nearly all the time. His addresses may be followed in Norman H. Baynes (ed.), *The Speeches of Adolf Hitler* (2 vols. 1942), to which should be added his important secret speech to German journalists, November 10, 1938, published in *Vierteljahrshefte für Zeitgeschichte,* VI (1958). The outstanding biography of Hitler—which includes an excellent account of the Munich crisis—remains Alan Bullock's, *Hitler—A Study in Tyranny*° (rev. ed. 1963), although the older work of Hermann Rauschning, *The Voice of Destruction* (1940) is still important, and so is the recent study of Günter Moltmann, "Weltherrschaftsideen Hitlers," in Otto Brunner and Dietrich Gerhard (eds.), *Europa und Übersee—Festschrift für Egmont Zechlin* (1961).

The memoirs of Nazi leaders, and those of former German diplomats, must be used with great caution. *The Ribbentrop Memoirs* (1954) omits most of the Munich chapter from the original German edition, *Zwischen London und Moskau—Erinnerungen und letzte Aufzeichnungen* (1953), which consists mostly of Ribbentrop's old half-truths and fabrications. His widow, Annelies von Ribbentrop, has published *Verschwörung gegen den Frieden* (1962), which adds new charges, half-truths, and fabrications.

Most German diplomats knew the record too well and kept quiet after the war. An important exception was Ernst von Weizsäcker, State Secretary in the Foreign Ministry at the time of Munich. His *Memoirs* (1950) are unctious and inaccurate. Paul Schmidt, *Hitler's Interpreter* (1950) reveals less than he knew.

Some of the German generals have also sought to defend themselves in print. Their books add little new however, and only serve to confirm their previous reputations. Some German historians, notably Walter Görlitz, have recently sought to defend some of these military leaders—see, for instance, his *Generalfeldmarshall Keitel, Verbrecher oder Offizier?* (1961). Wilhelm Förster, *Generaloberst Beck* (2nd ed. 1953) is a useful biography of the only high-ranking officer to resign in protest against Hitler's plans in 1938.

Most of the Sudeten Nazi leaders were executed or committed suicide at the end of the war. See, however, the apologia of Walter Brand, *Die Sudeten deutsche Tragödie* (1949), by one of Henlein's close associates. Some former Sudeten German leaders, journalists, and scholars have begun to make cautious —and, in some cases, not so cautious—appearances in *Sudetenland* and other West German publications. (See below, p. 198.)

Special Studies

The specialized literature on the Munich crisis is enormous and continues to mount. The first important survey of this literature, and a fine one, was Sigmund Neumann, "Europe Before and After Munich," *Review of Politics,* I (1940). There has been nothing like it since.

Among this large number of historical studies, the following are of special interest here: Martin Broszart, "Das Sudetendeutsche Freikorps," *Vierteljahrshefte für Zeitgeschichte,* IX (1961), which shows at some length how Nazi German guerillas violated Czechoslovak territory while Hitler continued to protest his peaceful intentions to Chamberlain and others; Hans Schiefer, "Deutschland und die Tschechoslowakei vom September 1938 bis März 1939,"

Zeitschrift für Ostforschung, IV (1955), and Heinrich Bodensieck, "Der Plan eines 'Freundschaftsvertrags' zwiechen dem Reich und der Tschechoslowakei im Jahre 1938," *ibid.*, X (1961), which show that Hitler never had any interest in the Sudeten Germans as such, and no intention of living up to the Munich agreement.

There is also now a substantial, and still growing, body of "revisionist" scholarship, most of it the work of former Sudeten German historians, writers, and publicists at present living in West Germany. The point of much of this "revisionist" literature, which in many ways is reminiscent of the "revisionist" scholarship of the 1920's and 30's, is not only to question the whole idea of national self-determination (upon which Czechoslovakia was largely founded), but to emphasize the misuse of Wilsonian principles at the Versailles peace conference, and to challenge Czechoslovakia's right to exist as an independent state.

Some of these Sudeten historians have gone so far as to argue, for instance, that Czechoslovakia was not deprived of the Sudetenland at Munich, that, on the contrary, President Benes had conceded most of the Sudetenland to Germany of his own volition—indeed, had asked France to assist him in getting his countrymen to accept this transfer—while other Sudeten German writers have claimed complete legality for the transfer of the Sudeten territory, arguing that Czechoslovakia accepted it "voluntarily," when she agreed to the Anglo-French demand to that effect on September 21st. For examples of such "revisionism," see the works of Wilhelm Turnwald and Emil Franzel, cited above (p. 192), to which may be added the voluminous writings of Kurt Rabl and Hermann Raschhofer, and the revealing symposium *Die Sudetenfrage in Europäischer Sicht** (1962), which also, however, includes contributions by such non-revisionist scholars as Professor Paul Kluke of the University of Frankfurt.

And there is still another school of "revisionist" historians—this one flourishing in East Germany, Czechoslovakia, and the Soviet Union. These historians seek to place most of the blame for the dismemberment of Czechoslovakia upon the Western democracies, who are accused of having had no intention of defending Czechoslovakia, but, on the contrary, of seeking to direct Hitler's aggressive interests toward the East, and especially against the Soviet Union. For examples of this kind of "revisionism"—now the official position in the Communist parts of Europe—see Andrew Rothstein, *The Munich Conspiracy* (1958), to which may be added M. Baturin, "The United States and Munich," *International Affairs* [Moscow] V, 1959; *Lectures on the History of Munich* (1959); Karl Obermann (ed.), *Die Hintergründe des Münchener Abkommen von 1938* (1959); and numerous articles in the East German *Zeitschrift für Geschichtswissenschaft*.

There have also been numerous important and interesting studies by scholars in Britain, France, and the United States. These include, on the background of the crisis, Macalister Brown, "The Third Reich's Mobilization of the German Fifth Column in Eastern Europe," *Journal of Central European Affairs*, XIX (1959); Gerhard L. Weinberg, "Secret Hitler-Benes Negotiations 1936-1937," *ibid.*, XX (1960); and William V. Wallace, "The Foreign Policy of President Benes in the Approach to Munich," *Slavonic and East European Review*, XXXIX (1960), based on study in the Czechoslovak archives.

On the crisis itself, see especially Bernadotte E. Schmitt, "Munich,"

Journal of Modern History, XXV (1953); Gerhard L. Weinberg, "The May Crisis of 1938," *ibid.*, XXX (1957); and for a discerning analysis of British diplomacy, Gordon A. Craig, "High Tide of Appeasement: The Road to Munich 1937-1938," *Political Science Quarterly*, LXV (1950).

The role of the British dominions is discussed by H. V. Hodgson, "British Foreign Policy and the Dominions," *Foreign Affairs*, XVII (1939), and D. C. Watt, "Der Einfluss der Dominions auf die Britische Aussenpolitik vor München 1938," *Vierteljahrshefte für Zeitgeschichte*, VIII (1960), which may be compared with the recent memoirs of Lord Massey.

Because their diplomatic archives have remained generally closed, there have been few important studies on the role of Czechoslovakia, France, Italy and the Soviet Union. On the first, see however the illuminating studies of Otakar Odlozilik and Eduard Taborsky, cited above; on the second, the impressive work of Pertinax (pseud. André Geraud), *The Gravediggers* (1943), the useful volume of Elizabeth R. Cameron, *Prologue to Appeasement* (1942), the critical survey of Maurice Baumont, "French Critics and Apologists Debate Munich," *Foreign Affairs*, XXII (1947), and the detailed study of Arthur H. Furnia, *The Diplomacy of Appeasement: Anglo-French Relations and the Prelude to World War II* (1960); on the third, the recent biography of Mussolini (1964) by Sir Ivone Kirkpatrick, who observed Mussolini at Munich; and on the last, the thoughtful essay of George Vernadsky, "A Review of Russian Policy," *Yale Review* (Spring 1942), and the more detailed account by Max Beloff, *The Foreign Policy of the Soviet Union, 1929-1941* (II, 1949).

There are a number of significant studies on German policy, and the diplomatic and military background of Hitler's actions. These include Gordon A. Craig, "Hitler and his Ambassadors," in his *From Bismarck to Adenauer** (2nd ed. 1965); D. C. Watt, "The German Diplomats and the Nazi Leaders 1933-1939," *Journal of Central European Affairs*, XV (1955), and two important German accounts, Rudolf Stadelmann, "Deutschland und England am Vorabend des Zweiten Weltkriegs," *Festschrift für Gerhard Ritter zum 60. Geburtstag* (1950), and H. K. G. Rönneforth, "Die Sudetenkrise 1938," *Zeitschrift für Ostforschung*, I (1958).

Much has been written also on the controversial role of the German resistance to Hitler and the part played by the German military leadership. See, for instance, Hans Rothfels, *The German Resistance to Hitler* (2nd ed. 1962), and the more detailed account of Gerhard Ritter, *Carl Goerdeler and the German Resistance Movement* (1958). The role of the German generals is discussed—critically—by Gordon A. Craig, "Army and National Socialism 1933-1945," *World Politics*, II (1950), and in his subsequent work *The Politics of the German Army 1640-1945* (1955); Telford Taylor, *Sword and Swastika* (1952); and Sir John W. Wheeler-Bennett, *The Nemesis of Power: The German Army in Politics 1918-1945* (1953), an important work unfairly attacked by many German historians.

Despite the growing emphasis on the importance of "Atlantic history," there have been few important accounts of the Munich crisis from this point of view. See, however, the revealing study of Gordon V. Haight, Jr., "France, the United States, and the Munich Crisis," *Journal of Modern History*, XXXII (1960), and the more detailed account in Roland N. Stromberg, *Collective Security and American Foreign Policy* (1963).

One of the most important aspects of the crisis remains the question of the comparative military preparedness of the two sides. On the state of German military plans and readiness, see the discerning study of Esmond M. Robertson, *German Prewar Plans and Preparations* (1963), but see also Gerhard Menck, *Hitler und die deutsche Aufrüstung 1933-1937* (1959), and Peter Graf Kielmansegg, "Die militärisch-politische Tragweite der Hossbach Besprechung," *Vierteljahrshefte für Zeitgeschichte*, VIII (1960).

The state of Western defenses is discussed at some length in R. J. Minney (ed.), *The Personal Papers of Hore-Belisha* (1960), the memoirs of Sir John Slessor and the diary of Sir Edmund Ironside, cited above (p. 195), and Denis Richards, *The Royal Air Force*, I (1953). See also the impressive volumes in the British official *History of the Second World War,* especially Basil Collier, *The Defense of the United Kingdom* (1957), Captain S. W. Roskill, *The War At Sea* (1960), and Sir Charles Webster and Noble Frankland, *The Strategic Air Offensive Against Germany,* I (1961). For the state of American preparedness—a not inconsiderable factor from Hitler's point of view—see the outstanding work of Mark S. Watson, *Chief of Staff—Prewar Plans and Preparations* (1950). No similar studies exist on the history of French preparedness, but see the interesting volume of Richard D. Challener, *The French Theory of the Nation in Arms 1866-1939* (1952), and the opening chapters of André Benoist-Mechin, *Sixty Days That Shook the West* (1963).

No student of the Munich crisis should ignore the impressive collaborative volume *The Diplomats 1919-1939** (1953), edited by Gordon A. Craig and Felix Gilbert, nor the superb collected essays of Sir Lewis Namier, *Diplomatic Prelude 1936-1940* (1948), *Europe in Decay 1938-1939* (1950), and *In the Nazi Era* (1952), which include some of the finest writing on the diplomacy of appeasement and the history of the Munich era.

The Era in Perspective

Munich was, of course, only the last but one of the great diplomatic crises of the 1930's. There is not yet a diplomatic history of this period comparable to Sidney B. Fay's classic work on *The Origins of the World War* (1930). For a general introduction to this troubled era, see Sir Winston Churchill, *The Gathering Storm**; Sir John W. Wheeler-Bennett, *Munich— Prologue to Tragedy**; Alan Bullock, *Hitler—A Study in Tyranny**; A. L. Rowse, *Appeasement—A Study in Political Decline**; to which may be added the volume on *The Diplomats** edited by Gordon A. Craig and Felix Gilbert and the collected essays of Sir Lewis Namier, cited above, as well as the powerful journalistic account of William L. Shirer, *The Rise and Fall of the Third Reich** (1961), the brilliantly perverse work of A. J. P. Taylor, *The Origins of the Second World War** (1961) and the dramatic narrative of Martin Gilbert and Richard Gott, *The Appeasers* (1963).

Two distinguished historians, in this country and in West Germany, have recently addressed themselves to the origins of the Second World War and the spirit of the times that produced the Munich crisis. For their thoughtful and balanced interpretation of these troubled years, see Hans Herzfeld, "Zur Problematik der Appeasement Politik," in Waldemar Besson and Friedrich Frhr. Hiller von Gaertringen (eds.), *Geschichte und Gegenwartsbewusstsein,* Festschrift für Hans Rothfels zum 70. Gebrutstag (1963), and Raymond J. Sontag, "The Origins of the Second World War," *Review of Politics,* XXV (1963).

LIST OF PERSONS

Attlee, Clement R., Labour Member of Parliament, and Leader of the Opposition, 1935–1940

Attolico, Bernardo, Italian ambassador to Germany, September 1935—May 1940

Baldwin, Stanley [Earl of Bewdley], British Prime Minister 1923–1924, 1924–1929, 1935–1937

Bechyne, Rudolf, Czechoslovak Deputy Prime Minister and Minister for Supplies 1932–1938

Beck, Colonel Jozef, Polish Foreign Minister 1932–1939

Beck, Colonel General Ludwig, Chief of the General Staff of the German Army, May 1935—October 1938

Benes, Eduard, Czechoslovak Foreign Minister 1918–1935; President of Czechoslovakia 1935—October 1938

Bevin, Ernest, British trade union leader

Blomberg, Field Marshal Werner von, German Minister of War 1933–1938, Commander in Chief of the German Army, April 1935—February 1938

Blum, Léon, leader of the French Socialist Party, and Prime Minister of France, June 1936–1937, March–April 1938

Bodenschatz, Colonel Karl Heinz, liaison man between Hitler and Göring

Bonnet, Georges, French Foreign Minister, April 1938—September 1939

Brauchitsch, Colonel General Walter von, Commander in Chief of the German Army 1938–1941

Bullitt, William C., American ambassador to the Soviet Union, 1933–1936; ambassador to France 1936–1940

Butler, Richard A., British Under Secretary of State for Foreign Affairs, February 1938–1941

Canning, George, British Foreign Secretary 1807–1809, 1822–1827; Prime Minister 1827

Carr, Wilbur J., American minister to Czechoslovakia 1936–1939

Cecil, Viscount, member of several British cabinets and delegate to League of Nation assemblies; recipient of the 1937 Nobel Peace Prize

Chamberlain, Hilda, sister of Neville Chamberlain

Chamberlain, Ida, sister of Neville Chamberlain

Chamberlain, Neville, British Prime Minister, May 1937—May 1940

Champetier de Ribes, Auguste, French Minister of Pensions and Veterans 1938

Churchill, Winston S., Conservative Member of Parliament

Ciano, Count Galeazzo, Italian Foreign Minister 1936–1943

Citrine, Sir Walter, British trade union leader

Cooper, Alfred Duff, First Lord of the Admiralty, 1937—October 1938

Coulondre, Robert, French ambassador to the Soviet Union, November 1936–November 1938

Cripps, Sir Stafford, Labour Member of Parliament

Crowe, Sir Eyre, British diplomat 1885–1925

Daladier, Édouard, French Prime Minister and Minister of Defense, March 1938—March 1940

Dalton, Hugh, Labour Member of Parliament

Dawson, Geoffrey, Editor of *The Times* (London) 1923–1941

Delbos, Yvon, French Foreign Minister, June 1936—March 1938

Dirksen, Herbert von, German ambassador to Great Britain, May 1938—September 1939

Doriot, Jacques, French political leader, founder of the Parti populaire français

Dunglass, Lord (now Sir Alec Douglas-Home), Unionist member of Parliament, Parliamentary Private Secretary to Prime Minister Chamberlain 1937–1939

Eden, Anthony, British Foreign Secretary, December 1935—February 1938

Eisenlohr, Ernst, German minister to Czechoslovakia 1936–1938

Flandin, Pierre Étienne, Member of the French Chamber of Deputies, French Prime Minister 1934–1935; Foreign Minister, January—June 1936

François-Poncet, André, French ambassador to Germany 1931–1938

Frank, Karl Hermann, Deputy Leader of the Sudeten German Nazi Party 1937–1939

Fritsch, Colonel General Baron Werner von, Commander in Chief of the German Army, May 1935–February 1938

Gamelin, General Maurice, Chief of the French Army General Staff, and Vice President of the Conseil Supérieur de la Guerre, 1935–1940

Goebbels, Josef, German Minister for Propaganda 1933–1945

Goering, Field Marshal Hermann, Commander in Chief of the German Air Force, 1935–1945, and Commissioner for the Four-Year Plan 1936–1945

Gort, Viscount, Commander in Chief of the British Imperial General Staff 1937–1939

Hacha, Emil, President of Czechoslovakia, November 1938—March 1939

Halifax, Viscount, British Foreign Secretary, February 1938—December 1940

Henderson, Sir Nevile, British ambassador to Germany, April 1937—September 1939

Henlein, Konrad, leader of the Sudeten German Nazi movement 1933–1938; Reich Commissioner for the Sudeten German territory, October 1, 1938

Henry, Jules, Official of the French Foreign Ministry, and chief of Bonnet's ministerial advisers

Hertzog, General James, South African Prime Minister 1924–1939; Minister for External Affairs 1929–1938

Hess, Rudolf, Reich Minister without Portfolio, and Hitler's Deputy, 1933–1941

Hewel, Walter, chief of the personnel staff of the German Foreign Ministry, and plenipotentiary of the Foreign Minister with Hitler

Himmler, Heinrich, leader of the SS 1929–1945, and chief of the German Secret Police 1936–1945

Hitler, Adolf, German Chancellor and Führer, 1933–1945

Hoare, Sir Samuel [later Lord Templewood], Foreign Minister 1935; British Home Secretary, May 1937—September 1939

Hodza, Milan, Czechoslovak Prime Minister, November 1935—September 22, 1938

Hore-Belisha, Leslie, British Secretary of War, 1937—January 1940

Hossbach, Colonel Friedrich, German General Staff officer and Adjutant to Hitler

Hull, Cordell, American Secretary of State 1933–1944

Inge, The Very Reverend William, Dean of St. Paul's 1911–1934

Jones, Thomas, Secretary of the Pilgrim Trust 1930–1945

Keitel, Colonel General Wilhelm, Chief of the High Command of the German Armed Forces 1938–1945

Kennedy, Joseph P., American ambassador to Great Britain 1937–1940

King, William L. Mackenzie, Canadian Prime Minister 1935–1948

Kirkpatrick, Ivone, First Secretary of the British Embassy, Berlin, 1933—December 1938

Kordt, Erich, Counselor of the German Legation in London, November 1936—February 1938; member of the Foreign Minister's staff, March 1938—February 1941

Kordt, Theodor, Counselor of the German Legation, London, April 1938—September 1939

Krejci, General Ludvik, Chief of the Czechoslovak General Staff 1934–1939

Krofta, Emil, Czechoslovak Foreign Minister 1936–1938

Kundt, Ernst, Deputy of the Sudeten German Nazi Party in the Czechoslovak Parliament

Lacroix, Victor-Leopolde de, French minister to Czechoslovakia 1936–1939

Lansbury, George, Labour Member of Parliament, and Leader of the Opposition, 1931–1935

Lebrun, Albert, President of the French Republic 1932–1940

Léger, Alexis, Secretary General of the French Foreign Ministry 1933–1940

Lindbergh, Charles A., American aviator

Lindsay, Sir Ronald, British ambassador to the United States 1930–1939

Litvinov, Maxim, Soviet Commissar for Foreign Affairs 1930–1939

Lorenz, SS Obergruppenführer Werner, representative for foreign policy questions on the staff of Hitler's Deputy

Lothian, Lord, Secretary of the Rhodes Trust 1925–1939

Lyons, Joseph A., Australian Prime Minister 1931–1939

Malkin, Sir William, Legal Adviser to the British Foreign Office 1929–1945

Mandel, Georges, Member of the French Chamber of Deputies, and Minister for Colonies 1938–1940

Masaryk, Jan, Czechoslovak minister to Great Britain 1925–1938

Masaryk, Thomas, President of Czechoslovakia 1918–1935

Mastny, Vojtech, Czechoslovak minister to Germany 1932–1939

Maugham, Viscount, British Lord Chancellor 1938–1939

Montgomery, Lieutenant General Bernard L., British General Staff officer, 1934–1937; infantry brigade commander 1937–1938

Mussolini, Benito, Italian Prime Minister 1926–1943

Namier, L. B. (later Sir Lewis), Professor of History, University of Manchester, 1931–1953

Necas, Jaromir, Czechoslovak Minister of Social Welfare 1935–1938

Neurath, Baron Constantin von, German Foreign Minister, June 1932—February 1938; President of the Secret Cabinet Council 1938–1939

Newton, Basil, British minister to Czechoslovakia 1937–1939

Perth, Earl of, British ambassador to Italy, October 1933—May 1939

Phillips, William, American ambassador to Italy, 1936–1941

Phipps, Sir Eric, British ambassador to Germany 1933–1937; ambassador to France, April 1938—October 1939

Pilsudski, Marshal Jozef, Polish Prime Minister, 1920–1923, 1926–1928, 1930; Minister of War and Inspector General of the Army, 1926–1935

Potemkin, Vladimir P., Soviet Vice Commissar for Foreign Affairs 1937–1940

Raeder, Erich, Commander in Chief of the German Navy 1935–1943

Reynaud, Paul, French Minister of Justice, April—November 1938

Ribbentrop, Joachim von, German ambassador to Great Britain 1936–1938; Foreign Minister, February 1938–1945

Roosevelt, Franklin D., President of the United States 1933–1945

Rothermere, Viscount, owner of *The Daily Mail* (London), and other newspapers

Runciman, Viscount, President of the Board of Trade 1931–1937; head of British mission to Czechoslovakia, July–September, 1938

Schmidt, Paul, Counsellor of Legation, German Foreign Office, and Hitler's personal interpreter

Schmundt, Major Rudolf, Hitler's Military Adjutant

Simon, Sir John, British Foreign Secretary 1931–1935; Chancellor of the Exchequer 1937–1940

Smuts, Field Marshal Jan Christian, South African Minister of Justice 1933–1939

Stojadinovic, Milan, Yugoslav Prime Minister and Foreign Minister 1935–1939

Strang, William, Counsellor in the British Foreign Office, 1932–1939; head of the Central Department, 1937–1939

Swinton, Viscount, British Air Minister, 1935—May 1938

Syrovy, General Jan, Chief of the Czechoslovak General Staff, Prime Minister and Minister of Defense, September 22—December 1938

Temperley, Harold M. V., University Professor of Modern History, Cambridge University, 1931–1939

Toynbee, Arnold J., Director of Studies, The Royal Institute of International Affairs and Stevenson Research Professor in the University of London, 1925–1955

Vansittart, Sir Robert, Permanent Under Secretary of State for Foreign Affairs, 1930–1938; Chief Diplomatic Adviser to the Foreign Secretary, 1938–1941

Vavrecka, Hugo, Czechoslovak Minister of Propaganda 1938

Weizsäcker, Baron Ernst von, Head of the Political Department, German Foreign Ministry, August 1936—March 1938; State Secretary in the German Foreign Ministry, April 1938—April 1943

Wigram, Ralph F., Counsellor of the British Foreign Office 1933-1937

Wilson, Sir Horace, Chief Industrial Adviser to the British Government 1930–1939; remanded to the Treasury for service with the Prime Minister 1935–1939

Wilson, Hugh C., American ambassador to Germany 1938–1940

Zay, Jean, French Minister of Education 1936–1939

Zeitzler, Lieutenant Colonel Kurt, staff officer of the German High Command, and Chief of the General Staff of the German Army 1942–1944